God

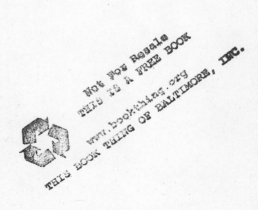

God

An anthology of fiction

**EDITED BY STEPHEN HAYWARD
AND SARAH LEFANU**

"It Had Wings" by Allan Gurganus first appeared in *White People*, published by Faber and Faber Ltd.

"My Stigmata" by Christopher Hope is from *Learning to Fly*, published by Minerva

"The Space Around God" by David Plante has been extracted from his novel-in-progress, *The Centre*

"Breaking It Up" by Bapsi Sidhwa has been extracted from her novel-in-progress, *The American Brat*, and is reprinted by permission of the Peters Fraser & Dunlop Group Ltd.

Library of Congress Catalog Card Number: 92-60143

British Library Cataloguing in Publication Data
Duffy, Maureen
    God
    I. Title   II. Hayward, Stephen
    III. Lefanu, Sarah
    823.0108 [FS]

    ISBN 1-85242-259-9

First published 1992 by
Serpent's Tail, 4 Blackstock Mews, London N4
and 401 West Broadway #2, New York, NY 10012

Typeset in Times by Contour Typesetters, Southall, London
Printed in Denmark by Nørhaven A/S of Viborg

Contents

Preface

Michèle Roberts   *God's House*   1

Tony Grist   *The White Lady*   20

Aamer Hussein   *Your Children*   28

Ursule Molinaro   *Doomed Survivors:*
    A Reconstruction in 2 Voices   48

Evelyn Conlon   *The Park*   58

Allan Gurganus   *It Had Wings*   71

Diana Hendry   *Mrs McCoy and Moses*   75

Gabriel Josipovici   *Can More Be Done?*   81

Elisa Segrave   *On the Subway*   98

James Morrow   *Bible Stories for Adults No 46:*
    The Soap Opera   106

Maureen Duffy   *The Last Priestess*   127

Lawrence Scott   *Leaving by Plane, Swimming Back*
    Underwater   134

Christopher Hope   *My Stigmata*   159

Judith Kazantzis   *God, An Untitled Story*   168

David Plante   *The Space Around God*   182

Joyce Carol Oates   *Work-in-Progress*   187

John Wakeman   *Sherry at the Rectory*   198

Bapsi Sidhwa   *Breaking It Up*   212

Jane Rogers   *Birds of American River*   234

Biographical Notes   244

Preface

If, ten years ago, we had approached almost any London publisher with the idea of a book of short stories about God, we would probably have been met with incomprehension. God? What an improbable theme. Religious issues were not much written about in the English-speaking world, except perhaps in a political or historical context. Was this the apparent end of religious history, the final, deadening victory of post-war Anglicanism? The church existed, but nobody took much notice of it. Only known 'religious writers' dealt with religious or theological themes, and those who did so were as likely as not to come from Catholic or Jewish backgrounds, members of minorities with notoriously eccentric preoccupations.

In the last ten years, however, religion has re-entered the public consciousness. The almost simultaneous rise of Solidarity in Poland, which put Catholicism back on the map in Europe, and the Iranian revolution, which placed Islam firmly on the world stage, can be seen respectively as responses to the failure of Soviet communism and disillusion with the promises of western capitalism. In the United States, meanwhile, the spectacular growth of uncompromising born-again Christianity is evidence of a profound unease with contemporary American values. Fundamentalism has reared its unattractive head in almost every religion, and throughout the world prelates and zealots are intervening, often successfully, in public debate about education, women's rights, the family and sexual mores. This re-emergence of religious power and influence necessarily raises questions both public and private.

For centuries religious issues have been the cause of, or have been used as an excuse for, warfare and persecution, and there seems little sign of that ceasing to be the case, whatever the fathers of the different churches may say. Some of the stories in this anthology deal with that aspect of religion: the pain and suffering it has caused both individuals and entire populations throughout history. Intimately linked to the recent resurgence of religious sentiment has been a revival of religious intolerance and, inevitably, its close relation, racial prejudice; this, too, is treated in some of the stories which follow.

The tradition of radical dissent has more or less fallen into desuetude in Britain, as it has in many other parts of the world, partly at least because the advances of technology and growing prosperity have created new points of significance in people's lives. Now that religion is experiencing a global revival, however, we believe it is important that this tradition should be rediscovered.

While some of the stories in this collection deal with the public face of religion, others are more private; not surprisingly, a number grapple with the questions of imminent death or recent bereavement, and also with mortality in a more general sense. It is not easy to define a religious theme, as religion is so all-encompassing and the major world religions are responsible for forming the way we view ourselves and our relation to the world, whether or not we are believers. Some of the stories which follow deal with possible alternatives to those major religions, others offer re-interpretations: some posit the existence of a god, others struggle against the consequences of religious faith.

Although some of the writers in this anthology are known for their treatment of religious themes, most are not; we nevertheless felt that all the authors assembled here would have interesting and thought-provoking ideas on the topic of religion, and we have tried to bring together a wide range of writerly responses on this most pressing of questions. We hope readers will find, in the pages that follow, writing which

....

provokes and stimulates them, intrigues and saddens them, even angers and amuses them.

Our thanks go to Pete Ayrton and John Hampson of Serpent's Tail, who were immediately enthusiastic about, and consistently supportive of, a project that might have been seen as unfashionable or, God forbid, uneconomic by many other another publisher. Thanks too to Suzanne Durbidge and Christopher Collins for their advice and support throughout. Most of all, of course, our thanks go to the contributors, who responded so keenly and creatively to our request for a story about God.

Stephen Hayward
Sarah Lefanu
1 April 1992

God's House

....

MICHÈLE ROBERTS

Inside the priest's house it was very dark. I flattened my palms against the invisible air then advanced step by tiptoeing step. I smelled dust and the dregs of wine. I'd left the heat outside. The curved edge of a stone doorway was cold, grazed my cheek. Groping forwards, I encountered glass, a metal catch. With a rattle and squeak of iron bars I undid the shutters, pushed them open. Light drowned me. I saw that I was in a kitchen, bare except for a cooker and oilcloth-covered table. Sunlight fell across glistening brown paint onto my hands. I turned around and leaned back against the windowsill.

I was a burglar. My first break and entry. I wasn't sure what I wanted to steal.

I was back with you, in our old house where I'd been born twelve years before. Now a verandah had been added on at the front, bellying forwards into the garden, and your bed had been put there under the dome of glass. Half in and half out. You sat up when you saw me come in, and held out your arms.

You haven't left yet then, I said.

The room behind us was full of relatives, a sort of party going on. You gestured towards me to come closer. You held all my attention: your lashless monkey eyes that were very bright, your translucent skin, your full, blistered lips, the outline of your head under its fuzz of curls. Everything that there was between

....

us concentrated into that look we exchanged. Above the glass roof was the red sky, the break of dawn.

For a while the road ran through the plain, along the poplar-lined Canal du Midi, and then it rose, as the land lifted itself and became hillier. A straight road, running between golden-green plane trees, towards Spain. The rounded hills, brown and dark yellow, took us up, and up. We swung off the main road onto a smaller one, and one yet smaller.

Our village was called Beauregard-du-Perdu. We turned, as instructed, by the wash-house and fountain, and drove up the main street lined with plane trees. A green tunnel pierced with bits of dancing light. At its top I saw the stone bulk of the church, a rounded doorway decorated with zig-zags. To the right, behind low gates of grey metal, was the house my aunt and uncle were renting from some French friends. We recognized it straight away from the photographs. I got out of the car and saw the other house, opposite. No. What I saw was the high wall enclosing it, the steps up to the padlocked wooden door in the wall, worn steps that curved sideways then went up to the church behind. A notice tacked to the door, just above the padlock, said A VENDRE. As I stared, the church bells began to clang out the hour and I started back from their dull, flat noise.

My aunt bent towards me.

Lily. Would you like to be the one to knock on the neighbour's door and ask for the keys? Show us how well you speak French.

I inspected the gravel under my new shoes that I'd bought for the funeral. The gravel was grey like the metal gates, loose chips under my stiff toes. I lifted a foot and scraped it along the ground.

No point, my uncle said: here she is anyway.

Our letter of introduction named her as Madame Cabazou, a widow. She came out of the alleyway opposite our house, below the wall with its wooden door and its FOR SALE notice. A blue enamel sign proclaimed that the alley was called Impasse des Saints. Madame Cabazou was as quick as one of the lizards on the hot wall nearby. Small and skinny, eyes black as olives in her brown face, grey hair cut short. Gold daisies in her pierced ears. Her marriage earrings, she told me later on: that she wore every day. Flick flick went her tongue in her mouth as she exclaimed and shook hands and pulled the key from her housecoat pocket and ushered us in. She darted off again with a wave of her hand, a promise to bring us a bowl of plums picked that morning from the trees in her field.

Our holiday home was a little house on three floors, its walls painted a cool blue-grey. Red speckled tiles underfoot downstairs, unpolished wooden floorboards in the two bedrooms. Up here the windows had white shutters that creased up like concertinas and let in long arms of brambles laden with roses, and tiny balconies, no bigger than windowsills, in white-painted wrought iron. The bed in my room was narrow and high, with a white cover. The chairs were old-fashioned, with curvy backs. They broke when you sat on them; they were just for show.

The garden was large considering it was in the middle of a village, my aunt said. It was mainly grass, with flowerbeds and tangly shrubs dotted about in it. The solid privet hedge surrounding it was such a dark green it was almost black. Over it reared the plane trees that lined the village street outside. Sage green, almond green, sea green, bottle green, those were the colours of the bushes and plants. The flowers were so bright with the light in them, mauve and pink. The sun dazzling down on the garden at midday made it white. Too hot to sit in without a hat. I felt scorched. I preferred the coolness of the broken-down barn with its earth floor, where swallows flashed in and out, quick blue streaks. On the first morning the swallows flew into my room when I was still in bed and I felt welcomed.

I was puzzled when the telephone rang. I hadn't seen one the night before. There it was, by the bed. I lifted the receiver and said hello.

Your voice sounded exactly as it always did.

Hello, you said back to me: how are you getting on?

D'you mean to say, I asked: that they've got telephones up there?

You laughed.

Of course we have. How else could we get in touch? Now come on, I haven't much time, how's your father managing, and how are you?

Oh he's doing fine, I said: more or less. You know. He's being extra careful when he drives the car.

Why did I say that? I don't know. Just then the church bells began to ring, battering the windowpanes, and your voice faded away under their onslaught.

My aunt and uncle were welded to their white plastic lounging chairs. Turned towards each other, they held hands and chatted. They were pink-faced, melting in the heat. I strolled past them with a wave, went out to explore the village.

The church door seemed locked. I shoved it with my shoulder but its resistance didn't yield. I wandered on past it, paused at an open pair of tall wrought-iron gates, went in.

I was in the cemetery. The village within the village. The houses of the dead neatly arranged side by side. The path ran all the way round, tombs on both sides. Some of the graves were just mounds of earth, with fragile, blackened crosses in crumbling iron at their heads. Others were doors laid down on the ground, thick polished stone bearing pots of pink and red porcelain roses, open porcelain books with gilt letters spelling out the names of the dead. Whole families seemed to be crammed into small tight plots. Some of the graves had photographs in black metal frames. Some had stone angels. One had a crucifix made of tiny black beads.

....

4

Madame Cabazou knelt by a shiny slab of white granite. She inserted mauve flowers, like the ones in our garden, into a black vase on top of it. I looked over her shoulder to read her husband's name carved into the stone. Emile.

He died three months ago, Madame Cabazou said: I'm not used to it yet.

She stood up and clasped my arm. Then she held my hand in hers. Water shone in her eyes, tipped over, flowed down her cheeks.

Just behind the graves the hills began, high and round, crusted with yellow sunflowers. The landscape crackled with their dark gold and black. The earth was a rich brown. We were high up in a wild and lonely place. From here you could see the Pyrenees, misty blue shapes against the blue sky.

Madame Cabazou wore a black housecoat printed with pink roses. She let go of me and fished a handkerchief out of her pocket. She mopped her eyes.

The village is dying, she said: we used to have vineyards up there but not any more. Only sunflowers now round here. So all the young ones have gone. Just us old people left. It's good your family has come to stay. You'll liven us up.

They're not my parents, I told her: they're my uncle and aunt.

Madame Cabazou whistled. An ancient beagle bitch trundled out of the bushes, panting, and followed us down the path. I winced away from her in case she snapped or bit.

Betty, Betty, good dog, said Madame Cabazou: oh she's a good dog my Betty, all the dogs in the village are good, none of them will harm you, they don't bite.

My mother's just died, I said in the loudest voice I could manage: so they've brought me away on holiday to be nice to me.

Madame Cabazou stood stockstill in the centre of the path and cried some more.

Oh poor child poor child poor little one.

She hung onto my hand again as she wept. Then she blew her

....

5

nose and shut the tall gates behind us. The church bells began to clamour out the Angelus. Bash, bash, bash.

Electronic, said Madame Cabazou: the old lady who used to ring the Angelus, because her father did before her, she died this spring. No village priest any longer, either. Just one who serves all the villages in turn. The presbytery's been empty for a long time.

She fingered the little silver crucifix slung round her neck on a silver chain and sighed.

The presbytery? I asked.

The priest's house, she said: there.

We were going down the stone steps from the side of the church, down into the well of green light under the plane trees. She waved her hand at the high wall beside us, the wooden door let into it. We paused there, on the corner of the alleyway, to say goodbye.

Oh this heat, she said: I do love it. And it's so good for my arthritis.

She tapped me on the cheek.

You must have faith. Your mother is with God. We must believe that. She's up there in heaven. She's alive for all eternity.

She hurried off. The old dog lurched along after her, slack-bellied, velvety nose in the dust.

You grasped my hand. We took off together with a swift kick, we whirred into the night sky. Holding on to you I was drawn along, buoyant, an effortless progress under the stars above the wheeling earth.

We flew into the mouth of a dark tunnel. I could see nothing, I gripped your hand, felt cold air stream over my eyelids. You knew your way. You carried us both along, our arms were wings.

I wanted to show you what dying was like, you said: I wanted you to know. Open your eyes. Look.

Below us, in the tunnel, were hospital beds crowded with sick

....

people. They lay still and silent, faces upturned as we flew past. Then they dwindled behind us, and we burst out of the tunnel back into the soft blackness of the night.

That was dying, you said: we've gone past death now.

Our curving flight traced the shape of the earth below. We swooped sideways, down. Another opening loomed. Another tunnel? I wasn't sure. The silvery stars rolled past. We were carried on the shoulders of the wind.

There's a lot more I've got to find out about, you explained: I've got a lot more to explore. Come on, let's go in here next.

A mosquito whined in my ear. I cursed and sat up. You were no longer there.

We ate lunch in the garden, beside the hedge, under the shade of a big white umbrella. Onion tart and tomato salad, bread and cheese, a plate of dark blue figs. My aunt and uncle drank a lot of wine. They went indoors for a siesta.

I sat on, idly looking at the bushes, the flowerbeds. All sun-drenched, glittering. The shutters of the rooms upstairs were only half-closed. I heard my aunt call out and laugh. Her noise rattled against my skin.

The dog Betty appeared in the farthest corner of the garden. She emerged from under the fig tree which grew there, began to toddle across the grass. She pursued her sedate, determined way as though it were marked out for her, pushing aside tall clumps of weeds that blocked her path, stepping delicately over the empty wine bottle my uncle had let fall. She didn't bother looking at me. I decided she must be on some private dog-road, some sort of dogs' short-cut via holes in our hedge we hadn't seen.

She flattened herself by the gate and tried to wriggle under. She was too fat to manage it. She whined and thumped her tail. I got up and opened the gate. She trotted through, then paused. She was waiting for me. I thought I would follow her to find out where she'd go.

....

7

She crossed the road and turned into the alley. Madame Cabazou's house, I knew, was the first one along. On the opposite side, on the corner with the street, was the priest's house behind its high wall. Betty didn't go home to her mistress. She nosed at a low wicker gate set into the wall near the end of the alley.

I tore aside the rusty wire netting stretched across the top of the gate and peered over it. A short path, overhung with creepers, led steeply upwards to a stone façade half-obscured by leaves. I understood. This was a back way into the priest's house, one not protected by padlocks and keys. In a moment I'd climbed through the netting and over the gate and dropped down on the other side. The branches of trees brushed my face and arms. Soft debris of dead leaves under my feet. I stood still and listened. The entire village seemed to be asleep. No sharp voice, no tap on my shoulder, pulled me back. I crept up the path. I forgot Betty: she'd gone.

The house rose up before me, wide, three solid storeys of cream-coloured stone under a red-tiled roof. Blank-faced, its brown shutters closed. Three steps led up to its double wooden door. On either side of this were stone benches with claw feet, and tall bushes of oleander spilling worn pink flowers along the ground. I didn't hurry working out how to enter the house because the garden laid insistent hands on me and made me want to stay in it for ever.

From the outside you couldn't see that there was a garden at all. It was hidden. A secret place. It was small and square and overgrown, completely enclosed by the towering walls that surrounded it: the house on one side, the neighbour's barn on a second, and the walls of the street and the alleyway on the other two.

Inside these walls the garden was further enclosed by a luxuriant green vine trained onto wires. What must have once been a tidy green plot edged by the vine, by bushes and trees, was now a thicket you had to push your way into. I crept into a little sweet-smelling box of wilderness. Just big enough to hold me. Just the right size. In its green heart I stood upright in the long grass and counted two cherry trees, an apple tree laden with fruit, more oleanders, a lofty bush of bamboo plumes and several of blackcurrant. I picked a leaf and rubbed it to release the harsh scent. There was an ancient well in one corner, fenced about with cobwebs and black iron spikes. I lifted its wooden lid, peered down at its black mirror, threw a pebble in and heard the far splash.

I was frightened of going into the house all by myself, so I dared myself to do it as soon as the church bells began to strike the hour. The doors were clasped together merely by a loop of thin wire. I twisted a stick in it, broke it. Then I pushed the doors open and entered the house.

Once I'd wrestled with the shutters in the kitchen and flung them wide, screeching on their unoiled hinges, I could see. The red-tiled floor, the white fireplace with columns on either side and a white carving of scrolls and flowers above, the stone arch I'd come through from the hall, the cooker black with grease, the yellow oilcloth on the table.

A corridor wound around the ground floor. I passed a store-room full of old furniture and carpentry things, a wine-cellar lined with empty metal racks, a poky lavatory with decorated blue tiles going up the wall. I picked my way up an open wooden staircase, like a ladder, to the salon and the bedrooms above. The salon was empty, grand as a ballroom but desolate. Striped blue and gold wallpaper hung down in curly strips, exposing the plaster and laths behind. The floor was bendy when I walked on it. The bedrooms were dusty and dark, falls of soot piled in their fireplaces. Old stained mattresses rested on broken-down springs, old books, parched covers stiff with dirt, sprawled face down on the lino, old chairs with cracked backs and seats were mixed up anyhow with rolls of lino, split satin cushions.

I put out my hands and touched these things in the half-dark. I draped my shoulders with a torn bedspread of scarlet chenille,

....

9

then passed my hands over the wounded furniture. I blessed it, I told it to be healed now, and that it was forgiven. Then I departed from those sad rooms, closing their doors behind me one by one.

I crawled up a second wooden stair, to the attic. Bright spears of light tore gaps in the walls and roof, pointed at a floor littered with feathers and droppings. A headless plaster statue leaned in the far corner. His hands clasped a missal. He wore a surplice and cassock. I recognized him, even without his head, as St John Vianney, the Curé of Ars. We'd done him at school. I looked for his head among the dusty junk surrounding him but couldn't find it. So I went back downstairs, into the garden again.

My bed in our old house was in the corner of the room. Shadows fingered the wall next to me and lay down on me like blankets. You'd draped a shadow over your face like a mantilla. You advanced, carrying a night-light. I was afraid of the dark but not of you, even though a grey cobwebby mask clung to your eyes and mouth and hid them.

You bent over me and spoke.

What a mess you've left everything in. Bits and pieces all over the place. Silly girl.

You whispered in my ear.

One day I'll tell you all the secrets I've ever known.

My aunt ladled cold cucumber soup from the white china tureen into white soup plates. We pushed our spoons across the pale green ponds, to and fro like swimmers. My spoon was big, silver-plated; I liked its heaviness in my hand. My uncle drank his soup heartily, stuffed in mouthfuls of bread, called for a second helping. My aunt waved the ladle at the moths butting the glass dome of the lamp she'd set on the table. It threw just enough light for us to eat by. The rest of the garden was swallowed by black night. From Madame Cabazou's house across the street came the sound of a man's voice reading the news on TV.

My aunt and uncle spoke to each other and left me in peace. I could lean against their chat like a pillow while I searched my memory.

No, my father said on the morning of the funeral: I don't believe in the afterlife. Though your mother tried to. Bound to, wasn't she, being a Catholic. We just conk out I think. That's the end of it. The end of consciousness.

My uncle's red cheeks bulged with bread. He caught my eye and lifted his glass to me. My aunt collected our empty soup plates and stacked them on one side of the table. My uncle swallowed his faceful of bread and fetched the next course. Stuffed red peppers. I lifted mine out of the dish onto my plate, inserted my knife, slit the red skin. The pepper fell apart easily, like a bag of thin red silk. Rice and mushrooms tumbled out, a strip of anchovy.

Overcooked, frowned my aunt: your fault, Lily, for coming back so late. Whatever were you up to?

I shrugged and smiled.

Oh we understand, she said: you're young, you don't want to hang around all the time with us middle-aged folks! And we trust you to be sensible. Not to do anything silly.

She began to toss green salad in a clear plastic bowl, moving the wooden spoons delicately between the oily leaves that gave off the fragrance of tarragon.

Of course you need some time by yourself, she said: especially just now. You want to amuse yourself, spend time by yourself, that's fine. Of course we understand.

It was early evening when I arrived at the house. Climbing the hill had taken me several hours. Now the sky at the horizon was green, as sharp as apples. The moon rose. A single silver star burned high above the lavender-blue sea.

The house was built into the cliff, at the very top, where the chalky ground levelled out, became turf dotted with gorse, sea-pinks, scabious. The front door stood open so I went in.

The whole place smelled of freshly sawn wood. Fragrance of resin, of cedar. Large rooms, airy and light. The walls and ceilings were painted a clear glowing blue. Beds were dotted about, manuscripts spilled across them. I wondered who they were, the people who lived here and strewed their papers over their beds. Then I saw the figure of a woman in the far doorway, leaning against the frame of the door, with her back to me. The owner of the house. Would she mind my presence? I was uninvited. A trespasser.

She turned round.

I'd forgotten that you'd ever looked like this. Young, with thick curly brown hair, amused hazel eyes, fresh unlined skin. Not a trace of sorrow or of pain. You were healthy. You were fully alive.

I'm living here now, you explained with a smile and a wave of the hand: in Brahma's house.

You walked me about the spacious blue rooms, up and down the wide, ladder-like staircases of golden wood.

Tell your father, you said: the cure for grief is, you have to sit by an open window and look out of it.

Your face was calm. No fear in it. You weren't suffering any more.

You look so well, I blurted out: and all your hair's grown back!

It's time for you to go, you told me.

You stood on the front steps and waved me off. My eyes measured the width of the doorway. I thought I'd slip through, stay with you. You shook your head, slammed the door shut on my efforts to break back in.

At eight o'clock prompt each day a siren wailed along the main road. That second morning, Madame Cabazou leaned over our gates and called.

....

The bread van. Hurry up, girl. It doesn't wait long.

I stumbled after her, half-asleep. She dashed along on nimble slippered feet, a thick cardigan thrust on over her white night-dress. The dog Betty trailed us, folds of fat swaying.

Down by the fountain we joined a queue of old people who all smiled and exclaimed. Madame Cabazou introduced me, made me shake hands all round. Once I was part of them they went on swopping bits of news. Madame Cabazou was the lively one. Her chatter was staccato, her hands flew about like the swallows that zigzagged between our house and barn.

My wretched grandchildren, she cried: they hardly ever come and see me. Children these days. Oh they don't care.

I bought a bag of croissants and a thick loaf, one up from a *baguette*, that was called simply a *pain*. I walked slowly back up the street to the house. The voices of the old people rose and fell behind me, bubbles of sound, like the splash of water in the fountain. They were recalling the funeral they'd been to the week before. A young girl, from a farm over by the lake, had been trapped by her hair in her father's baling machine and strangled. The voices grew high and excited, like the worrying of dogs.

After breakfast my aunt and uncle drove off in the car to visit the castle at Montségur. I waved them goodbye, then prowled about the kitchen, collecting the things I needed and packing them into a basket. I shut the grey metal gates behind me and crossed the road into the alleyway.

Madame Cabazou was working in the little vegetable patch in front of her house. Her thin body was bent double as she tugged weeds from the earth. Today she had on a blue housecoat, and she'd tied her straw hat on like a bonnet, the strings knotted under her chin. I slunk past while her stooped back was turned and hoisted myself over the wicker gate.

Once inside the priest's kitchen I opened the shutters and the windows to let in light and air. I swept the floor with the dustpan and brush I'd brought, dusted the table and the

....

13

fireplace and the windowsills. I laid a fire, with sticks and bits of wood from the storeroom. I'd brought a small saucepan to cook in. I had a metal fish-slice and one wooden spoon. For lunch I might have stewed apples, using the fruit from the tree outside. I might try mixing up some grape juice. I had three plastic bottles of mineral water in my basket, a croissant saved from breakfast, a blue and white checked tea-cloth, and a couple of books. I left all this equipment on the table in the kitchen, and went outside.

I dropped into the garden like a stone or a plant, taking up my place. The garden had been waiting for me. I belonged in it. I had discovered it and in that act had been accepted by it. Now I was part of it. Hidden, invisible. The long grass closed over my head, green water. The bushes stretched wide their flowering branches around me. The bright green vine walled me in with its jagged leaves, curling tendrils, heavy bunches of grapes. Around the edges of the garden rustled the tops of the trees.

I had plenty of time to get to know the garden. I had seven whole days in which to stare at the ants and beetles balanced on the blades of grass next to my face, to finger the different textures of stems, to listen to the crickets and birds. I rolled over onto my back, put my hands under my head, and stared at the sky through branches and leaves. My hammock. I swung in it upside down. It dandled me. I fell asleep and didn't wake for hours.

Over supper my aunt and uncle told me about the castle of Montségur, perched on top of a steep mountain. They'd climbed up the slippery rocks. They'd eaten their picnic in the lofty stronghold where the Cathars had held out against St Dominic's armies come to smash them and drag them down to the waiting pyre.

God how I loathe the Catholic church, cried my aunt: God how I loathe all priests!

My uncle poured red wine into tumblers.

Nice day, Lily? he asked.

....

I nodded. My mouth was full of cream-laden spaghetti scented with rosemary and sage. I had the idea that if I kept on eating the memory of my mother wouldn't be able to climb out of my silence, out of the long gaps between my words, and disturb me. So I held out my plate for a second helping and bent my head over it. I concentrated on the pleasures of biting, of chewing and swallowing, the pleasure of feeling full.

I was in bed but I wasn't asleep. The room was dark, and very warm. Gold glow of a lamp in one corner. Rain beat against the window, I heard it shush-shush through the curtains. Around me was folded the softest and lightest of quilts. Like being tucked up in a cloud. Or held in your arms. For you were there, a dim presence by the lamp, humming to yourself while you read a book about gardening. Peace was the physical knowledge of warmth, of your familiar profile, your sleeve of dark pink silk resting on the plump arm of your chair, the dim blue and gold pattern of the wallpaper.

You repeated to me: you're safe now. Safe now. Safe now.

Our last day, Lily, smiled my aunt: are you sure you don't want to come out with us for a drive? I can't think what you find to do on your own here day after day.

I shook my head.

Well, she said: if you don't, you don't, I suppose. You could make a start on your packing, in that case.

Her words jolted me. For seven days I'd been in retreat, in my private green world. I'd ceased to hear the church bells banging out the hours overhead. Hunger was my only clock. A week, in which I'd lain on the grass reading or daydreaming, had flowed past without my knowing or caring what day it was. Back home my schoolbooks waited, and a timetable ruled into squares.

I had an ache inside me. A sort of yawn that hurt. A voice in my stomach that wanted to scream. I felt stretched, and that I might topple over and break in two.

Back home I'd enter an empty house. My mother was dead. If

....

only that could be a fact that was well past, something I'd dealt with and got over. Recovered from. I didn't want to embark on a life in which she'd go on and on being dead, on and on not being there. I didn't want to let it catch up with me. I shut the grey metal gates and hurried across the road.

Madame Cabazou was sitting on her front step, picking fleas out of Betty's coat. She nipped them between her fingernails until their little black backs cracked. Crack! Crack! She brushed the fleas from her fingertips like grains of black sand.

Do you want some melons? she asked: I've got far too many. Even with this tiny patch I've grown more, this year, than I can use.

She waved her hand at the tidy rows of tomatoes, melons and courgettes. The earth between them was spotless, fine as sieved flour. She scowled at it.

We used to have proper fields of crops, and the vineyard. Not like this. This pocket handkerchief of a garden. Oh I do miss all that, I can't tell you how much.

Perhaps one melon? I suggested: we're leaving tomorrow morning early. We could have melon tonight.

Come and fetch it later on, she sang out: I'll pick you one that's really ripe.

She shoved Betty's nose off her lap, and got up. She put her hands in her pockets and gazed at me.

She jerked her head towards the wicker gate in the wall.

Some German people coming to view the house this afternoon, she remarked: with a lady from the agency.

I tried to sound indifferent.

Oh really?

The man who drives the bread-van told me, she said: this morning. His brother-in-law works in the café next door to the agency in Carcassonne, he heard them talking about it when they came in for a beer. Didn't you hear him say so down at the van this morning? You were off in some dream.

Coldness clutched me inside. I stared at Madame Cabazou.

....

If I were you, she said: I'd come and fetch that melon this afternoon. You dream too much, it's not good. Better wake up. Otherwise you can be sure you'll be in trouble. Too much time by yourself, that's your problem.

Her words hurt me like slaps on the face. I swung away without saying anything. Tears burned my eyes but I wouldn't cry while she was watching me. I heard her front door close, then her voice drifted through the window, scolding Betty, breaking into song. She was cold-hearted. She didn't care how much she'd upset me. She didn't know how it felt to be told I'd got to leave this house and this garden for good.

I'd believed for a whole week that it was my house, my garden. I'd hardly believed it even. I just knew it. I'd just been part of it. The garden had seemed to know me, had taken me in without fuss. Leaving it, going outside and not coming back, would be like having my skin peeled off. I might die. Something was tearing me apart inside. It frightened me. I was a piece of paper being slowly ripped in two. I staggered, and fell onto the little patch of tangled grass under the vine. I started crying and could not stop. The crying went on and on, and the pain. It twisted me up, it sawed me, it squeezed my heart so I could hardly breathe. The worst thing was feeling so lonely, and knowing I always would.

Just before my mother died, the night before, I was with her. It wasn't her any more, this tiny person so thin under her nightie I couldn't bear to look at her, with clawlike hands and a head that was a skull. Her eyes were the same, that was the only part of her left that I knew. She looked out of the darkness she was in and recognized me. For a couple of minutes she fought her way up from the morphine and tried to speak. She looked at me so trustfully. My father had said I should say goodbye to her but I couldn't.

You're not going to die just yet are you, I said loudly: you're not going to die just yet.

Her cracked lips tried to smile.

Oh yes I am, she whispered: oh yes I think I am.

That night I dreamed of her bed in the glass conservatory, half in and half out of the house. I woke up at dawn and saw the sky like red glass. My father came in and said my mother had just died.

I could think of her being alive. I could think of her being dead. What I could not bear to think of was that moment when she died, was dying, died. When she crossed over from being alive to being dead. I couldn't join the two things up, I couldn't connect them, because at the point where they met and changed into each other was pain, my body caught in a vice, my bones twisted and wrenched, my guts torn apart. I gave birth to her dying. Violently she was pulled out of me. I felt I was dying too. I could hear an animal howling. It was me.

I lay on the grass exhausted. I felt empty. Nothing left in me. I was an old sack used then thrown away. Now I was low as the grass, low as the ground. Flattened. I was worn out. As though a mountain had stamped on me.

A yawn possessed me and I looked up. My eyelids felt swollen like car tyres, and my nose too, and my mouth. I licked the salt tears off the corners of my lips, blew my nose.

I lay staring at the gnarled trunk of the vine, the weeds and grasses stirring about its root, the yellow flowers mixed in with them whose name I didn't know.

Then it stopped being me looking at the vine, because I dissolved into it, became it. I left me behind. Human was the same as plant. This corner of the garden, the earth: one great warm breathing body that was all of us, that lived strongly, whose life I felt coursing inside me, sap blood juices of grass. Love was the force that made things grow. Love grew the vine, the weeds, me. I started crying again because of the joy. It swept through me. The knowledge of love. Such sweetness and warmth inside me and the vine and the grass under the light of the sun.

Madame Cabazou whistled for me as though I were Betty.

We both came running. I carried a melon home under each arm. She kissed me on both cheeks to say goodbye, instructed me, if I wished to be well thought of, to write to her. She snatched me out of my garden, shook me, set me upright, told me to go home now. She pushed me off.

Next morning I slumped in the back seat of the car as we drove out of the village and headed for the motorway. I wanted to take the road back, to go the other way, to stay. I cried as we left the high golden hills and descended onto the plain. The wind from the sea, that Madame Cabazou called the *marin*, blew strongly. It meant the end of summer. It sang an elegy for my mother. She was dead she was gone I had lost her she would never come back and live with us again.

Every cell in every leaf had had a voice, which spoke to me.

Of course I am here. Where else should I be but here. Where else could I possibly be.

The White Lady

TONY GRIST

A thunderous midsummer afternoon — the air thick, the heat insufferable; the congestion of westward-flowing holiday traffic had turned the narrow, low-lying high street of Sullis Hill (an ugly small town on the English side of Offa's Dyke) into a sump of bad air. The vicar, Lawrence van Harlem, returning from attendance at a death-bed in the cottage hospital, plunged across the street with scissor-man strides to avoid Mrs Beckett.

The skirt of his cassock snagged on the bumper of a stalled and simmering Fiesta. He didn't notice it rip. Forty years of sexual and professional frustration had given him the look of a well-preserved pharoah — gaunt, leathery, furious.

He always did his best to avoid female parishioners — and Mrs Beckett in particular. Her gluey chat about her good friend Jesus disgusted him. His own God was elusive and terrifying, an abyss of diamond light, not something to be bantered over at street corners.

Emma Hartley, a member of his Parochial Church Council, was coming out of Leila Ambrose's antique shop. And Father van Harlem, who had decided to camouflage his flight from Mrs Beckett as the sudden desire to study the bits and pieces in Leila's window, nearly ran into her.

She was in her late thirties, an unmarried schoolteacher, slim, businesslike, with short black hair and a severity about her that masked nerves. The vicar had long since defined her to his own satisfaction as "that damn women's libber".

They smirked at one another.

"Bell-ringers tonight?" she asked.

Emma never would address him as "Father", though he expected it of all his parishioners. The omission was arrogance and bad manners. It flustered him.

"Yes." He consulted his watch. "I should be hurrying along."

"Have you filled the vacancy yet?"

"Well, I've been making enquiries . . ."

"Jane Morrison is interested. You know that."

"Yes, well; we'll have to see . . ."

He had been seeing about it for over a month now — ever since old Ted Evans had been carried off to Milton Keynes by a dutiful daughter who wanted him where she would be able to keep her eye on him. It was proving impossible to find a replacement. Jane Morrison, the only volunteer, was a sixth former at Emma's school.

And of course, being a girl, she was totally unacceptable. In Father van Harlem's church the women baked cakes and gave out hymn-books — as Mrs Beckett did — and that was that. Even the choir was all male. Emma had tackled him at the P.C.C. over what she called "this blatant discrimination" and he had told her, in a strangulated voice, that Christ hadn't chosen women as his disciples, and she had said, "what about Mary Magdalen?" and one of the wardens had swiftly and skilfully diverted the discussion back to the question of what colour the new choir robes should be.

Ever since that encounter a couple of months back, Emma and Father van Harlem had been a little afraid of one another. He smiled now in a way that was meant to be conciliatory but merely struck her as grim — at which point Leila Ambrose put her head round the door-frame behind Emma and grinned at him with witchy charm. Her teeth were gappy and all over the place. She was an enemy. "I'll see you at Mass," he coughed, then looked at his watch again, grimaced as though he were really sorry to have to tear himself away, and stepping round Emma, went scissoring up the street once more in the direction of St Bride's. Fat Mrs Beckett, with her shopping bag in one sweaty hand and the youngest of her five children tugging at the other, watched him wistfully. "Poor man," she thought.

"Poor bastard," said Leila Ambrose with tolerant contempt. Leila was a left-over hippy who had come to the village in the late 60s in search of magic mushrooms and then stayed on because she dug the vibes. Middle-aged now, she wore her iron-grey hair in a page-boy bob and jingled all over with cheap jewellery. She had just sold Emma a pretty little dish in imitation Chinese porcelain. The two were friends.

Emma was embarrassed by the intervention of an outsider into what was, after all, a family dispute. She felt suddenly protective towards her vicar.

"He's all right," she said, apologetically, but without great conviction.

"No, he's not," replied Leila; "he's an arrogant, patriarchal prat. So what's all this about bells?"

Emma put aside her scruples of loyalty and told her.

"Typical," said Leila; "he came in here once and I tackled him — the way you do — about women priests. He told me God was a man — or words to that effect. I told him God was a woman long before She was a man and gave him a lecture about Sul and the Ladywell. He's never spoken to me since."

The Ladywell was a natural spring that rose a stone's throw to the north of St Bride's church. Leila had a theory that it had once been sacred to the prehistoric eye Goddess, Sul — hence the name of the town. The little pond created by the spring had been haunted for as long as records went back by a ghost known as the White Lady. Leila explained her as a folk memory of the Goddess.

Emma was never sure just how seriously she was supposed to take Leila's Goddess worship. Had she taken it on board to irritate the pious or was it a real religion?

....

22

"But surely Sul is make-believe," she had protested once.

"Precisely," said Leila.

Now she asked, "Isn't God beyond sex?"

"I hope not," said Leila decisively. "I like sex. I wouldn't want a God who rises above it."

"You know what I mean. Doesn't God include male and female?"

"Yes. Fine. So how come we're only allowed to call him HE?"

"It's a convention." It was offered tentatively.

"It's an instrument of oppression."

"So — what would you want to call Him? It?"

"No. He or She, depending on the context. But then I'm not a Christian. I'd prefer to have lots of different Gods and Goddesses."

"But that's paganism. It's going backwards . . ."

"Who says? The Church says. The Christian propaganda machine."

"No. I say. The whole progress of religion has been from polytheism to monotheism."

"And from religious tolerance to wars of religion. Christianity has been the most violent, the most oppressive, the most totalitarian . . ."

Leila paused, searching for a final, sledgehammer adjective. Emma suddenly found their earnestness quite funny. "You're a bigot," she interjected.

Leila caught the new, bantering tone. "Yes," she replied, jauntily cheerful, "But they started it. I'll tolerate Christians, if they'll tolerate me."

"I'm a Christian. I tolerate you."

"Yes; you're a love." Leila reached out her hand, a silver ring on every finger, and lightly touched Emma's upper arm.

Mrs Beckett was waiting for Emma, two doors down outside the Post Office. "What's she done now?" she asked, nodding in the direction of Leila's. "Did she say something to upset the vicar? She's a Satanist, isn't she? It shouldn't be allowed."

Father van Harlem strode up the churchyard path. Parts of St Bride's were arguably Saxon, but the bulk of it was Victorian reconstruction — and that included its most striking feature, the tall, finicky, overdecorated spire.

He was feeling more than usually agitated. Emma, who saw him as an institution not a man, would have been surprised to learn how much she had rattled him. She might even — like Mrs Beckett — have pitied him. Father van Harlem lived in fear of the forces "out there" who regarded him as a medieval relic. He was constantly expecting them to move in for the kill.

It would be half an hour and more before the bell-ringers arrived. He fumbled the gaoler's bunch of Gothick Revival keys out of his cassock pocket, unlocked the door to the spiral stairway in the corner turret of the tower, and began to climb.

His only motive was restlessness. The stairwell was almost completely dark and smelled like an aviary. He trod gingerly, in fear of putting his foot down on something soft. Two complete turns took him to the bell chamber and another quarter turn to the platform above it. The bell chamber was full of shadows and its sleeping dragons made him feel uneasy, but the platform above was an airy loft, with eight foot high, unguarded Gothic windows looking out to the four quarters. He thought of it as his oratory.

The pigeons panicked, beating furiously round the walls. They found the windows and the dust subsided. The hollow interior of the spire rose to a fabulous height above him. He crossed to the northward facing window.

It was very still. The sky was a sickly orange-grey. He was facing the hill that gave the town its name — Sullis Hill — a low, gently-contoured hill, with lower slopes under cultivation and its grassy crown given over to sheep. The farmhouse to the west belonged to the Becketts. To the east, at the edge of their land, was the Ladywell, a near circular pond some fifty foot across. There was a copse at the back of it, enclosing the spring.

....

The window came down to within six inches of the floor. Very carefully, bracing his arms against the sides, he stepped up onto the ledge.

He wasn't going to kill himself; he never actually would; but on occasion — as now — he liked to take himself to the brink. It was his favourite temptation — indeed the only one he ever permitted himself. He explained it as a religious exercise, a way of disdaining the body, of contemplating God.

For God was an abyss like the one he teetered above, only endless, without dimension. He tightened his grip on the stone and leaned out further.

Death was very close now. He looked down. It was nearly a hundred feet to the ground. In his mind's eye he saw, as if he were a spectator on Sullis Hill, his own black-cassocked figure dropping, straight and true as a diver, below the level of the tops of the churchyard trees.

There came a bass note of very distant thunder. He shut his eyes and drew a deep breath, fronting infinity, waiting for the rain.

It bit his ear.

What did?

It did — something that flew past him with the zip of tearing paper. He put his hand to the hurt place and withdrew it with his fingers wet with blood. He swayed in the aperture, panicking, stepped back, and felt his foot catch in the skirt of his cassock. The lunge forward was involuntary. He beat the air with his arms and pedalled with his feet like a pioneer birdman in a Pathé newsreel — but retained enough of his dignity not to scream.

Emma walked up to the boy who was crouching on the short-cropped turf beside the Ladywell. "What *are* you doing?" she asked in her best classroom drawl.

He started. It was pretty obvious what he was doing. He had his elder brother's high-powered air rifle pointed at the church tower. He was one of the Beckett children, a tousled nine-year-old in shorts and his dad's old army surplus pullover.

"Don't you think the pigeons have as much right to life as you do?" she admonished.

He stared at her, wide-eyed. He had just seen something astonishing: a black figure standing in the topmost window of the tower. He had fired at it and it had come flapping out of the window like a gigantic bird of prey. He was shocked and frightened. He couldn't lie.

"There was a Dracula," he said, "I shot him."

She disregarded the obvious untruth, and told him to go home, threatening to tell his mother if she caught him at it again. "And the vicar," she added as an afterthought, remembering that the boy sang in the church choir.

There was a bench beside the pond, and she sat herself down on it as she watched him trail off along the blackberry path to Beckett's Farm, then, satisfied that his retreat was not merely tactical, she turned round to face the water. The spire of St Bride's was quivering at her feet.

Then a tiny breeze, outrider of the coming storm, broke up the reflection. And the bells began.

The slight hiccough that occurred every time the peal jumped over the missing bell reminded her of the injustice to Jane Morrison, of the vicar's icy embarrassment, of his angular figure stalking up the high street, and she thought, "We make God in our own image."

Then froze inwardly, realising that something momentous had happened. The idea took hold of her. Was it something Leila had once said or something she had read or something she had originated herself? She didn't know, but the effect was as if she had tipped over the first in a chain of dominoes. Detached, impassive, she watched the others go down, one by one, changing her life.

Father van Harlem's God is a reflection of Father van Harlem.

I don't like either of them.

....

Yet I give them my support.

Because I am a conformist.

An edgy conformist.

Living up to other people's expectations.

Not any more.

But what would my own God be like?

What am I like?

The pale stonework of the spire stood out against the black sky with surreal clarity. It was a perch for vampires, an aggressive, spiky object in a landscape that rolled, dipped and folded like a woman's body. It was a dagger clenched in a fist, pointing upwards, it was reversed lightning, an emblem of ambition and violence, alien to her now.

She took her purchase from her bag and unwrapped it. The rising wind carried the paper away. She knelt at the edge of the pond and very carefully set the little dish down upon its surface, where it floated, tremulously, like a lotus, her offering to the White Lady. Then the rain began; big, single drops at first and then a battering downpour. The dish rocked, shipped water, tilted and went down.

Your Children

....

AAMER HUSSEIN

I

When my son came home that Wednesday night with the bottle
of blessed water and insisted that we drink a few drops of it each
morning, I threw a fit. For weeks we'd been hearing about our
filthy eating habits, he'd forbid us to eat at Chinese restaurants
and European hotels, he'd lament our lack of hygiene because
occasionally we'd take a soak in salts and no shower after. Not
that I minded any of that. After all, the University's young were
turning *en masse* to more conservative religious forms in
emulation of our always more orthodox neighbours. They'd
say they needed some radical ammunition to combat the cumu-
lative effects of Imperialist-Capitalist-First World-Hegemony
and our own jaded brand of feudal mysticism just wasn't good
enough. But this? Wasn't it too much like the mumbo-jumbo
that I'd seen my mother furtively toy with, huddling in corners
with her maids and her stepmothers? All that religious zeal was
bad enough: I remembered my late father — before his
defection with the bright-eyed Eurasian from Manado —
laughing at its early manifestations. How petit bourgeois can
you get, he'd say, in my town only the bloody shopkeepers said
their prayers and locked up their wives. But this? Indigenous,
perhaps, but downright lower class. — Where, I said, did you
get that, Narto?

I didn't even have to ask. Trimurti, of course, or Ilmuddin
Salam as he calls himself these days. Sheikh Ilmuddin Salam. In
revenge for my having rebuffed him during college days,

because he was the son of a minor concubine of a minor Rajah's son by a minor concubine and I, — in spite of my Dutch veneer — was after all a daughter of the Tjondrokironos?

— Why do you dismiss the Sheikh out of hand, Mama? said Narto. The least you could do is give him a chance.

A chance, to Trimurti? I'll give him this much, he fought his way up through the Department of Letters and got his chair in Arabic philosophy — read esoterisms — but this pose of his, finger wagging and eyes flashing, just doesn't — oh, never trust a Javanese in disguise. Semar playing Krishna, tell me another tale. Two months in Cairo and God and his Holy Angels got him by the throat.

I never drink — well, hardly — but I got up from the table, walked to the cabinet where I keep liqueurs for European arrivals, and retrieved a bottle of Tia Maria that Helge, my translator, had got me from some airport on her last trip along with all the other useless — and alcohol-laden — stuff she always brings to Jakarta. I poured out a thimbleful and gulped it down despite a burning throat. Rather some of this, I said, why don't you join me with your Mahaguru?

— Why, Mama, must you always mock and trivialise?

Yati? My Yati? Screaming at Mama?

Little Yati?

If you haven't read a book by me, you may know me from your TV screen — I'm always on prize-giving and award-donating panels, I've chaired literary quizzes and answered letters from the love-lorn, writing the letters and the answers, let me tell you. My novels, say the young gynocrit-squad ladies at the U, bridge the gap between the feminine romance, the local oral forms, and the Contemporary Western Feminist Novel. Me, I prefer to call my self post-everything. Post-modern, post-colonial, post-feminist. In Paris, I attended seminars by Barthes and Lacan and Levi-Strauss. All men, you might say, but they certainly got the women going with their critiques — phallogocentrism, I think they called it, and I'd go home and tell Hartono that I loved logos more than — we still used to laugh in those days. The children were only tiny then. Yes, you've guessed, you read about it in my novel *The Travails and Trajectories of Dewi Sri*.

Yes, you're right. I'm Sundari Tjondrokirono. At the height of my husband's career I left him because he went off — no, not with another woman, that happened later. Some nascent revolutionary dream or the memory of the patriotic songs of his childhood got to him and he filled the pockets of some radical group that called itself — no, I'll delete that, there may still be relics of those idealistic moments about and I've never been a squealer. He didn't really wait to get into trouble, he just up and skipped off to Holland, I suppose he'd always dreamed of going back since his student days and at the time it was still vaguely fashionable to be Javanese. So I made my life alone, brought up the children on good books, good food and good thoughts, sent them off to Holland every few years to keep in touch with their father and his new Dutch wife Elleke, and relegated my fantasies and my youth to my novels and just got on with living. Sometimes I think it's all in the past, that wild and sometimes wanton dreaming and that yearning and that calling out a name, any name, Hartono, Hartono, with the children sleeping and the Seine outside and some story or the other unfolding somewhere — but I don't think much about it. I'm secular, rationalist, though I confess to a vague curiosity about astrology.

As for God, well. Well, well. He used to be for the old and the poor, now the young and the rich seem to want to acquire him by the bottle.

Yati? You, too?

Did I go wrong somewhere?

Brother and sister chanting in Arabic and swigging holy water and fasting and praying all night. Their sweet tongues

....

corroded with those guttural Arabic sounds. Narto, I'd say, how could you, you know she's always followed your lead. That was when she came home with the veil.

Pale green, soft, really, nothing like those horrors you see on certain women, she'd draped it lightly around her head and you could see the hair on her forehead and her temples. I cover my head sometimes, too, when I'm cold, but this — it has connotations.

I died.

— Mama, says Narto, where have you been living? Yati found the Sheikh. She took me to see him. She said we had a hole in our lives that called for faith. You should hear him, some time, Mama. He says that all faiths are one and they all lead to one face — His. He says that the Imperialists have lost the way because their systematic exploitation of the weak has sapped their morality. He says the Buddhists have turned away from the violence of war by denying its reality and their own collusion and participation in this reality. They've turned inward to contemplate the void but the nature of serving God is to love your neighbour by serving him or her with your life if you have to make the world a better place. He says that the Muslims too have suffered a loss of faith because we've battled each other and compromised and betrayed our beliefs but there's always the One Text and the Words of the Saints to guide us back to the real road. He says that each one of us can find salvation in his religion and our religion, Mama, is Islam. He says that the blind can't read the Koran until a sudden light illuminates the text and then those cryptic words that hide their truth from us become clear.

— Old gods with new faces, I retorted, old shadows on a new screen.

— You're so good at making fun of everything you don't believe in, said Yati. That's the way you handle your liberalism — with mockery and despair.

....
31

That night I had a strange dream. I saw the back of a man in a green turban, standing in my living room, looking at the books I'd brought home from my father's house in Yogyakarta. I stood behind him for a moment: he was oblivious of me. Tri, I said, or should I call you Ilmuddin? Why do you want to take my children away?

Your children are not your children, I heard a voice saying, but it didn't seem to be his, it seemed to emanate from the walls. I knew the words from somewhere, some half-forgotten and unfashionable philosophical tract, perhaps, but something stopped me from delving into the streams at the outer edges of my consciousness to retrieve the floating paper memory. Trimurti turned. But it wasn't Trimurti at all: in the half-light, I could have sworn that the face on that tall, swaying body, so different from his, was my son's, but before I had time to cry out, I was awake and sweating.

The next morning I knew what I had to do. Hartono had been pestering me for ages to send the children to Europe: it wasn't, he said, that he wanted to keep an eye on them in their early adulthood, but with his resources and with Elleke teaching at the University (she taught classical Javanese, would you believe) and so on, he couldn't understand why the young ones shouldn't spend some time under his auspices, perfecting their English and checking out the colleges and the courses they had on offer. I'd always said that our country was developing and its universities needed all the support they could get: if the children went out later to do post-graduate degrees, they'd not only show how far we'd gone in terms of educational progress but also have the firmer, truer sense of that perplexing, demanding reality that our somewhat one-sided education had denied us. Then, of course, there was the problem of the language; studying in English would certainly be an incredible advantage to them, but wasn't it necessary for our rapidly expanding national language to be absorbed at a higher level, so that its students, while learning its neologisms, could also help in its growth and extension? Like any man he held that I wanted to keep them close to me and that I didn't even bother to deny, it was at some level true, but hadn't I given them the opportunity to expose themselves to all sorts of opposing and contradictory ideologies, they could after all have become capitalists or communists and not embryonic religiosos.

Well, now was the time: they could always go out for a year to study English at some theoretical and advanced level. Yati hadn't ever got on very well with her father and cordially despised her stepmother, but surprisingly she was the one who seemed most sanguine about the proposal, and Narto followed her lead, in that strange and baffling reversal of their normal emotional contract that seemed to be evident now.

II

Mama:
When I think of home, it's not Jakarta I remember, but grandfather's home in Yogyakarta. That chicken we used to eat with our fingers, soaked in the taste of jackfruit, sticky rice we licked off our fingers and those small hot chillies to balance the sweetness. The food here is terrible, but we've found a Malay hostel where we can get a decent meal — not marvellous, but all right. Elleke doesn't cook much. On the third night after our arrival she said she'd make some Nasi Goreng and we were curious to see how she'd handle it. Yati went into the kitchen to see if she could help her — which she doesn't much like, anyway — and she was decorating the rice with slices of meat from a cellophane packet. What's that, asked Yati. Ham, of course, came the answer. But we don't eat ham, said Yati, or any other form of pork — So move it, said Elleke, and eat the other stuff. There's lots of prawns and vegetables and egg in there.

We couldn't do that.

....

Papa said in Bahasa, as if Elleke couldn't understand — Come on kids, it won't kill you, your mother used to feed it to you when you were kids — Is that true, Mama? Did you feed us pork in Paris?

We have the same sort of problem in the lavatory. There's no bidet and I took an old vinegar bottle I'd scavenged from the kitchen so that we could keep ourselves clean but in a day or so it had disappeared. I found another one and hid it behind the loo. Elleke decided to have it out with me. This isn't Jakarta, you know, she said. There isn't anyone here to mop up your spills. I kicked that last bottle over, drenched the carpet and nearly broke my leg. Can't you just have a bath if you're so fastidious about your body? God knows you aren't a terribly tidy pair.

She says everything with a sort of indulgent smile and I can see her point in a way I suppose, but Mama, there isn't a shower in the bathroom and you have to soak yourself in a bath. I can get away with sneaking a glass in to wash my body off with after soaking but she's got some sort of obsession about water. One drop anywhere drives her crazy. And Yati's veil. You should see how she handles that. On Sunday morning she came down to breakfast in jeans with a plain white scarf on her head and Elleke gave her that saccharine smile and said: Yetty (that's how she pronounces it), Yetty darling, you should lose some weight before you put on such tight things. Your bottom is far too big and when you wear that scarf — it looks so incongruous and it does rather defeat the point somehow, don't you think?

Yati handles Elleke far better than I do. She's found some sympathetic 'sisters' in college and a girl from Kelantan took her to an Indian shop where she bought herself yards of stuff which they stitched up into an adapted *sarong kebaya*, matching and loose and flowing, so you should see Yati now, she looks a bit like a colourful nun. She says she feels good about it, distinctive somehow, as if she's painted on the parameters of her identity and people know how far to go with her. She calls it her gentle armour.

Yati's generally more resourceful than I am. She's found herself a prayer group and a discussion group and she attends classes in history and political theory because she says faith should be intellectual as well as visceral and in any case this ex-centre of empire segregates discourses and it's all-important for us as Javanese and Indonesians to introduce ourselves into the discussion rather than to hide in corners pleading cultural distinction or adopt Arab gestures and rituals in some kind of false identification of Arab culture with Islam. You should see the debates that go on in abandoned college classrooms, in cafés and in hostels and even on the pavements on the street. We were used to hearing our Muslim companions criticising the capitalist way as detrimental to spiritual progress: here you can meet people who praise dictators and kings who squash their poor because they deal in the letter of the law and follow the precepts of the faith. Our Shaikh always called those leaders semi-infidels; he said they were just as much to blame for our plight today as those radical innovators who told us to throw away all our good beliefs along with the old superstitions and pushed the kind of nationalism down our throat that fostered isolation from our brothers and identification with satanic powers. Of course in Ilmuddin Salam's terms satan — I emphasise the small s — is only a metaphor for those powers we carry within ourselves that reflect and continue the evil powers contained in the universe and released through acts of war and injustice and violence.

Other groups analyse Islam in terms of politics of a semi-Marxist sort, picking up the flaws in all debates and filling in the gaps with enlightened sayings from the Koran and other, later texts. Sometimes I feel they sound too much like the bigots they criticise, but I can see their point; they say that since economics determine our wordly consciousness, we're trapped in a prison

....

of spiritual poverty that is a symptom of our abject position in the hierarchy of power.

After one meeting — we were addressed by a European scholar — I met a Swedish girl who's doing her PhD in Islamic studies. She asked me out for a coffee because she wanted Indonesian perspectives on Islam. We fell into the way of meeting once or even twice a week and the third week she said she'd cook something for me. I went to her house — a hundred miles away from Papa's house, it seemed, in a suburb of unpainted doors and untrimmed hedges. She laid out some dips that were tasty and filling though they were cold and I felt like something hot, but then she brought out some meatballs with nuts in them that were quite delicious. We drank coffee and she told me the story of her life. She's in her late twenties and already divorced.

I spoke a little bit about our life at home, Mama, about you and Yati and the house and the college and Rendra's recitals. When I came to the situation here at Papa's I hesitated: you know how you've always said that I seemed to be more grandmother's child than yours with my Javanese reticence whereas you and Yati had inherited some gene that made grandfather such an outspoken extrovert. But talking about one's intimate experiences hurts; and Europeans have a way of picking up what's unsaid and assuming somehow that you're hiding it all from your self, which of course I'm not. She spoke of my life in terms of paternal deprivation and maternal domination and said that I longed for order and authority and that was the reason I'd become a neo-Muslim, but the natural gentleness of my personality took me towards a father substitute who was less abrasive than the beliefs he represented. I've never really looked upon Ilmuddin as a father substitute and her interpretation — it's what the Sheikh would call over-interpretation, or the danger of agnostic theory — somehow seems to leave out Yati and her reactions which are similar at least in their essence to mine.

It was midnight when we finished talking. She said I'd better stay the night and began rummaging in her cupboard for blankets while I, in some trepidation of their reaction, dialled Papa and Elleke's number — I'd never stayed out so late before and certainly never all night. Elleke answered. Her tone was irritated but tolerant. She said that Papa'd begun to panic because he thought that in these rough times and rough places I might have been taken for an Indian with my dark skin and attacked by hoodlums. She said she'd explained to him that I must be hanging out with one chapter or another of the Muslim brethren and decided to stay over. I wish, she said, that you'd find a girlfriend — I almost wondered whether she'd guessed that I was with a girl.

Viveca — my friend's name — called out to me to help her carry out some pillows from her bedroom. She'd already changed, she wore pyjamas, so unlike your silk nightgowns or Yati's. Her bed was unmade and littered with clothes. She's not very tall for a Scandinavian but Mama, she's almost my height. As I reached for the pillows she stood behind me I could feel her brown hair brush my face and her breath, too.

— If you like, she said, you can just pop into my bed.

I always thought popping in meant dropping in to visit someone. I suppose that's what I did. I visited her. A strange country. Her eyes are green and big. She was surprised that I had hair on my chest and legs because my hands are nearly hairless and she'd thought that all Javanese were smooth. At first I was nervous, too impetuous to cover my inexperience, but she saw me through. In the morning I was shy of her but she was already in the kitchen spreading the remains of last night's supper dips on biscuits and toast. Hi, she said when I walked in, The kettle's boiling. Just take down some cups and make some coffee. There's tea, too, if that's what you prefer.

It's funny, Mama, she always says: would you prefer some coffee? Would you prefer a biscuit? without adding another clause. I can't correct her, her English is otherwise so much

....

better than mine. But you've passed on your love of words to me, Mama, of sentences and their structure and syntax. It's the meanings that I worry about now, though, and I can't seem to get to the meaning of this relationship. We certainly don't have a future. At the moment I'm not even sure I want to stay on here to attend college when I've done my English certificate. So I keep on writing to you in my head or on scraps of paper or in this notebook that I keep by my pillow with the title *Letters to Mama*, knowing these are things I can't admit to you in the formal Javanese missives you seem to receive from me every Wednesday morning, but telling you about them seems to clear my head, even though you may not know what I'm talking about. Because I know that you would have an answer that would help me to decide even in contradiction to you.

What do they say in Jakarta about this war, Mama? You should hear the students at school, in the cafeteria, in the mosque. Some of them believe Saddam is our friend, our brother, even our saviour. Others defend America: after all, they say, whatever its reasons, you can't justify the invasion of a tiny country by a superior power and America has at least led the world to fulfil its moral obligations. Brothers fight with each other over the ethical and the political issues of the war. I wonder what our Ilmuddin would say: sometimes I feel that his lessons were too gentle, too mild, and I have to search within myself for answers. One thing's for certain: it isn't a Muslim war. You should hear the different Arab groups in conflict with each other, not to mention the Iranians and the Indians and the Pakistanis.

When I first went to the mosque, I found it strange to say my prayers surrounded by so many different races. There's a massive group of Africans and you can see Lebanese and Cypriots and Syrians so blond and blue-eyed I took them at first for European converts to Islam. Then I thought of it as a kind of universal fraternity of Muslims and suspended that nagging historical question I'd always asked myself: Is it our

....

religious beliefs that have exposed us to ridicule, subjugation, decadence, and loss of identity? And I opted instead for a waking dream — perhaps this fraternity, paralleled by the sorority I see among Yati's group of Muslim women, veiled and unveiled, black, brown or white — I thought that may be the answer; no, not the answer but an answer, the suspension of national and ethnic differences in search of common causes, united within a newly-defined frontierless land of Islam, an Islam free of the despotism derived from centuries of subjection and distortion.

But what can you say when after our Friday prayers the groups separate — the Gulf people and the pro-America Egyptians and some Lebanese, walk away swearing at the Iraqis and damning the Palestinians? Even the Arabs themselves — the thinking ones — accept however quietly the abdication of their peoples from the leadership of the Muslims. The Muslim dream, Mama, has no country, except in our hearts. Mama, this isn't even a question of religion — it touches for me the question of the very nature of God. In our arguments — Yati is always more vociferous than I am — the Chinese and the Indians seem to be more logical than some of us. Then, again, divided in their opinions, but I'm talking about the ones who stand against the war. It's a Third World Cause, they shout, it could be us tomorrow, and loving Saddam doesn't come into it, he may be the butcher he's said to be but surely he's a creation of these very monsters that are now out to destroy him? So. It's a question of nations and peoples and economics but our faith seems to be trapped in the middle of it all. You should hear some of the stuff on television, Mama, even Papa nearly got sick the other night into his whisky when an interviewer rounded up some Muslims and pushed them to reject the reasons for war — and you know what the outcome was? Over-interpretation again. You should have heard the men they chose, Mama, none of them defended Saddam, but the interviewer announced at the end that there was an Islamic fifth column in the heart of this country that was out to subvert the very basis of its democratic and egalitarian rules. And all they'd said was that the systematic destruction of any country by an amassed confederacy of superpowers was excessive in these times. It was wrong to bring religion into it, Mama, wrong of this man and wrong of the warmongers who call upon us to kill each other in the name of God.

We have learned to confuse countries with their ideologies and the spirit of people with the doctrines of their rulers, Viveca said. She supports my ambivalent stand against the war, though she says it has as much to do with her own European guilt about the cold use of advanced technology in the name of just causes as it does with her fascination with the heritage of Islam and the Arab culture and language that she still holds lie at its centre.

As for me, Mama, I continue to believe in that dream enclosed in the song you used to sing to us, about a world without nations or borders, but while these borders exist what can we do but shoulder the distinctions imposed upon us by history and race and culture and all those externals beyond our control, what can we do but examine them and extract from them what we can to make sense of our lives? I don't know if my religion is part of my identity or my identity has been written into my religion so long ago that it's impossible to extricate myself from its demands without tearing myself apart.

Mama:
Ours is a group that has united in spite of its differences to call out for an end to war. The snow is thick on the ground and yet we stand here in protest against injustice. Today we stand together under the banner of what some of us may choose to call the message of the eternal God and others may defend as the abstract principles that we believe emanate from Him. But today, Mama, it doesn't matter. Do you remember those old Javanese poems that spoke of the dwelling-place of God? Viveca showed me a strand running right through the utterances

of the mystics that say there's no need to visit the Holy Places, no need to kiss the Black Stone of Mecca, if he lives in your heart.

Mama, the speakers come from all walks of life, there's a Kurd asking us not to use his people's name as another tool of exchange, and a Christian woman with an accent I can hardly understand whose main concern is the survival of the children and a youth from the North of this country whose seventeen-year-old brother has gone to the war and may die. Suspend ideologies, they seem to say even as they dissect the beliefs that fuel these conflicts and the materialistic non-beliefs that lie behind them. Viveca is weeping. Yati has clapped so hard that her brown face has reddened with emotion. The snow flakes fall on our bare heads as we seek shelter under dripping trees. The city is almost silent — snowdrifts so deep have formed that walking is a hazard. And yet we walk, and yet we stand, and we stand here in the biting wind and we march to light a fire of justice and to extinguish the fire of war . . .

There's a large gang of men approaching, Mama. We can hear their voices in the distance, coming closer, at first we think it may be a chant against the war but it sounds like a drunken litany of names, it's menacing somehow, threatening, they come closer, it's a group of men, some of them carry bottles and flags, there's a strong smell of drink emanating from them, they're drinking, Mama, and shouting the names of some places I don't know, Viveca grips my arm, her fingers are urgent, I can make out some of their words now, it's a confused diatribe, Butchers, Wogs, Muslims, Sodom, Sod'em, Fuck black bastards, Ay-Rabs, we don't want your sort here.

Who began the fight, Mama? They're attacking us with bottles. The Palestinian group has taken charge of us, they're forming a barricade against the intruders. Members of one of the left-wing

....

41

groups have moved forward too, parrotting the ugly sounds of the green-clad gang with new words. Two men have gone down already, and there's a strange knot of three men on their feet, heads together, entangled hideously. A bleeding youth has grabbed his adversary's bottle and is attacking at random, determined to draw blood for blood. Where are the upholders of the law, Mama? Are they on some hidden margin of our small demonstration, protecting some other splintered group? Our assailants have grabbed a girl, Mama, and torn off her scarf. She's struggling but from where I am I can smell her fear. I move forward. Viveca restrains me. Stop, screams the pressure of her fingers. But Yati's broken away, she's running towards her friend, she's kicking at an attacker, look, Mama, she's bleeding, I've got to go, there's a knife flashing somewhere, I've got to go, Viveca's with me though I try to push her back, I'm nearly there, Mama, Yati, O, Yati, she's bleeding, someone has me from behind, I don't know whose bodies these are, pressing against me, I push against them at random, here I am, Mama, nearly there, a hand grabs my hair, someone's stinking mouth on my face, take this, wog bastard, a kick in the small of my back, I'm struggling, a fist in my teeth, Mama, something's bursting, I can hear the explosion in my head, I smash at my adversary, feel hard bone splintering under my fist, help me, my sister's pinned under one of them on the ground, bottles fly all around us, a knee in my belly, in my ribs, I'm face to face with my killer, yes Mama, I'm bleeding inside, a bitter liquid fills my mouth, Mama, Yati, Viveca all fading, I fall into someone's arms, I recognise her smell, Mama, I'm gone

III

When you heard the news, Sundari — when you heard the news, did you weep, did you hold your belly and cry, did you call for your son or your daughter or your dead mother? No,

....

Sundari, you were encircled, the servants were around you and you strangled your grief, spoke in the cold sombre tones you knew so well from your mother, and told them the young golden master was dead, your only son dead by violence, and your choked tears flowed from the eyes of the old cook you had brought with you from Yogyakarta, and you had to comfort her.

When you are alone, Sundari, what do you do, do you mourn, do you moan, do you ask yourself what you did wrong, will you turn to the spirits of the trees or your dead or the ancestors or that God you never called out to for succour? No, Sundari, strong Sundari, there are preparations to be made, prayers to be murmured for the peace of the dead, strangers or intimates to be fed at feasts, you must stand, don't sit down, when they weep you must hold them, strong Sundari.

If the woman from your son's life comes to you, Sundari — you know she has travelled here in search of the relics of her lost lover — if she comes to you, will you receive her, will you take her in your arms, will you stand across the room and ask for the true story from her reddened eyes, will you ask her if by some small chance she carries your son's last breath in her body, will you beg fortune to let there be a child?

And you must tell your own story, Sundari. You must write it all down. My voice — maybe I'm the woman from the North, carrying your son's words to you in a language I have translated from the gaps and the silences that surrounded him. Or maybe I'm the daughter who hasn't come back to you, compelling you to drown in the rejected rituals of your past, which you must follow because you have no other choice. Or maybe I'm the man who led your son away, come to tell you that your daughter is waiting for you at the door, begging you to take her in your arms, to accept her pain, to let her comfort you — my voice can only echo the hollow centre of your echo, none of us can tell your story, Sundari, only you can.

....

43

The man you used to call Trimurti came to see you. You were calm; you met him with your mask so close to your skin that your bones beneath it were on fire. Sundari, he said, I have come with my condolences. I know how you must feel, that your son's body was buried in a foreign country, so far away. You know how much I loved him, he was like a son to me. You know you can say he died a martyr's death. Fighting the evil Kauravas who were tearing off Draupadi's veil. He died with the name of Allah on his lips. (How Javanese. Even in the midst of his exhortations to prayer — yes, I knew they would follow his condolences — he weaves a garland of *wayang* allusions around his words, you said to yourself.)

— You must say a prayer for his soul, Sundari, he said. It doesn't matter if you don't remember the words or know their meanings. It will give you release.

— Your holy men have done all that, you said. And all the prayers in all the holy texts wouldn't give me peace. I can't even face the anger that's ripping me into shreds. An innocent boy beaten to death because his skin is a shade too dark. How can I understand? Is this what the All-Powerful does for his children?

— He died for his beliefs, Sundari. For insisting on believing when all avenues were closed. You should talk to Yati, she'll tell you. After all, they're your children — ask yourself where their conviction came from . . .

Yati?

— My Yati? Here in Jakarta?

— Yes, Yati is with me, Sundari. She doesn't want to live abroad and she doesn't want to study, at least not for now. She's going to teach for a while in my garden school.

— But how can she teach when she can't even speak Arabic or read the Koran?

Trimurti smiled. — She doesn't teach religious texts, he said. Though believe me she makes a perfectly good job of reading them. I'd been teaching her for a while before she left and when she was away she made some progress with a Malay group. But

....

she's not going to teach the Koran, not now. There are women who come in from the villages to study along with their children. They just want to learn to read. Yati's path, she says, is service, to women and their children, and you can help her by understanding her. Each one of us has our own path to follow: illumination lies in finding it within ourselves and tracing its trajectory in the world. Narto found his, and Yati . . . (First he sent your son to madness on his path, and then he steals your daughter. If you weren't in so much agony you'd remain silent, but you can't.)

— Yati is young enough to be your daughter, you say. You should be ashamed of yourself. Is that what you wanted all along?

— Take a hold of yourself, Sundari, she is like a daughter to me, and only one of many. Think deeply. When you were her age you used to think that the radical parties would show us all the light and even Java could be abandoned in the name of their ideologies. Even today you cherish most of your old beliefs while you call them by new names. Look at Yati. The language is ancient — or new — but what she wants, is it really any different from what you wanted? And as for my influence in their lives, Sundari, it's significantly less than yours. Both of us are only the reflections of their dreams, you and I, and in the end less than nothing.

That night you dreamed that you were following Narto in a field, he was far ahead of you but his feet had left a trail of blood that glowed so red in the darkness you could trace his path. Your feet were torn and you were tired. Every so often he would look around but when you waved he didn't see you, he seemed to be searching for someone behind you. He walked on. You were sweating, weeping with fatigue. You must have walked miles.

You followed him to the sea, to the rocks above the sea. He walked on. Was he looking for a boat? Would he . . . Narto, you

. . . .

can't swim, you tried to call to him, but he didn't listen. Fully dressed, he strode into the waves, without looking back.

When you woke up you were exhausted on some alien shore, drenched to the bone in salt spray, old before your time. Your urban bed had become a burning beach.

Then one day your daughter finally came to see you: your Yati, thin now, a woman. She was living in Trimurti's establishment; she was teaching her women and their children, basket-weaving, pottery, painting, reading, English. Dressed in the clothes of your region, she'd loosened her veil so that her appearance was less severe than the plump, white-scarfed visage of the girl to whom you'd said goodbye.

You offered her tea and biscuits. You didn't know what you could say to her; she faltered when she spoke to you. Both of you so Javanese, able to communicate in ritual gestures, until the cook came in. Seeing the withered face, Yati's lips trembled; when she left the room Yati wept, for her dead brother and all the dead in the riots and the curfews and the partitions and the wars and for the mothers and sisters and brothers and fathers and lovers who'd never wanted them to go, she wept for herself and for you.

You took her in your arms. You had to. When she stayed with you in your bed that night you knew you'd been cast again in that role of comfort-giver, sorrow-bearer, love-dispenser. In your dreams you'd waited for her to come and be your mother, to hold your grief in her arms, to cradle you.

But that didn't happen. And she stayed on with you: travelled to her villages for a day or two, went to her religious groups and her prayer meetings, read her books, fell into her old routines. At home she'd even wear her old skirts and jeans and walk about with her hair loose, forgetting her scarves in her bedroom.

She never talked about Narto. You wondered if she ever saw Viveca: you imagined she was still here though she'd never

....

attempted to contact you, and you knew Yati must have been familiar with her, if not intimate, for Narto's sake. A last link, to those misspent European winter days. But for you, the dead and Saddam and the war were never to be approached in words.

It was a Tuesday. Forty days tomorrow since the hatred and innocence took your son's life on that terrible foreign evening. Yati came to you: she said Mama, will you pray with me for him? You know he'd want that.

Narto?

Can you hear me?

Walking through the rocks into the waves and the green of the fields gleaming with the red of your dreams?

You were moved. Not the Sheikh, but you. The mother-renegade who'd forgotten how to pray, if she'd ever known.

— You'll have to tell me what to say, you said, I don't know the words.

She draped her head in green. She read the prayers out loud and you sat beside her: her voice was low and soft as she said the alien words that you couldn't even read and you parroted them, remembering them from some forgotten time of mindless repetition, unaware of their significance.

Suddenly, from some ancient depths, her voice:

All things come from the One, and to the One they will return. And then you wept, Sundari, and your daughter, your double, your twin, your Yati, I took you in my arms and I wept with you as our faces in the mirror of our story became one.

Doomed Survivors:
A Reconstruction in 2 Voices

URSULE MOLINARO

I know I've come to Mexico to get myself murdered. By 1 or several of the local men I sleep or slept with. Whom I outrage when I demand the same one-sided fidelity they demand of me. Of any woman.

They'd be more outraged if they knew that I compare the length/diameter/coloring of their penises the way they compare the slits & tits of all the *gringas* whose fiancé they claim to be, for each turn of a screw.

My comparisons are more interesting than their boastful inventories. They're better worded, & I write them down. Miniature profiles of Mexican society, based on parallels between these men's treatment of me & other *gringas* & the attention they lavish on their instrument.

Spiced with a touch of humor. Which is considered blasphemy by the priests of phallus worship. They don't know that I send amusing descriptions of my miserable love life off to friends in New York, but they sense my irreverence, & it fills them with a dark rage.

The same primal indignation that may have killed the much maligned Malinche, the native interpreter of Hernán Cortéz. Who called her his "tongue".

Perhaps.

Probably. What but a rub-out killing can explain the silence that suddenly cloaks her life, or her death, after she turns 24?

After nearly a decade of blatant news coverage.

Not by Cortéz, who vaguely mentions *una india* in his careful letters to his king. Whose immense national debt he was paying off with the spoils from a devastated distant civilization. But Moctezuma's reporters — her "own" people — depict her tirelessly. Standing beside or behind Cortéz — taller & larger than Cortéz, i.e. more important than Cortéz; to them — pointing an interpreting finger toward intent Aztec messengers who stare at her from the gaping mouths of jaguar heads. Listening to her rephrase the many promises Cortéz makes & the many reasons he gives for breaking them during his rodeo conquest of Mexico.

& her command of Spanish is tirelessly praised by the priests who accompany Cortéz on his Christian mission. & save the Christian conquerors from the mortal sin of copulating with heathens by hurriedly baptizing the native women who are given to them as appeasement presents. Or who are part of the spoils.

The future interpreter is 1 of 20 such appeasement presents, when he first lands. She is 14, & beautiful. & the only one who speaks Nahuatl (Aztec) as well as Mayan. She learns Spanish, *el lenguaje divino*, in 2 weeks.

I refuse to learn Spanish. Why should I learn it? I'm too old for that sort of thing. Besides, not speaking the local language makes me seem exotic. As well as open season.

I learned very proper English in America. After learning very proper French in France. I refuse to become tri-lingual to make mono-lingual macho fiancés feel more at home. They might respect me more — become more faithful? — if I could speak Spanish with them, but I'd lose my foreign-lady-traveler mystery veil. I'd become like their own less accessible women. It would accentuate my flaw.

Cortéz has his interpreter baptized: Doña Marina. The

eloquence of beauty, rising from collective memory on a giant seashell. A brilliant tongue riding an ear.

Perhaps Cortéz had his tongue silenced by his faithful captain Juan Jamarillo — the lawful husband he assigned to her after he himself tired of sleeping with her — because he feared her eloquence at his trial in Spain. Before his now-again-solvent, most-Christian king, who was showing less gratitude than might have been expected. His "tongue" had witnessed every step of his laborious triumph. Every hanging he had ordered. Every burning alive. Every cut-off pair of hands &/or feet. Every gem in his loot.

— Perhaps even the alleged murder of his first allegedly asthmatic wife, whom jealous stay-at-homes rumored he had choked to death.

I was flawed as a little Jewish girl during the Nazi occupation of France. My mother walked out on me, into the ovens, after shoving me inside a closet when she heard boots coming up the stairs.

My father was out at the time. When he returned, he rolled me into a blanket, & walked with me for what seemed days, deep into the countryside, to the house of a peasant family who promised to hide me. Because: they said: I was beautiful, & bright, like the Christchild who had also been a little Jew.

Malinche survived the devastation of her country as the interpreter of that devastation. & has been accused of "malinchismo" ever since. A word coined for her alleged betrayal of "her own people" to an alien power-beast. A centaur with hair on his furrowed larva face, whose "whore" she allegedly became.

Who are your "own" people, Malinche? Doña Marina? The Aztecs who took Cortéz to be a Toltec god, returning in anger, displeased with the Aztec brutalization of his worship? Which stipulated the number of cactus thorns to be pushed through the tongue of a sinner.

A returning god who killed populations in order to eradicate individual human sacrifice.

Your parents named you Malinali. Which your father caressed into Malinche. The name of your snow-capped northern volcano.

A name of respect which your own people extended to their conqueror, the man they always saw by your side. They called Cortéz: Don Malinche.

& they called the Spanish soldier whom Cortéz assigned to guard you your 24-hour jailer, who watched you sleep & wash & shit & menstruate; except when Cortéz ordered you to his bed; which he didn't do right away Juan Malinche.

It was winter. I caught a cold that developed into an ear infection. That made me scream so wildly, the peasants feared we'd be discovered. They silenced me with warmed-up *gnole* (onion brandy), while my father went in search of penicillin.

An illegal shadow, who would be scooped off to the death camps if spotted, trying to buy a scarce new drug reserved for the infections of the occupying conquistadores. By the time he returned, my infection had made a handsized indentation into my left cheek. I'm still beautiful on the right, & scarred & deaf on the left.

& very bright in between. Brighter than he was: my father kept repeating to me. To challenge my self-disgust with the obligation to "survive."

You're more intelligent than he was at your age: your father tells you. He wants you to study the administration of the land, in order to succeed him as a *cacique*. Since he has no son. & yours is 1 of the rare 16th-century communities that lets women be almost the equals of men. It also lets them do almost all the

....

51

work. But then he walks out on your life, when he dies of a snakebite, when you're 11.

Your mother teaches you to sew feather capes. The dusty smell of dead feathers nauseates you. She disciplines you for mismatching colors. Because she loves you, & wants to teach you her taste.

After your father dies, you feel like a stranger in the house where you were born.

Still, you're shocked when your mother tells you that she has made arrangements to sell you into slavery. To which she feels entitled. She made you. You're her property.

Meanwhile she has also made a son, with your father's brother. A baby *cacique*, who is to succeed your father.

You're flawless merchandise. A 12-year-old virgin. Ideal to have your heart cut out, & offered, still beating, to the sabre-toothed Chac-Mol.

However, human sacrifice is not practiced in your region. Paynala is far away from Moctezuma's City on the Lakes. Where human sacrifice increases as the prophets announce the return of an angry Toltec god.

Your mother is not particularly religious. She is practical. She needs the cocoa beans she has been offered for you by a Mayan farmer, who is the *cacique* of Tobasco.

Your new owners welcome you. In Mayan. They tell you that they love you like the daughter they would have liked to have. You quickly learn what they are saying. You need to understand the masters of your life. You please the wife, sewing feather capes. She praises your subtle feeling for color. You please the father, whom you help with the administrative duties of a *cacique*. He praises your intelligence.

& your beauty, as you please him also in his bed. How can you refuse to please him. You are his slave.

You're 14 now, & you also please your owner's son. Who pleases you back. & wants to marry you.

Which does not please your owner. Who also owns his son, &

sends him away to fight intruders from a hostile tribe. You wait
for his return, until you hear that he has died.

You also hear that alien beast-men with hairy faces have
landed on your shores. & that they may be messengers from a
dissatisfied god.

The wife who loves you like the daughter she would have
liked to have takes you to them. In secret. Behind her husband's
back. She's giving you your freedom: she tells you: The rest of
your life is up to you.

I was born unfree, as a Jewish baby in an antisemitic land &
time. I've never felt free anywhere since, despite my criticized
"free" lifestyle.

The peasants who hid me were kind enough. I guess I was a
meal ticket, but they were risking their own freedom for me.
Their farm. Maybe their lives. The woman even claimed that
she loved me like the daughter she would have liked to have.
But I was stuck in their house like a prisoner, watched over by
the woman's old father. A toothless skull with frog eyes, above
a caved-in torso that made baby motions with its arms & hands.

In America I was hailed as a survivor. & solicited as an object
of much tolerance & compassion. A worthy cause. Until I
discovered sex, which became my only if only temporary relief
from survival pains, & my initially enthusiastic teachers began
begrudging the refugee nymphomaniac her brilliant grades.

Still, I graduated with honors. & an unsuspecting faculty
quickly offered me a job as a teacher. — Who was soon
suspended, however, for failing to appreciate that sleeping with
one's students remains a male prerogative.

& Mexico is just another prison. Though of my choosing.
Staffed with judges, & censors, & righteous matrons.

This morning I was at the market, buying forbidden fruit —
apples, which are supposed to stop diarrhea — when a woman
crossed herself at the sight of me. Perhaps because of the blouse
I was wearing. Black silk, strewn with white geckos. Geckos are

considered good luck here, but they may have looked like ghosts to the woman. The ghosts of little dead children.

Unless, of course, she was crossing herself at the sight of my cheek. Although flaws seem to shock Mexicans less than Americans, or Europeans.

Even the local studs don't make me feel free. Although I'm their sex vacation. Actually, *they* are *mine*. Which I've been tempted to tell them sometimes. So far I haven't.

You are 1 of 20 women & girls led to the beast-men who may be gods. You watch them from behind a cluster of bushes. You see the top part of 1 of the creatures rear up & jump to the ground. & walk beside the 4-footed bottom part, on 2 very human-looking legs & feet. With the intelligence that surpasses that of your father you deduce that: they are 2 separate creatures. 1 beast, 1 man.

Bestial men, perhaps. With hair in strange places. But not all that different from the men of your "own" people. Although they neither speak nor understand Aztec. Or Mayan. You're not particularly religious, but enough to know that they can't be gods, because gods speak & understand all languages.

Then you reconsider when you hear 1 of them say something in Mayan. But to an Aztec, who can't understand him. You giggle, & come out from behind your bush to tell the Aztec what the strange man is saying in Mayan. Which you translate into Aztec, your treacherous mother tongue.

You've drawn attention to yourself. The Mayan-speaking stranger takes you to his leader. A hollow-eyed man who inspects you with pursed-lipped interest. & finds you potentially useful. He signals another stranger in a robe who pours water over your head. The leader says: Marina. The robed stranger repeats: Ma-ri-na. Ma—ri—na.

Meanwhile, another stranger has been watching you. With a different interest. He looks younger than the leader, especially around the eyes. Which have a touch of laughter as he claims you as his concubine, wet hair & all, & hoists you up on his beast.

Perhaps the laughing Spanish captain Puertocarrero feels like an adventure to you. Rather than a new master. Unlike your Mayan master, whose pleasure was a part of your chores. Or even his abruptly deceased son.

Perhaps.

You're Marina now. That's what your new lover calls you. You're a new person, in a new Spanish dress, which he puts on your body, playfully, as though you were a doll. You quickly learn his language as you ride with him. Or lie beside him during long hours of pillow talk. You point to your hands your nose his mouth, & he tells you the Spanish word, & kisses you as you repeat & retain it. He is proud of you. & of his teaching. You are the only *india* to speak *el lenguaje divino*. Which may have felt like your language of love. He takes you to Cortéz to show you off.

& instantly regrets it. With Spanish you have become a real "tongue". Now Cortéz can use you directly, without the intermediary of his only-Mayan-speaking Spanish interpreter. He sends your lover on a mission back to Spain, & keeps you by his side. You are his parrot, obediently repeating your conqueror's words. You never see your lover again.

Eventually you also share your conqueror's bed. & make a son with him. Cortéz's first son Martín, named after his father. Later, he makes another Martín, with a legitimate Spanish wife. His second wife, after the choking to death of the asthmatic first one.

By then, you, too, are legitimately married. To your conqueror's most loyal captain Juan Jamarillo. Who may or may not have strangled you to death, on January 24, 1529. After 5 years of conjugal cohabitation.

You're 24, & you're never mentioned again.

Centuries later, certain historians claim that you betrayed "your own people" out of your mad passion for a brutal genius.

....

They make your brief life into a love story, because senti-mentality is the other face of violence.

Or else they claim that you became an ardent Christian. & did what you did because you wanted to convert "your own people" to the true faith you had found. Which you could not have done without "betraying" them first.

Lately, a few are coming to your defense. They call you the great maligned Malinche. A linguist, inadvertently yoked to a maniac, whose words would have been the gesticulations of a deaf-mute, without the help of your tongue.

Which you were in no position to withhold, unless you wished to die another one of the many torture deaths your conqueror made you rationalize to his victims.

Perhaps you were a survivor.

Perhaps you also took pride in your craft.

I have wished many times that my mother had not saved me. For the horrible ear infection at the peasants' house.

Or that the ear infection had not stopped short of my brain. Saving me for star-billing in this freakshow that is my life.

But I'm a survivor. Against historical odds. & my own half-hearted attempts at sabotage. I hate the word: Survivor. What's so desirable about more of the same?

The only time I don't mind being alive is when I have an orgasm. & even then, my survival-programmed mind spoils the precious moment by trying to make it last.

The slain body of a foreign woman in her mid-thirties was discovered behind a cluster of bushes by a trucker early yesterday morning, when he stopped his vehicle to relieve himself. The left side of the face was badly marred, but medical examination determined it to be a scar at least 25 years old. There were no signs of a struggle. Police have no motive, or suspects.

Author's note:
I remember leaning against the rear wall of an elevator in some public place   perhaps the UN, or a publisher's building,   when a tall slender woman stepped inside, loudly chatting with 2 shorter, fatter ones. I remember freezing at the sight of a hand-sized indentation that disfigured the left side of her face like a brown slap. I tried not to look at her, but her eyes found mine & held them during 6 floors of defiance.

The Park

EVELYN CONLON

Apparently my blood pressure is the same as everyone else's, that is just below boiling point. The fat which, during the last few years, had wrapped itself like a tight hug around my arse has begun to disappear. Where does fat go when it falls off people? Are there chunks of it floating around the air in the exact spot where people have got thin, and where is the exact spot, and do people breathe it in and does it damage their lungs? My nerves are no worse than they ever were, and I sleep well. These things surprise me but they don't surprise Brigid. Nothing surprises her, that's why I love her, and her eyes are grey.

Brigid was going through a bad time, doing her best to get through each day without making an ass of herself. Her boyfriend (she would call him a lover, because she has confidence like that) was away. Again. But this time there was an eeriness about his absence, a banging insistence, that seemed to be trying to tell her something. She was finding it difficult to put her days in, days based on promises, particularly since, as she had begun to admit to herself, the promises had never actually been put into words and said. She had a notch up from a middling job in the Corporation and the sort of car that a woman like her can afford in a country which eleven years later was to miss the point completely and interview the staple diet of men on the night that Mary Robinson was elected President. She was driving home in this car wondering, and trying not to, if there would be a letter from him when she got home. More of those flags had appeared, this area had been coming down with flags for the past week, new ones sprouted every evening as if there had been multiple births all day long when people who had work were at it. A local festival she presumed, a very spready local festival by the looks of it.

There was a long letter from him that said nothing but wished she was there which was something. She bit the inside of her lip, wondering again, until it bled, she walked around her flat in a disarrayed fashion, picking things up and putting them down somewhere else. Rosaleen rang her up and asked her if they wanted to come to dinner tonight.

"It's for Macartan McElwaine, he's emigrating next week lucky divil."

"There's no we, only me," she said.

"Ah is Diarmuid away again? Well come yourself."

Because something is better than nothing she went. She took the poor route bus into town, the quickest journey, the one that makes no effort to avoid the desolate patches. She tried not to hear the tightly packed sounds of poverty. Not tonight.

"Your perm's still in."

"It'd need to be, I only got it done a month next Thursday."

The restaurant was perfect, it could dismiss the outside world in a matter of seconds. It had the right consistency, enough ordinary to be relaxing, slightly exotic so Brigid could be interested, a little conservative so she could count herself exotic in contrast. This hanging between realities made her dizzy with satisfaction. The others came together. There was Jacinta, a long term student, who always had money from somewhere and who was more used to spending it in pubs than in restaurants, Rosaleen, an indifferent clerk in the Norwich Union Insurance Corporation, a dedicated Northerner whose mind was sharp as razors, Macartan, dreamy and absent always, but even more so tonight because he was already drinking fast drinks in

Manhattan and Padhraig Copeland whose father, a Connemara Gaelgeoir, had married a Basque woman who sometimes spoke Spanish with an overlay of longing. They fussed and hugged and sat down and ordered wine and made plenty of noise. They were of the runaway generation, Brigid too. There were no family heirlooms, even cheap ones, in their sitting rooms because none of them had been forgiven, not yet anyway. Perhaps later they would be, when the death of a parent might force reconciliations on the one left behind. As teenagers they had bit and sniggered at everything and when they got to be twenty they didn't have to swallow their words because things were better for a while then.

Brigid liked staring at people, she was mesmerised by their hair, their faces, their clothes, she could see sloppy sewing through an overcoat. Looking at these people what could she see? Jacinta never had to seek first attention because she had carrot magenta hair. Since the sixties when it was first allowed that red could be matched with pink, or other reds, or any colour, Jacinta had started wearing shocking blood lipstick. She wore it still, even though the time had not yet recome when thinking women could paint themselves. Padhraig Copeland was far too good looking, there should be a law against anyone having such a perfect face and mouth. No one ever noticed what he was wearing. Macartan McElwaine had a startled face, a crooked nose, and hair so straight it looked wet. Rosaleen was so puny, she nearly had no face at all therefore her voice came always as a surprise, a big deep thing that had its way perfectly curved around difficult ideas. She had fed her intelligence well. Brigid would have a good night after all.

Rosaleen was concerned about the impending visit of the pope to Ireland.

"It will knock us back years," she said.

So that's what all the flags were for. Brigid wondered to herself where the people got them, had they had them all the time in boxes, away with the Christmas decorations waiting, in case the pope ever did come to Ireland, or was there a factory somewhere spewing them out of machines at the rate of knots or did the women sew them up at night in their individual homes and pretend that they had them all along.

"Look how much damage he particularly of all the popes has done, in how many years? How long has he been pope now?"

Jacinta remembered. Exactly. Because she was picked out of a crowd on the night of the first Reclaim the Night march in Dublin by a TV personality and asked if she would come on his programme and say how she could defend not letting men go on the march in support of the women's demand that they should be able to walk safely down the streets at any time day or night without men. Well that's not the way the TV personality put it. She said yes. When she got there her knees were knocking together with fright and she had forgotten that television was in colour so her clothes were all wrong (how could she have thought that, her and her shocking blood lipstick?). But she was saved because the first Polish pope ever had just been chosen and Today Tonight had spent all evening scouring Dublin for a Polish priest. By the time they got one all the Polish priests were paralytic on vodka. So there he was, his English not the best in the first place, slurring his way through his interview. In comparison to him, Jacinta sounded like a professional. Rosaleen was so concerned at the assumption that we all wanted him here she said that something should be done about it.

"WE should do something," she said.

And that led to a long discussion about what they would do, what they couldn't do, what they could do and what they dared to do.

And so by the end of the meal they had decided to paint slogans so that people would know that there was some opposition in the country. They believed that to be important. Nothing too drastic like "Fuck the Pope" because that could be taken up the

....

wrong way, twice, nothing too obscure because people would just knit their eyebrows and not know, something simple like "No Priest State Here". They would do it on the road from Maynooth to Dublin. "Maynooth," Macartan said dreamily, turning it on his tongue like a child would repeat a word to itself knowing that it meant something but not knowing what. "Maynooth, where priests are made."

Brigid was given the job of driving down and up to Maynooth once or twice over the next few days to calculate how many Special Branch cars were cruising the route. "Branch cars! How will I know them?"

"You'll feel them on the back of your neck," Rosaleen said.

During the week, Brigid dreamt that she was a bird flying into people's kitchens, into canteens, on to building sites, switching the bloody radios off as they built up cosy pictures of the wonderful preparations for the wonderful man, the way a radio voice can.

The night came, the night before he was to come. Brigid felt nervous in an alert way, pleased that they were doing at least some little thing. She had plenty of petrol, oil and water in the car, she had cleaned it while she was at it, the tins of paint were in the boot. She was clean herself, spruced up in a pair of jeans that had zips where no zips were needed, a royal blue light jumper, a white shirt collar peeping up around the neck.

They had decided to leave her flat after midnight, the later they painted the slogans the more chance that they would remain unnoticed until morning when people would see them on their way to work and be outraged or smile gleefully with relief. It was a long evening. At twelve o'clock or thereabouts Rosaleen and Macartan arrived, by half past twelve it was obvious that Jacinta and Padhraig had had second thoughts and were not in favour of pursuing a wildcat decision taken in a restaurant when there had been plenty of wine drunk, because

Macartan was emigrating, oh! yes leaving the place, but brave
enough to do one last thing for the oul sod before he abandoned
it altogether, easy for him, and as for Rosaleen she'd think
better of it when she remembered her job and as for Brigid she'd
never.

So Macartan, Rosaleen and Brigid set out and drove through
the early autumn night. Sometimes they checked to see if
Brigid's calculations of the Branch cars were correct — every
eight minutes, every five minutes, that's not one, oh it is, it is I
can feel it, but mostly they behaved as if they were out on a
mid-afternoon Sunday drive.

The first one was the hardest. They reached the spot that Brigid
had picked out before they had decided who would do it so it
was too late because dithering might bring notice on them.
They shouted at each other and jumped around in their seats as
if a flea had bitten them. But they calmed down and decided
that Rosaleen and Macartan would do the first ones in rota
while Brigid sat at the wheel and started the car up again when
they got to the second last E. If they were getting on well she
could have a go when they got to a quieter spot. O.K. here goes.
"No Priest State Here" in luminous white paint, lucid in the
dark, as if it has been there for all time. They had to tear
themselves away, they could have stood around for hours
chatting, taking the odd long admiring look at it, remarking on
how well the letters were done, smelling the paint, watching the
moon watching it. The second one, a mile from Maynooth,
lacked originality, didn't look as pleasing but maybe that was
because of the bad background wall, it didn't show the letters
up terribly well. The straight stretch of characterless road took
away from it too. Still it was done. And a third. By now the
rhythm was flawless, they had the paint and brush and painters
out and in again in one minute.

They were concentrating so hard on the fourth, enjoying

....

63

themselves so much, making the letters flourish more, that they didn't hear the car coming until it had rounded the corner ahead of them. Quick as a flash Brigid switched on the engine and moved forward. The driver would think he had only imagined that the car had been stopped. Macartan and Rosaleen jumped across the hedge, scratching their legs on thorns. Rosaleen got stung by a nettle. They sat in the ditch listening to their hearts drumming one long beat in their ears. Brigid drove around the corner, switched off the engine, listened, and when no sound came she reversed back to the spot.

While the two were extricating themselves from the ditch and getting into the car Brigid, bold as brass, finished off the "Here".

"Phew! If that had happened with our first one we would have scarpered home."

Because of the fright they turned left at Lucan and took the Strawberry Beds road, "just as good for commuters in the morning and far safer for this business and more beautiful anyway," they consoled each other with something near love, born from the fear that was rising up in their voices.

They looked at the road, its tall trees crowded together in places gossiping, its houses perched dangerously on the edge of steep hills leaning over to hear. Brigid's mother had walked dogs along this road, once when she worked as a doctor's housekeeper. The dogs were well fed. Had Brigid's mother ever wondered about the trees? Was she asleep at this moment having a peculiar dream about the time she worked in Dublin for that doctor? The drive was so pleasant it was hard to remember that they had stops to make.

Did Brigid's car stop at the very places where her mother had taken a rest with the dogs, listened to the river whispering and making music? Who knows. She couldn't quite remember how many they had done on the Beds road, five at least, she had got to do two herself. The one that stretched across the road, that's the one she liked best, it was under a thick black tree and the RE

....

64

ran into the roadside staining the grass as it broke up. It was that grass you can whistle on if you cup it properly between your hand and lips.

They drove through the park talking louder now, laughing a lot at nothing, relief beginning to take them over. They drove up Oxmantown Road, down the North Circular, left at Phibsboro, getting further away, getting nearer a door they could close behind them. For some reason, they couldn't let it go, this night-time artistry, and stopped to do one last one opposite the gates of Glasnevin Cemetery. Funny, that was the one that stayed the longest. A garda car passed them as they drove off.

"Shit we nearly got caught," Macartan said.

"Nearly pregnant never did anyone any harm," Rosaleen said.

When they got to Brigid's flat they were ravenous. Macartan and Rosaleen checked the car for stray splashes of paint and washed the brushes. Brigid made fried egg, tomato and mushrooms on toast. Macartan stayed the night.

In the morning they switched stations on the radio. One news bulletin mentioned that some vandals had daubed a protesting slogan against the pope's visit.

"A slogan, only ONE, is that so," Brigid said sleepily as she fiddled with the tuner.

"The pope this, the pope that, and the pope the other," she muttered and switched it off. By the time they got up, the country was in full swing, children bathed and dressed already, if they were travelling far to the park, cars washed, minds battened down, bus tickets secured and picnics packed. People who lived in the city were out buying their plastic chairs.

Hawkers were converging on the park. The last stones of the park's inconvenient walls were being tipped into the dump, they had to go to make room for all the cars, guards, priests, mothers, bankers, the few radicals who had decided to make a fortune selling periscopes, councillors, fathers, poets and musicians who had finely tuned themselves to receive the Body

....

and Blood of Jesus Christ. Those who thought otherwise, were, simply, invisible for the day. By nine o'clock in the morning no amount of floodlights could have picked them out. (It took a certain kind of flash violence to make so many disappear, there are bruises left, there are sounds of strangling, but there you go . . . choking sounds, well that's only to be expected, it couldn't be avoided . . .)

Brigid's doorbell rang. She went to it slowly because she was feeling the effects of erasure, and the small gurgling of anger in the pit of her stomach was not enough antidote. She opened the door to her smiling brother and his careful girlfriend, her cousins and their friends. They had come early so as to get a good view and to buy some of those chairs if there were any left and they would park their cars here if she didn't mind.

"We thought we'd get our tea here too as I'm sure there's no place open," her brother said moving into the hallway. Brigid felt as if they would crush her if she didn't step aside. She backed into the kitchen, the last one closed the door behind him. They were standing now around her boyfriend's packed luggage. She hated them doing that. That was all she had of him, as long as his belongings were packed in boxes here, here in her room, there was hope. If these pope visitors hung around his things for long he might never come back. Look at that big ignorant mouth leaning his dirty arse on Diarmuid's stereo. Now that she had woken a little, flashes of anger were skittering through her, shaking her up and strengthening her legs. She said "I'm not making tea for anyone on their way to see the pope." They all laughed. "I'm not," she said. They laughed again. "No really," she said as the laugh died down. Her brother said "You were always great crack. I was just saying that recently. We miss your crack in Mullingar, we could be doing with it especially on a Monday morning. Right, who wants tea, who wants coffee?" Brigid went to the door, opened it, and said, "I'm serious. No one on their way to the park is welcome here. The whole country is at your disposal today so why are you bothering me. I'll have enough trouble all day keeping that creep out of my mind without having to feed his followers on their way . . . Enough said, I won't insult you, just get your tea and your posters and your rosary beads somewhere else."

They did leave, well what else could they do, their hearts wincing at the only blow struck against a believer that day. How well it had to be them! Brigid couldn't believe they had actually gone. The triumph left no taste of ashes in her mouth. She said "Whoopee," and went back to bed with Macartan where she curled her bare body as close to his as possible, merging her chest into his so that their hearts might beat together. He wasn't Diarmuid but he was there. A few hours later they heard a cheer go up from the street. Her neighbours were all hanging out upstairs windows waving yellow and white flags at a speck in the sky that must be your man's helicopter. Brigid lifted the nearest black garment to hand which happened to be a nightdress, attached it firmly to her window, and got back into bed again where she tried to shut out the noises of belligerent piety.

At half past eleven she and Macartan decided to go to Newgrange, the most pagan place they could think of. They drove alone along roads that wove through North County Dublin townlands, roads that skirted the pope's evening journey to Drogheda, meeting the odd Branch car, the occupants of which pinned eyes on them — what could those two people be doing, where could they possibly be going, Mass was on in the park by now, wasn't it? The pope had already told the people in icy sharp tones what they must not do and nor must you and you must not and also . . . It would take the people years to recover from the things being said in such a way on such a day. As a million and more people genuflected, creaking their knees within a quarter of a second of each other, Macartan put his feet up on the dashboard and sighed the way people do when making love has satisfied them beyond what they think they deserve. The pope raised the host, the people bowed their heads. Brigid wondered if that was her period starting now. The people filed in straight lines to get communion, some shuffling, some stamping as they edged their way confidently towards heaven, Brigid shivered in a flash of cold. People had started opening their flasks in the park by the time Macartan and Brigid reached the gate. CLOSED DUE TO THE POPE'S VISIT. They said nothing just caught each other's hands tight and started looking for an opening in the hedge. They climbed through a slit in the ditch and jumped onto the hard ground. Macartan felt as if his hip bones had been pushed up to his ribs with the impact. The people swayed and sang "He's got the whole world in his hands". (Eleven years later, when some of the poison was leaving, a few people sang "She's got the whole world in her hands" to Mary Robinson as she drove through the park gates. They giggled low down knowing where they'd heard it last.) Macartan and Brigid reached the stone wall. Brigid caught Macartan's face and stuck her tongue down his throat. Across the city that they had just left odd souls longed for the comfort of a warm body, the big crook of an arm to bury their faces in, a chest to lie on, a mouth to kiss, anything to take their minds off it.

Brigid and Macartan went into town that night to have a drink. It was the worst thing they could have done for their hearts, because they met too many people who had gone to the park, people they expected more from, were surprised at, and there was a strange sound, or was it a smell, lurking in the shadows. The streets were full of rubbish as if an army had trampled through today and left a wash after it. If that was so Brigid and Macartan were swimming precariously on the edge of it, being watched by the backs of the people on deck. They met Padhraig and Jacinta who were now furious with themselves for not

....

having gone painting. They had spent the day sitting on a bed together but they didn't get into it because Padhraig was gay, much to Jacinta's disappointment, not always, but on this day! They waved homemade flags at the screen and shouted "Up the pole, Up the pole!" They all had a drink. The four of them whispered together hoping to draw some consolation from each other but it didn't feel enough.

At the airport Rosaleen, Brigid, Padhraig and Jacinta hung around at the back while Macartan's parents went through the emotions. Macartan's mother looked furious with grief. She would wait six months or more before sending him postcards of the West, of pubs in the West, of musical instruments under blue skies, of valleys pinpointed by intimate rivers and lakes in the West. She would wait. Brigid couldn't kiss him properly, his parents didn't turn their heads for long enough. In the toilet Rosaleen and Brigid decided to go out together painting once more. Why? There was no need. It must have been the airport, the sense of people fleeing. It must have been. They didn't tell Padhraig or Jacinta, it was too serious.

They drove to the park in the early darkness and painted IF MEN GOT PREGNANT CONTRACEPTION AND ABORTION WOULD BE SACRAMENTS on the monument built for the pope's visit. There were a lot of letters, Brigid did fifty of them, hers looked sudden and fluid, Rosaleen's seven were non-runny and perfect. In the paper the next day you could tell that there had been two people. The worst part of it all was doing what Rosaleen said they had to do afterwards, go to the nearest pub, pee on their hands, and then wash them under the tap. The worst, but she was right. It got rid of the paint from around their fingernails. Rosaleen then told Brigid that she too was emigrating. Brigid said "Aw God no", missing her like death already.

Brigid got caught painting a harmless slogan seven years later, one year after the passing of the statute of limitations. "It may be a harmless slogan your honour, but the vandalism of the papal cross in the park wasn't." The judge's eyes widened into white. "Six months," he said. I got caught. I had a standby job taking in the lottery ticket money in my local shop any time the lottery reached seven hundred thousand pounds or more. A customer left half the receipt one night, the winning numbers were marked on it. Not knowing (I should have) which receipt was needed to claim a prize, I chanced my arm and brought the docket in. By an odd coincidence a hundred pounds went missing from the till the same week, not me, I wouldn't have the nerve. "A hundred pounds may not be a lot of money your honour, but attempting to fraudulently procure eight hundred and sixty thousand two hundred and ninety two pounds is." "Six months," he said.

We're getting out next week and Diarmuid is throwing a party for us.

It Had Wings

. . . .

ALLAN GURGANUS

For Bruce Saylor and Constance Beavon

Find a little yellow side street house. Put an older woman in it. Dress her in that tatty favorite robe, pull her slippers up before the sink, have her doing dishes, gazing nowhere — at her own backyard. Gazing everywhere. Something falls outside, loud. One damp thwunk into new grass. A meteor? She herself (retired from selling formal clothes at Wanamaker's, she herself — a widow and the mother of three scattered sons, she herself alone at home a lot these days) goes onto tiptoe, leans across a sinkful of suds, sees — out near her picnic table, something nude, white, overly-long. It keeps shivering. Both wings seem damaged.

"No way," she says. It appears human. Yes, it is a male one. It's face up and, you can tell, it is extremely male (uncircumcised). This old woman, pushing eighty, a history of aches, uses, fun — now presses one damp hand across her eyes. Blaming strain, the luster of new cataracts, she looks again. Still, it rests there on a bright air mattress of its own wings. Outer feathers are tough quills, broad at bottom as rowboat oars. The whole left wing bends far under. It looks hurt.

The widow, sighing, takes up her blue willow mug of heated milk. Shaking her head, muttering, she carries it out back. She moves so slow because: arthritis. It criticizes every step. It asks about the mug she holds, Do you really need this?

She stoops, creaky, beside what can only be a young angel, unconscious. Quick, she checks overhead, ready for what? —

some TV news crew in a helicopter? She sees only a sky of the usual size, a Tuesday sky stretched between weekends. She allows herself to touch this thing's white forehead. She gets a mild electric shock. Then, odd, her tickled finger joints stop aching. They've hurt so long. A practical person, she quickly cures her other hand. The angel grunts but sounds pleased. His temperature's a hundred and fifty, easy — but for him, this seems somehow normal. "Poor thing," she says, and — careful — pulls his heavy curly head into her lap. The head hums like a phone knocked off its cradle. She scans for neighbors, hoping they'll come out, wishing they wouldn't, both.

"Look, will warm milk help?" She pours some down him. Her wrist brushes angel skin. Which pulls the way an ice tray begs whatever touches it. A thirty-year pain leaves her, enters him. Even her liver spots are lightening. He grunts with pleasure, soaking up all of it. Bold, she presses her worst hip deep into crackling feathers. The hip has been half numb since a silly fall last February. All stiffness leaves her. He goes, "Unhh." Her griefs seem to fatten him like vitamins. Bolder, she whispers private woes: the Medicare cuts, the sons too casual by half, the daughters-in-law not bad but not so great. These woes seem ended. "Nobody'll believe. Still, tell me some of it." She tilts nearer. Both his eyes stay shut but his voice, like clicks from a million crickets pooled, goes, "We're just another army. We all look alike — we didn't, before. It's not what you expect. We miss this other. Don't count on the next. Notice things here. We are just another army."

"Oh," she says.

Nodding, she feels limber now, sure as any girl of twenty. Admiring her unspeckled hands, she helps him rise. Wings serve as handles. Kneeling on damp ground, she watches him go staggering toward her barbecue pit. Awkward for an athlete, really awkward for an angel, the poor thing climbs up there, wobbly. Standing, he is handsome, but as a vase is handsome.

When he turns this way, she sees his eyes. They're silver, each reflects her: a speck, pink, on green green grass.

She now fears he plans to take her up, as thanks. She presses both palms flat to dirt, says, "The house is finally paid off. Not just yet," and smiles.

Suddenly he's infinitely infinitely more so. Silvery. Raw. Gleaming like a sunny monument, a clock. Each wing puffs, independent. Feathers sort and shuffle like three hundred packs of playing cards. Out flings either arm; knees dip low. Then up and off he shoves, one solemn grunt. Machete swipes cross her backyard, breezes cool her upturned face. Six feet overhead, he falters, whips in makeshift circles, manages to hold aloft, then go shrub-high, gutter-high. He avoids a messy tangle of phone lines now rocking from the wind of him. "Go, go," the widow, grinning, points the way. "Do. Yeah, good." He signals back at her, open-mouthed and left down here. First a glinting man-shaped kite, next an oblong of aluminum in sun. Now a new moon shrunk to decent star, one fleck, fleck's memory: usual Tuesday sky.

She kneels, panting, happier and frisky. She is hungry but must first rush over and tell Lydia next door. Then she pictures Lydia's worry lines bunching. Lydia will maybe phone the missing sons: "Come right home. Your Mom's inventing . . . company."

Maybe other angels have dropped into other Elm Street backyards? Behind fences, did neighbors help earlier hurt ones? Folks keep so much of the best stuff quiet, don't they.

Palms on knees, she stands, wirier. This retired saleswoman was the formal-gowns adviser to ten mayors' wives. She spent sixty years of nine-to-five on her feet. Scuffing indoors, now staring down at terry slippers, she decides, "Got to wash these next week." Can a person who's just sighted her first angel already be mulling about laundry? Yes. The world is like that.

From her sink, she sees her own blue willow mug out there in the grass. It rests in muddy ruts where the falling body struck so

....

73

hard. A neighbor's collie keeps barking. (It saw!) Okay. This happened. "So," she says.

And plunges hands into dishwater, still warm. Heat usually helps her achy joints feel agile. But fingers don't even hurt now. Her bad hip doesn't pinch one bit. And yet, sad, they all will. By suppertime, they will again remind her what usual suffering means. To her nimble underwater hands, the widow, staring straight ahead, announces, "I helped. He flew off stronger. I really egged him on. Like *any*body would've, really. Still, it was me. I'm not just somebody in a house. I'm not just somebody alone in a house. I'm not just somebody else alone in a house."

Feeling more herself, she finishes the breakfast dishes. In time for lunch. This old woman should be famous for all she has been through — today's angel, her years in sales, the sons and friends — she should be famous for her life. She knows things, she has seen so much. She's not famous.

Still, the lady keeps gazing past her kitchen café curtains, she keeps studying her own small tidy yard. An anchor fence, the picnic table, a barbecue pit, new Bermuda grass. Hands braced on her sink's cool edge, she tips nearer a bright window.

She seems to be expecting something, expecting something decent. Her kitchen clock is ticking. That dog still barks to calm itself. And she keeps staring out: nowhere, everywhere. Spots on her hands are darkening again. And yet, she whispers, "I'm right here, ready. Ready for more."

Can you guess why this old woman's chin is lifted? Why does she breathe as if to show exactly how it's done? Why should both her shoulders, usually quite bent, brace so square just now?

She is guarding the world.

Only, nobody knows.

Mrs McCoy and Moses

DIANA HENDRY

Being between lusts and mellow fruitfulness, Mrs McCoy had decided upon a day of piety. Or rather a day of piety had decided upon her, for Mrs McCoy's cholers came and went as they so pleased and she suffered their arrival and departure as best she could.

Either she was a woman of infinite variety, or she was possessed by the cast of the Royal Shakespeare Company, or else her nature was akin to a computer that plays its one programme *ad nauseam*. Who can hazard at the truth? But Mrs McCoy favoured the last of these theories on the grounds that whoever she was, she was not herself. In the main she felt like one who has studied meteorology for decades and is still unable to predict the morrow's mood of rain, hail, sun or storm.

So did this day of piety catch her without her umbrella, so to speak, when with a moment's retrospect it would appear easy enough to have predicted it.

The vicar had been to call. Now although he was an ungodly man, fond of a liberal use of the Anglo-Saxon, still some incense-odour lingered about his person. He had brought her a book about Thomas Merton and Nowness. And then, as if it were a signal for Mistress Piety to begin her speech, the picture of Moses, coloured by Mrs McCoy's daughter, unsellotaped itself from the window pane, slid through the slit in the radiator and lay in sin upon the floor.

Apart from all this, Mrs McCoy was fair sated with love, sex, death and poetry and it was a Monday, the washing machine broken and the weather of unmitigated greyness. Mrs McCoy's computer program was limited to the afore-mentioned topics plus God. This observed, it should have been a matter of great simplicity to predict a day of piety.

She would have liked to wallow in the guilt of her meteorological failure but piety would allow no such indulgence. Mrs McCoy set to, contemplating first Moses, then the breakfast dishes, then Nowness.

Clearly Moses could not be left on the floor. Mrs McCoy picked him up and studied him. The portrait had been made on tracing paper so that when coloured and sellotaped on glass, produced, if poorly, the effect of a stained glass window. Moses, courtesy of Mrs McCoy's daughter, had a red and blue war helmet, a purple robe, a yellow face (scrolls to match) and bright green eyes. Under his nose was a kind of doctor's mask, inexplicable to Mrs M.'s daughter who did not know that Moses's face to face encounter with God had left his own fizzog so shining, so aglow, that he had had to hide it from the common multitude. A little of Moses's beard protruded from under the mask. He had been on the window about a year. A grey oblong (and four sellotape marks that would be tedious to remove) bore witness to that.

Mrs McCoy found herself full of jealous hatred for Moses and resentful of his veil. Why, having had such a rare privilege, did he keep it all to himself? What harm would a quick shuffti at glory do to anyone? What were the Israelites afraid of? One look might have melted their software and selved them solid. She was tempted to crumple Moses into the bin but wished to do so with indifference. Angry blasphemy was only next door to faith. Mrs McCoy was not stupid.

She put Moses down and began on the dishes and Nowness.

They were of comparable difficulty, there being several burnt pans and each Now as unholdable as water. She had to continually yank herself back from time past and time future into time now — if there was such a thing, which she began to doubt.

As for the pans — Mrs McCoy reminded herself of a lover who had once been given a quantity of such pans to scour and had survived the occasion by chanting "The Buddha is in the pot! The Buddha is in the pot!" Mrs McCoy tried it. But the phrase evolved, as phrases will, and became "Sod God".

Though it lacked originality, Mrs McCoy was pleased with it. Indeed she thought about leaving the pots and telephoning X who, she was sure, would enjoy "Sod God", for only last week he had advised her that for the sake of her health she should say "Fuck the Pope" three times a day.

However, such was the piety upon her that she decided not to telephone X. Instead, the dishes finished, she stood, broom in hand, mind travelling the length, depth, breadth and cobwebbed height of this domicile which, due to her formal upbringing, required of her that she clean and tidy it.

It was a gloomy prospect and she shied at it but Christian valour was at her heels that day and telling herself that eternity was in a grain of dust, she began to sweep the floor, wondering all the while why, if she were to live in the Now, she could not be given a more interesting Now to live in? (She bore, it will be apparent, a great grudge against the mysterious ways of Our Lord and refused altogether to traffic with Christ, finding his descent to earth lacking in propriety.) Mrs McCoy was stolid Old Testament, liking the virility of an angry, jealous God, one with a penchant for drought, famine, fire, flood and pestilence — all matters which she felt to be proper for a God. Gentle Jesus lacked machismo.

Finding it impossible to nail any thought to the Now, Mrs McCoy began talking aloud, itemising the possessions about her. For some minutes this proved an interesting occupation.

There, on the shelf, were old blue and brown bottles salvaged from the dump by Mrs McCoy's husband, Tom. Was she not fortunate to have a husband who raided the inarticulate and brought forth blue Milk of Magnesias, brown Schweppes, one delightful ink bottle labelled "Field's Ink and Gum" — all now numinous with age? On the dresser was a mug with a rainbow handle given to her by X. It was rare indeed to find a lover who possessed soul and sexuality in more-or-less equal degrees. In fact, as she looked about her, it came upon her that this room was peopled (by way of teapots, jugs, pots and mangles) by a positive horde of friends and relations. Nowness had revealed it to her. Here she was, balking at the duster, blind to the animate symbols of love and of history.

But the sop and sentimentality of this "count your blessings" attitude only sufficed to put her in a passion. So what? she cried. So what? (Give the woman her due, her contempt for Christ was equalled by her contempt for false comforts. She was a proud bitch and it is possible that the Great Jehovah intended to give her the Job-treatment so that she grovelled for any comfort).

However she fought Him gamely. In her younger days she had aspired to such profanity as would cause Him to strike her dead. Maturity had taught her that no amount of abuse would provoke the Bastard. That determined, she decided that no platitudes about Nowness would reduce her to doing the housework with sweetness and joy. She was not, in fact, prepared to do it at all. Dung and death, dust and decay. What was the point? (She lacked the humour to suffer futility gladly.)

Piety, however, was not yet defeated. It delivered The Sermon on the Mount, recalled to mind various paths of enlightenment, reminded her that she must go by the way wherein there is no ecstasy and concluded with a homily on moderation and the still centre of the turning world where is the dance.

All this was somewhat wasted on Mrs McCoy, but then God was an Infinite Wastrel. Mrs McCoy knew well enough that moderation and the middle path was the Right Royal Way but it was impossible for her to take it. She had no middle to her nature. She was programmed to alternate longings for ecstasy or oblivion.

And therefore Mrs McCoy prayed to God to cast her into the

darkest pit so that from there she might try to sing. (The logic of this is hard to find and there is probably no more to it than that it was more interesting to sit, with coffee, cigarettes and anger, contemplating the possibility of pure joyous song springing from purgatory than it was to wield the broom).

God being indisposed as usual, Mrs McCoy took to Eliot's *Four Quartets* as a substitute for her craving. Now although she had read these before, on that particular day they spoke to her condition — as the Quakers will have it. In particular she was hauled ashore by the lines about waiting without hope, love, faith or thought. Such positive negation had her enraptured. She found it an immense relief to abandon all four, pronto.

She memorised the lines, lay on the sofa and listened without love, hope, faith or thought, to the Brandenburg concertos (which suffered as a consequence) while quietness and peace invaded her various zones.

It was all a cod of course. Piety had won the day and cast its spell upon her so that Mrs McCoy quite forgot the thousand and one times she had hung her life, like her coat, on the peg of man, beast, poem or philosophy.

She had fought and lost and therefore now lay in a sort of deluded trance (which was possibly necessary for her physical survival) believing that she had now truly found the answer to life and was prepared to wait, simply wait, gallantly and for a lifetime.

In the event she lasted three days during which time she went about with an air of serenity admirable to behold. She also wrote to most of her friends telling them that she had no wish to see any of them at the moment as she was waiting without etcetera etcetera — an action she was soon to regret.

Her insincerity might have been detected by the fact that Moses remained where he was, neither on the window nor in the bin, neither in the to nor in the fro.

The cause for Mrs McCoy's lapse from piety is of course inexplicable. Either her computer program moved on or else the peg, the frail branch on which she had hung her tonnage, snapped. Whatever the cause, Mrs McCoy grew tired of waiting. Explosively tired. She wanted action. Love, sex, poetry or death action. Any action. Futile action.

At which point in the Now she opened up shop again and cast her myopic orbs on that small portion of the universe given unto her.

Moses she took out of limbo and with fresh sellotape set him up again. There was nothing to be afraid of. An English sun illuminating a portrait of Moses would not be too blinding. And anyway, she'd lived with him for a year — or was it a lifetime? — and still found his bright green eyes irresistible.

Can More Be Done?

GABRIEL JOSIPOVICI

All who saw him climb unsteadily into the pulpit knew at once that the end they had so long feared had come at last. "Many of them thought," wrote a contemporary, "he presented himself not to preach mortification by a living voice; but mortality by a decayed body and a dying face."

The text he had chosen for this sermon, delivered at Whitehall before the King himself in the beginning of Lent (February 25) 1631, was taken from Psalm 68: "And unto God the Lord belong the issues of death." "Many that then saw his tears," the chronicler goes on, "and heard his faint and hollow voice, professed they thought the text prophetically chosen, and that the Dean had preached his own funeral sermon."

Having gathered himself together for the effort (he had refused to comply with the fervent wishes of his doctor and his friends that he cancel the engagement), he found, after a few uncertain seconds, that the power of his voice was barely diminished by his recent illness, and that the old excitement of performing — on whatever stage, but pre-eminently on this one — had quite driven away any doubts he might secretly have entertained as to his ability to accomplish this, his final public duty. He had always liked to start strongly, both in the poetry he had once written and in the sermons that had now by and large taken its place. If the foundations are securely laid then the building, no matter how elaborate and fanciful, will give little trouble — that had always been his principle, and he had been fortunate in having a gift for the strong opening. Today was no exception. Indeed, the first image was precisely that of a building and what keeps it from falling down:

> Buildings stand by the benefit of their foundations, that sustain and support them, and of their buttresses that comprehend and embrace them, and of their consignations that knit and unite them. The foundations suffer them not to sink, the buttresses suffer them not to swerve, and the consignation and knitting suffer them not to cleave.

And now for the application:

> The body of our building is the former part of the verse: It is this: He that is our God is the God of salvation: *ad salutes*, of salvations in the plural, so it is in the original; the God that gives . . .

He found it difficult to make out his congregation as anything more than a blur. Too much reading had caught up with him, that hydroptic thirst for knowledge to which he had confessed, though he had always been able to do without spectacles. But he felt their presence, felt their extreme attention — he had always been acutely aware of his audience, that had been one of the reasons for his success as a preacher, whether in the open air of Paul's Cross or in the great echoing space of the Cathedral, in the humble parish church of St Dunstan's or here before the King at Whitehall.

> For the first foundation of this building (that our God is the God of all salvations) is laid in this: That unto this God belong the issues of death, that is, it is in his power to give us an issue and deliverance, even then when we are brought to the jaws and teeth of death, and to the lips of that whirlpool, the grave . . .

....

That death was the mouth of the old enemy was a commonplace, but even in his present condition he felt the old familiar thrill of pleasure at the way he had brought the period to its close, moving rapidly from the key word, *lips*, to *whirlpool* and then to *grave*. That had always been his mark, this ability to change direction at speed, barely giving the reader or listener time to adjust to a new focus before altering it again. As he threw the sentence out into the great hall he rejoiced once again at the way he had found to flesh out the common tropes before consigning them, with a single final pause after *whirlpool*, to oblivion, by ending with that most ordinary word, now made new and startling by the fantasies that had preceded it — *the grave*.

Not much longer though. This time he had known at once that there would be no escape. Of course there had been alarms before, in his great sickness eight years earlier, or that other, many years previously, in Mitcham. But the attacks then had been sudden, violent, as though a force had seized him from without and immediately rendered him powerless. This time though it had come upon him slowly, and from within, helped on by another bout of fever and then by the death of his beloved mother in her eightieth year, not five weeks since. That had finally sapped what little strength remained to him, and without further ado he had made his will and sat down to compose this sermon. He had written it out carefully, afraid of the tricks even his phenomenal and well-trained memory might play upon him, afraid of the effort it would cost him to learn it by rote.

As he delivered the text now, glancing up occasionally to see how the King, in his raised chair facing him across the hall, was taking it, but unable to make out his features at that distance, his mind, always liable to wander when he was well launched on a sermon, flickered this way and that before settling on the thought that had struck him so forcibly while he was preparing the sermon and making sketches for his monument, that sermon in stone whose place in the Cathedral he had already reserved.

....

Unto God the Lord belong the issues of death, that is, the disposition and manner of our death: what kind of issue and transmigration we shall have out of this world, whether prepared or sudden, whether violent or natural, whether in our perfect sense or shaken and disordered by sickness . . .

The thought was this: Why, even at such a time as this, do I still so much enjoy the idea of acting out a role? Why am I thrilled, even now, by the thought of standing up in the pulpit, a man so obviously dying, and preaching to them about death? Why does my heart beat faster at the thought of sitting for my last portrait clothed in nothing but a shroud? Is it not time to put aside these childish things and to compose myself in the right spirit of humility for what must come?

First then, we consider this *exitus mortis*, to be *liberatio a morte*, that with God the Lord are the issues of death, and therefore in all our deaths, and deadly calamities of this life, we may justify hope of a good issue from him . . .

He had always felt a little uneasy with this propensity of his for play-acting. And yet, at the same time, when it came to it, he had never been able to resist the impulse, had felt, indeed, that he only came alive when he threw himself into the part of the cynic, the wounded lover, the humble petitioner, the husband, the father, the penitent, the preacher . . .

But then this *exitus a morte* is but *introitus in mortem*, this issue, this deliverance from that death, the death of the womb, is an entrance, a delivering over to another death, the manifold deaths of this world . . .

Had not God put us on earth for a purpose, he wondered, hearing his voice echoing round the great hall, had He not made us in His image for a reason? If this was how God had made him would it not have been sinful to deny it? And he felt again in his guts his old anger at the Jesuits for trying to force martyrdom on those born in the Catholic faith. His uncle had been made to suffer imprisonment and exile for the cause. And were they not responsible for his brother's death as they had been responsible for so many needless deaths? Either an apostate or a martyr, they had insisted. But the choice was a false one. He had refused to submit to their blackmail. Even though (as his mother never tired of reminding him) he was a descendant of the greatest English Catholic martyr of them all, Sir Thomas More. More More More. Always More. She had never let him forget. But he had held out. Had escaped the Jesuit clutches. Had made his way alone, determined to live out to the full the life God had blessed him with. As He would surely have wanted him to. For what use to God was a brain like his, a spirit like his, a thirst for knowledge and a gift for words like his, if he was to be hanged and disembowelled before he had had a chance to put those gifts to use?

And yet, what had he done with them? Read a great many books. Written a little poetry. Fallen in love rather too often. Made many friends. Seen service as a soldier. Travelled. Married. Become a father to umpteen children. Become a priest. And then a widower. And all his life, it seemed, since he had made that conscious decision to reject the false Jesuit alternative, all his life he had been searching for something solid, for firm ground under his feet that would enable him to jump up and seize his rightful reward, to rise up and become fully himself. But instead everything slipped from his grasp, crumbled in his hands as soon as he grasped it. Was it for this then that he had denied the faith into which he was born? Was it for this he had refused the martyrdom that had been his for the taking? *Here*, he heard himself saying to the assembled congregation:

....

here we have no continuing city, nay no cottage that
continues, nay no persons, no bodies, that continue . . .
Even the Israel of God hath no mansions; but journeys,
pilgrimages in this life . . .

Why had God done this to him? Why had he filled him with this
immoderate thirst for knowledge, for experience, if it was only
to thwart him at every turn? And his anger, as he pitched his
voice to the furthest reaches of the enormous chamber, turned
once more against God. Not against his mother, not against his
brother, not against the Jesuits — but against God, who had
put him in this impossible position, filled him with these
contrary desires. *That which we call life*, he heard his voice
proceeding, and he had been in the pulpit often enough to know
instinctively how to give the words just the right inflexion, just
the right weight, though his mind, by then, was far away:

That which we call life is but *hebdomada mortium*, a week
of deaths, seven periods of our life spent in dying, a dying
seven times over and there is an end. Our birth dies in
infancy, and our infancy dies in youth, and youth and all
the rest die in age, and age also dies, and determines
all . . .

He had sought for employment that would ground him
solidly in the world, but it was not forthcoming. He recalled the
many letters he had written from Mitcham: "I would fain be or
do something: but, that I cannot tell what, it is no wonder . . .;
for to choose is to do; but to be no part of any body, is as to be
nothing; and so I am, and shall so judge my self, unless I could
be so incorporated into a part of the world, as by business to
contribute some sustentation to the whole." But nothing had
come of such letters.

He had dreamed of a perfect union which would at least

provide a focus for his many desires, and he had even celebrated it in verse:

> Twice or thrice had I loved thee,
> Before I knew thy face or name;
> So in a voice, so in a shapeless flame,
> Angels affect us oft, and worshipped be;
>   Still when, to where thou wert, I came,
> Some lovely glorious nothing did I see,
>   But since my soul, whose child love is,
> Takes limbs of flesh, and else could nothing do,
>   More subtle than the parent is
> Love must not be, but take a body too,
>   And therefore what thou wert, and who
>   I bid love ask, and now
> That it assume thy body, I allow,
> And fix itself in thy lip, eye, and brow.

He had always despised the idealism of the sonneteers, known that his dream of a union not just of spirits but of bodies too was infinitely more interesting, more satisfying, than the abstract love they celebrated. Besides, his dreams had always come clothed in flesh, and flesh, he knew, was the home of the spirit:

> As our blood labours to beget
>   Spirits as like souls as it can,
> Because such fingers need to knit
>   That subtle knot, which makes us man:
>
> So must pure lovers' souls descend
>   T'affections, and to faculties,
> Which sense may reach and apprehend,
>   Else a great prince in prison lies . . .

And then one day he had found her. Another More. Anne

More. He had married her, thirteen years his junior, still a minor, and so had risked prison for her, as if to prove to himself that here at last he had found something truly worth suffering for. But nothing had changed. His life had not been transformed, except in so far as he had found his prospects in the world destroyed for ever. So they had retired to the damp cottage in Mitcham and she had given birth to child after child, as God had willed. But still his all-consuming thirst was unassuaged. The new situation merely made time pass more slowly and exacerbated his sense that more was due to him than he was receiving, that life, his life, the only life God had given him, could not simply be this, a loving wife and a damp cottage far from the centre and the feeling that time was passing and he had nothing to show for it.

He had been stricken at her death. It had forced one of his finest poems out of him, that "Nocturnal Upon S Lucie's Day" which he would still exchange for almost any of his other poems:

> 'Tis the year's midnight, and it is the day's,
> Lucy's, who scarce seven hours herself unmasks,
>   The sun is spent, and now his flasks
>   Send forth light squibs, no constant rays;
>   The world's whole sap is sunk:
> The general balm th'hydroptic earth hath drunk,
> Whither, as to the bed's feet, life is shrunk,
> Dead and interred; yet all these seem to laugh,
> Compared with me, who am their epitaph.

Perhaps its quality derived from the pain that had forced it out of him. At the same time there was no denying the pleasure that had spread like a gentle flame through his body as the image of the bed's feet came to him. It did not drive away the pain but co-existed with it.

....

But for us that die now and sleep in the state of the dead, we must all pass this posthume death, this death after death, nay this death after burial, this dissolution after dissolution, this death of corruption and putrefaction and vermiculation and incineration, of dissolution and dispersion in and from the grave, when these bodies that have been the children of royal parents, and the parents of royal children, must say with Job, Corruption thou art my father, and to the worm, thou art my mother and my sister, and my self. Miserable incest, when I must be married to my mother and my sister, and be both father and mother to my own mother and sister: when my mouth will be filled with dust, and the worm shall feed sweetly upon me . . .

There it was again, that lingering on dissolution, disintegration, annihilation. *Absence, darkness, death; things which are not*, as he had put it in the "Nocturnal". Was it sheer morbidity on his part? And why did his spirit quicken at that "sweetly" which had not quickened at the mention of the resurrection itself?

He is, he realises, in particularly good voice today; his words are ringing out powerfully and he can sense his audience straining forward in their seats, caught once more as he has so often caught them in the past.

He had married a More and found that he could never have done with Donne. And it was as if the more he pleaded with God, argued with Him, threatened Him even, to remove that burden from him, the heavier it grew. For even the pleas and threats seemed to become a kind of game, a kind of play-acting, under his hand:

> Batter my heart, three-personed God; for, you
> As yet but knock, breathe, shine, and seek to mend;
> That I may rise, and stand, o'erthrow me, and bend
> Your force, to break, blow, burn, and make me new.

. . . .

I, like an usurped town, to another due,
Labour to admit you, but oh, to no end,
Reason your viceroy in me, me should defend,
But is captived, and proves weak or untrue,
Yet dearly I love you, and would be loved fain,
But am betrothed unto your enemy,
Divorce me, untie, or break that knot again,
Take me to you, imprison me, for I
Except you enthral me, never shall be free,
Nor ever chaste, except you ravish me.

Curious the pleasure those lines had given him. As if even the assertion of his desperate state were itself one more proof of his betrothal to the enemy. Was this then what he had refused martyrdom for, the old serpent's first last trick? *That monarch*, he read from his text, and looked straight across to where he knew the King to be, on his raised seat above the throng,

That monarch, who spread over many nations alive, must in his dust lie in a corner of that sheet of lead, and there, but so long as that lead will last, and that private and retired man, that thought himself his own for ever, and never came forth, must in his dust of the grave be published, and (such are the revolutions of the graves) be mingled with the dust of every high way, and of every dunghill, and swallowed in every puddle and pond: This is the most glorious and contemptible nullification of man, that we can consider . . .

"O think me worth thine anger, punish me," he had entreated God in that Good Friday poem written as he rode from Polesworth to Montgomery Castle. "Burn off my rusts and my deformities," return me, in other words, to my first self, to what I was like before Adam's transgression and fall, when I was made in your image and nothing had yet happened to tarnish

. . . .
90

that image. For from that time on we are condemned to wander far from the truth, encrusted with that which is not ourselves, lost in a labyrinth of games. Games. Always games. Even here, at the end of this poem of entreaty, he had found himself playing games with God: "Restore thine image, so much, by thy grace, That thou mayest know me, and I'll turn my face." If you do that, he had said to God, then I will do the other. If you remove Adam's sin from me, restore me to that self in which you first made me, then, and only then, will I turn to you. Be able to turn. Be inclined to turn. The poem had led him into that challenge. The words themselves had, as always, taken over. Not that he did not stand by them. As he wrote he felt the pleasure of the ambiguity. But all that showed was that he was still clothed in corruption, still incapable of feeling what he ought to feel, of speaking as he ought to speak — and how then could he expect God to listen?

And so it had always been. Even in his great sickness, after his wife's death, after ten years in the habit of a priest. Even then he had found that his way of talking to God was itself the sign of his distance from Him. For this way of talking did indeed give him a deep and perverse pleasure, even as he recognised that pleasure as the sign of his damnation. That had been the poem in which he had tried to sum up his life, the poem in which More and Donne had played hide-and-seek through the lines and he had, while composing it, quite forgotten what he had set out to do, so engrossed had he become in the actual doing:

> Wilt thou forgive that sin where I begun,
>   Which was my sin, though it was done before?
> Wilt thou forgive that sin, through which I run,
>   And do run still: though still I do deplore?
>   When thou hast done, thou hast not done,
>   For I have more.

Wilt thou forgive that sin which I have won
   Others to sin? and, made my sin their door?
Wilt thou forgive that sin which I did shun
   A year or two: but wallowed in, a score?
     When thou hast done, thou hast not done,
      For I have more.

I have a sin of fear, that when I have spun
   My last thread, I shall perish on the shore:
But swear by thy self, that at my death thy son
   Shall shine as he shines now, and heretofore;
     And, having done that, thou hast done,
      I fear no more.

But, as so often, the last verse was much less convincing than
the others. For what, after all, did it say? Only that *if* God
swore, then he would fear no more. But there was no guarantee
that He would ever do so — indeed, He had not talked to men
since the days of the Prophets. So, even after the poem was
finished, God had not Donne; only Donne had Donne — more
and more Donne. More and more. And there would always be
more. There was no end to it.

  He became aware that there was a shuffling and a rustling in
the assembled congregation. He had stopped speaking as he
recalled the poem and its circumstances, and faces were looking
up at him, wondering at his silence. Hurriedly he found his
place and pressed on:

This death of incineration and dispersion, is, to natural
reason, the most irrecoverable death of all, and yet,
Domini Domini sunt exitus mortis, unto God the Lord
belong the issues of death, and by recompacting this dust
into the same body, and reinanimating the same body with
the same soul, he shall in a blessed and glorious
resurrection give me such an issue from this death, as shall
never pass into any other death, but establish me into a
life that shall last as long as the Lord of Life himself . . .

         . . . .

Now there was a sigh from those below him. This was the fulcrum of the sermon, this was what they had come to hear. He had paused at precisely the right place, as though even in his distraction his old dramatic instinct had been in control.

But what did the words mean? What did *he* mean by the words?

He hurried on:

> The tree lies as it falls it's true, but it is not the last stroke that fells the tree, nor the last word nor gasp that qualifies the soul. Our critical day is not the very day of our death; but the whole course of our life. I thank him that prays for me when the bell tolls, but I thank him much more that catechises me, or preaches to me, or instructs me how to live . . .

A didactic point, a preacherly point, but perhaps it meant more than he had understood it to mean when he penned the lines. Our critical day is not the very day of our death but the whole course of our life. That was what he was beginning, but just beginning to understand. He had always written about sudden change, about moments of total transformation, and when the poem was over nothing at all was changed. But perhaps he had misunderstood himself. Perhaps there are no sudden changes. Perhaps there is no critical moment — but the whole course of our life. "I wonder by my troth what thou and I/Did, till we loved?" he had written.

> Were we not weaned till then,
> But sucked on country pleasures, childishly?
> Or snorted we in the seven sleepers' den?
> 'Twas so; but this, all pleasures fancies be,
> If ever any beauty I did see,
> Which I desired, and got, 'twas but a dream of thee.

GABRIEL JOSIPOVICI

But we are never weaned, we go on snorting in the seven
sleepers' den for the whole of our lives, all beauty is but a dream
of beauty. That is what life is, he thought. That is what beauty
is. There is no life of wakefulness elsewhere, no true beauty
round the corner. And that is as it should be.

His mind was suddenly alive with his earlier verse:

> Busy old fool, unruly sun,
> Why dost thou thus,
> Through windows, and through curtains call on us?
> Must to thy motions lovers' seasons run?
> Saucy pedantic wretch, go chide
> Late school-boys, and sour prentices,
> Go tell court-huntsmen, that the King will ride,
> Call country ants to harvest offices;
> Love, all alike, no season knows, nor clime,
> Nor hours, days, months, which are the rags of time.

What had filled him with pleasure had been his ability to assert
the triumphant escape from time even as he marked its work in
the very rhythm and pace of the verse. No one had done that
before him, not Dante, not Spenser, not Shakespeare or
Jonson. *Nor hours, days, months, which are the rags of time*. The
rags of time. He had found a way to do it, or perhaps it would be
truer to say that he had been forced to discover a way by the
pain of his frustration, the constant and debilitating sense of
time passing. "Grief brought to numbers cannot be so fierce,/
For he tames it that fetters it in verse," he had written in another
poem, and that, in the end, was what it all came down to.
Though perhaps the grief remained equally fierce but alongside
it an equally fierce joy was brought to life.

But it was more complicated even than that. Fettering his
grief in his time-bound, earth-bound verse had the effect,
paradoxically, of releasing him. Without these fetters a great
prince — his essential self — in prison lay. Yet fettered, he rose

....

94

up, a new Samson, no, not a destroyer like Samson, but a new, yes, a new Adam.

It was as if a huge and diffuse weight, which had been crushing him all his life, had suddenly been lifted from him. He saw with great clarity that poetry was not of the Devil but of God. Our critical day is not the day of our death but the whole course of our life. Truth is not on the further side of language but in language itself. This was God, life, the resurrection even. His error had been to look for that which would be stable, which would lie outside time, change, the ageing of the body and the vagaries of language. He had looked for it in women, in God, in the Church. But there was no stability. There was only life. He had wanted to have done with confusion, uncertainty, the horrors of waste and change. And the more he had wanted it the less he had found it. His Anne, Anne More, had known better, as she bore him child after child. But he had been blind to it. God is not outside the world, aloof, disdainful, cunning and deceitful. He is in the ever-changing fabric of the world. And so language, and poetry, are not an aberration, an instrument of the old enemy, but the very form of the Godhead.

Somewhere at the back of his mind, as he went on speaking to the assembled court — he thought he saw the King nodding in sleep now that he had turned the corner of the sermon and come to the glorious resurrection — somewhere at the back of his mind, as his voice faltered and then found a new strength (he felt the thickness of the remaining pages of his sermon between the thumb and forefinger of his right hand and realised with a mixture of sadness and relief that he had come almost to the end of his last public performance) — somewhere at the back of his mind words were forming:

> That the green leaves came and covered the high rock,
> That the lilacs came and bloomed, like a blindness
>   cleaned,
> Exclaiming bright sight, as it was satisfied,

....

> In a birth of sight. The blooming and the musk
> Were being alive, an incessant being alive,
> A particular of being, that gross universe . . .

He knew they were not his words and could never be his words, yet they hovered in his mind as though one day he would speak them:

> These leaves are the poem, the icon and the man.
> These are a cure of the ground and of ourselves.

All his life he had looked for the rock, he now saw, and never realised that there is no rock but only leaves. And yet he had known: These leaves are the poem. These are a cure of the ground and of ourselves.

Later, as he lay dying, the picture of himself in his shroud on the wall before him, the words echoed in his mind, and he knew that his violent and unnatural thirst had been the result not of a lack but of a gift. Now his boat was setting out,

> The boat was built of stones that had lost their weight
>   and being no longer heavy
> Had left in them only a brilliance of unaccustomed
>   origin,
> So that he that stood up in the boat leaning and
>   looking before him
> Did not pass like someone voyaging out of and beyond
>   the familiar,
> He belonged to the far-foreign departure of his vessel
>   and was part of it,
> As he travelled alone, like a man lured on by a syllable
>   without any meaning,
> A syllable of which he felt, with an appointed sureness,
> That it contained the meaning into which he wanted to
>   enter,

. . . .

A meaning which, as he entered it, would shatter the
   boat and leave the oarsmen quiet,
As at a point of central arrival, an instant moment,
   much or little,
Removed from any shore, from any man or woman,
   needing none.

Or, as a contemporary put it: "Being speechless, and seeing
heaven by that illumination by which he saw it; he did as St
Stephen, look steadfastly into it, till he saw the Son of Man,
standing at the right hand of God his father; and being satisfied
with this blessed sight, as his soul ascended and his last breath
departed from him, he closed his own eyes; and then disposed
his hands and body into such a posture as required not the least
alteration by those that came to shroud him."

Thus did John Donne, poet and preacher, pass out of this
life. But the fruit of his gift lives on.

On the Subway

ELISA SEGRAVE

I am waiting at 59th Street West for the A-line subway to take me downtown to Canal. It's 10.30 a.m. I've already waited twenty minutes. I must be back before my friend Rachel wakes up. She's got cancer and is going to have chemotherapy today. I said I'd be back before she woke up at 10.

As I wait a woman comes to sit on the seat beside me and starts writing frantically in a notebook. I look over her shoulder. This is what she's writing:

"Life is hard for others. I know. They have told me. I am very scared. Please God help me!"

She writes the word VISION in capital letters then her train comes. I look quickly at her. She's young with very long blonde hair, probably bleached, a very pale face and dark brown eyes. What she's written seems like a direct message from my friend, something she doesn't say.

"I am very scared. Please God help me!"

When I get back to the apartment my friend's very tired. She wishes she hadn't had a glass of whiskey the night before. She walks several streets on her own through Chinatown where she sees a healer, and comes back looking much better. She says this woman healer puts her into a relaxed state, like a trance except she doesn't lose consciousness. She's able to remember her early childhood which she can't do normally.

When I was a child I believed in God. I was sent to Catholic instruction at a convent near the town where we lived. The two nuns who met me at the front door seemed scared, running about like little mice.

I was seven. The nun who taught me was Sister Camilla. She led me past a picture of Christ with his bleeding Sacred Heart into a cold sitting-room with ice-blue walls. The catechism was blue too. I had to learn the whole catechism by heart. I learned it quickly in bed at night while listening to Radio Luxembourg.

"Why did God make you?"

"God made me to know Him, love Him, serve Him in this world and be happy with Him forever in the next."

I imagined God as a bald man sitting in the sky.

Jesus himself, with his long hair and weak expression, did not appeal to me.

My friend Rachel doesn't believe in God. Would it help her if she did? She won't admit to me how scared she is.

The night she's in hospital having chemotherapy I'm alone in the apartment with her orange kitten. There's only one small bedroom where she sleeps; the rest of the room is an enormous loft. I feel exposed sleeping in a small bed in the middle of this enormous room. The kitten drags something out from under the bed, some big bit of yellow fly-paper with something on it. I don't pay much attention and the kitten pushes it back under the bed.

Next morning Rachel returns from the hospital earlier than she said. She looks white and desperate. I make her bed for her. She puts on a white nightdress and goes to bed.

But she has to keep going across the loft to the bathroom to be sick. The fact that she looks so strong normally — a tall woman with wiry black hair and almost black eyes — makes her weakness seem worse.

She tells me to go out if I want as she'll sleep most of the day. Will I bring some food back about five? She suggests something

....

99

digestible, like a small Cornish chicken from the local delicatessen.

I walk to a bookstore in Spring Street and open a copy of *Interview* magazine. By chance I open it on the page where there's an interview and photograph of a man I think I am in love with. He has just published a book. This man, who abandoned me after leaving all his possessions in my house for eight months without getting in touch, resembles my father, who died aged sixty-two of cirrhosis of the liver, and also my brother, who died on his twenty-fourth birthday. The man I think I am in love with is supposed to be very religious. He is a Catholic like me and became more religious after being tortured in South America.

How can a religious person behave so callously?

A few minutes later going up on the subway towards Lexington and 89th Street, I start to cry. Is it because of this man reminding me of my dead brother or am I crying with pity for Rachel? A man sitting opposite me in the subway carriage looks at me.

When I get back to Rachel's around five she seems better. It's Good Friday. I'd like to go down to Greenwich Village this evening where Almodóvar the Spanish film-maker is giving a talk but Rachel doesn't want me to go. She wants us to have dinner together and insists on making it herself. She takes out glasses, mats, a bottle of white wine and even candles.

Just before she starts cooking I go over to my bed in the middle of the room and the kitten's dragged the large yellow fly-paper out from under the bed. I ask Rachel what it is and did she put it there?

She did not put it there and what's more has never seen it before although she's had the apartment two years. Not only that, she immediately points out that this weird American mouse-trap — because that's what it is — has a disintegrating mouse-skeleton on it.

Rachel admits she finds it gruesome but at the same time

shows a strong nerve. She does not admit, to me or even to herself perhaps, what this reminds us of — her death. I admire her bravery.

My brother committed suicide on his twenty-fourth birthday. He took an overdose of sleeping pills. He was in London; I was in New York. I was staying in Rachel's apartment in the mid-thirties, where she lived with her husband. They're now divorced.

I flew back to London that night in time for Christmas, but my brother was dead. I did not see him. I never saw him again.

A year later, Rachel's mother committed suicide in New York. We have this in common, this horrible tie.

I couldn't pray for my brother and now I can't pray for Rachel, who I think is dying. I have forgotten how to pray.

While the chicken's cooking I become very restless and say I'm going out for a short time. Rachel goes back to bed.

I walk north, through SoHo, then through Washington Square where I once met a drug-dealer who'd spent time in both Italian and German prisons. (He preferred the Italian, which was cosier because the Italian families brought in food.)

I find myself in a church at the beginning of Fifth Avenue.

The Passion of Christ on the Cross is being read out by the priest. Even my grandmother, who was agnostic, said, about the Crucifixion: "That poor man. Even if it's not true, it's such a sad story."

When I was a child I used to pray alone at night, looking at the crucifix at the foot of my bed. The body of Christ was white on a dark Cross. I prayed for a canary I had seen in a poor village in Spain where my mother had taken me on holiday. I prayed that this bird would escape. Please God let the bird be free.

When I went to the dentist I summoned the image of Christ on the Cross so that the pain was easy to bear.

Now in this church on Fifth Avenue I can't concentrate on the words, and the image of the man I am in love with, who looks like my dead brother, keeps appearing before me. When we get to the Agnus Dei, 'Lamb of God who takest away the Sins of the world, grant us Peace,' tears run down my cheeks. But I am restless in the church, I can't pray and I leave early, walking quickly back to Rachel's apartment.

Rachel in her white nightdress and white dressing-gown is in command of the supper. She wants to do it herself. She says: "That man who looks like your brother. He just appeared on the television news."

I am upset by this.

The man who looks like my brother came to church with me once in London. I asked him to go to a movie with me the night before but he preferred to go to a Memorial Service with me the next day.

In the church, this man went down on his knees in front of me. I was aware that he knew how to pray, or thought he did, and I didn't. I sat behind him, thinking how hideous the church was.

At the same time I wanted someone to help me.

Now that man's abandoned me, like my brother, and it's as though these intimate things between us never happened.

Rachel thinks that when someone close to you commits suicide, you find another person like them, that reminds you of them, and try to play out the ending you never had with the person who died.

The next day I have to fly back to England. Before I go, we have another candle-lit dinner. Rachel's ordered a cab to take me to the airport. It arrives early, driven by a young Israeli. She tells me to make him wait. She wants to go on talking, about love. What is it?

I say it's a feeling of intense happiness. She replies: "But then it's incredibly painful if it's not reciprocated."

....

I'm impatient to get into the cab but she leans across the table and looks at me intently. She asks if I think she will get better. As she asks this, she becomes like a little girl. She says: "All my other friends say I will."

I can't say she'll get better because I don't know. Or maybe I do, that's why I can't say it. I murmur inadequately that I don't know why some people have to suffer more than others. Then I have to leave.

I hug her awkwardly at the gates of the elevator, or she hugs me, as I'm holding two bags. This is the last time I see Rachel.

Nine months later I'm going to her burial. It's in a small village in Connecticut. It's January. I drive up there in a rented car with my American friend Carla and her ex-husband.

We drive over the Hudson River, past high-rise blocks in Harlem, but find we've gone the wrong way and have to turn round. Then we get on the right road north and drive up through Connecticut, past other rivers, enormous icicles hanging from banks, and huge pine trees. We're going to the cemetery where Rachel's mother's buried, where Rachel will be buried herself.

The cemetery's on a small hill, and the coffin's already there, beside the grave, with some flowers on it. About fourteen people are there, including the Vicar.

A friend of Rachel's reads out a passage from the book Rachel was writing about her mother, describing how she had had to find this graveyard for her mother several years earlier, and buried her between two women, Constance and Beauty, because she liked the names. This seems to me the saddest thing of all, that she had to find an unknown place to bury her mother, instead of a family graveyard, as they had no proper family.

The Vicar says we can throw bits of earth into the grave if we want. Some of the friends do this. I have a strong resistance to it.

....

A flashback of childhood memory comes to me — I am with my mother in Avila, a walled town in Spain. I am seven. We visit a church with some Spanish children. Inside the church we're supposed to put our hands down a hole to touch this relic of a saint. I refuse to do this.

Now, at Rachel's grave, I feel I'm involved in an obscene primitive rite in being asked to throw in earth or touch the coffin and pretend the thing in there is Rachel. A woman in front of me is sobbing but I can't bring myself to comfort her. I stand there shifting from foot to foot, not knowing what to do.

At the lunch later in a local restaurant my friend Carla, who's sitting next to the Vicar, asks him: "What is the current theological teaching on Heaven? I want to know where Rachel's going."

He doesn't give a satisfactory answer. He says he's never known such confusion over a funeral.

Carla explains that there was no proper family to organise it. She adds: "All the people here were in love with her."

Next day in New York I go on my own to St Patrick's Cathedral for Sunday Mass. A famous American Archbishop O'Connor is preaching. I find his ranting against AIDS and sex before marriage obscene and un-Christian. He seems to love the sound of his own voice.

During the Mass they play the hymn "Amazing Grace". The soothing words and tune bring tears down my cheeks and I feel completely lost. However I don't or can't pray.

I see two people who look like junkies, in pop-stars' clothes, singing vigorously as I leave the church.

A few months later I have a dream in which I have to be alone with Rachel's dead body in her loft. It's very frightening. She's involved in some voodoo rites from Haiti, in which your body is reunited with the earth. She's trying to leave her coffin. I am supposed to help her. But I can't. I don't want to be alone with her.

When I tell a Catholic friend of mine my dream she says it means I'm supposed to pray for Rachel's soul. How on earth would I do this? I have no idea.

Nine months after Rachel's death, I'm told I have cancer myself.

As I have the first chemotherapy injection, the image of Christ on the Cross suddenly comes before me, as it did when I was a small child at the dentist, to help me bear the pain.

Now at last I know how to pray. Now the words come to me very easily, the words the woman wrote in her notebook on the New York subway that day.

"I am very scared. Please God help me!"

Bible Stories for Adults
No 46: The Soap Opera

JAMES MORROW

*The curtain rises on a vast pile of excrement and refuse. As
dung heaps go, this one is actually rather appealing, a hypnotic
conglomeration of ash, trash, discarded toys, cast-off utensils,
coffee grounds, egg shells, orange rinds, feces, and 55-gallon
drums, not to mention the refrigerator, washing machine, toilet
bowl, food processor, and VCR, plus the two TV sets and the
large Whirlpool clothes dryer. Our initial impression is of a
huge mound of aspic in which some demented chef has
suspended characteristic chunks of the twentieth century.*

*Two wooden poles bracket the dung heap, a high-tension line
slung between them. In the middle of one pole sits a jerry-
rigged transformer, furtively siphoning electricity from the
cable and feeding it to a long strip-plug swaying above the trash
like a pendulum. About half the machines are connected to the
plug, including the 40-inch Zenith TV, stage left, and the 30-
inch Sony TV, stage right.*

*Enter our hero, Job Barnes: ageless, beardless, spry. He
wears an Italian silk suit that cost more than the present
production. Like a masochistic mountain climber, he slowly
ascends the eastern slope of the heap. Reaching the summit, he
brushes bits of garbage from his coat and trousers and speaks
directly to the audience.*

JOB   No way to treat a two-thousand-dollar suit, huh? Don't
worry, I've got plenty more back home. God gave me a
whole *closet* full of suits. (*beat*) Fifteen closets full of suits,

actually, along with a seventy-five-room mansion to keep the closets in.

He starts down the western face of the heap.

JOB   Will you permit me a bit of vanity? When my book made the rounds in New York, nine major publishers bid on it. *The Job Barnes Story: How I Suffered, Suppurated, and Survived.* My agent and I decided to go with St Martin's Press. The name had a certain spiritual ring, plus they came up with three million dollars. (*wanders toward the Zenith TV*) Random House offered as much, but I'd had quite enough *randomness* in my life by then. (*taps on the TV*) My agent betrayed me. She said there was a movie deal in the works, then turned around and sold the thing to television: *One Man's Misery*, the world's first soap opera set on the edge of the Arabian desert in the fourth century B.C. Pure trash, but people are eating it up. Last season, we left *Ryan's Hope* in the dust and nearly blew *General Hospital* off the air.

He slips a vest-pocket King James Bible from his suit and opens to the Book of Job.

JOB   You all know the basic concept. (*reads*) "There was a man in the land of Uz, whose name was Job — and that man was perfect and upright, and one that feared God, and eschewed evil. And there were born unto him seven sons and three daughters. His substance also was seven thousand sheep, and three thousand camels, and five hundred yoke of oxen, and five hundred she asses, and a very great household." (*closes Bible*) An old story, really. Man finds perfect life, man loses perfect life, man regains perfect life.

Unseen by Job, a tattered quilt rises from the western slope of the dung heap. Underneath we spy Franny Fenstermacher, a middle-aged, female Pangloss, the sort of person who'd note the protein value of the worm you just consumed with your apple. Bent with osteoporosis, wracked by emphysema, she wears a ragged chemise, a ratty apron, and a red kerchief tied around her head like a bandage. As she yawns and stretches, we get intimations of her vanished vibrancy and former beauty.

JOB   Yes, but is our hero truly content after that? Does he come home every day and admire his new sheep, count his new oxen, kiss his loyal wife, soak in his hot tub, and take his Mercedes out for a spin? (*plucks a yellowing newspaper from the dung heap*) For the first millennium or so: yes, he does. But then, gradually, doubt overtakes him. He wonders if he's been exploited. He wonders if he should retract his repentance. He even wonders if he should ask God to . . . apologize. (*reads*) "Two hundred die in Miami jetliner crash." (*turns page*) "Mudslide buries ninety-five thousand in Lisbon." (*turns page*) "Ethiopian famine claims half a million." (*turns page*) "Dear Abby: My first grandchild was born with spina bifida . . ." (*turns to comics*) "'What's that lump, Blondie?' 'I can no longer hide the truth, Dagwood: I've got breast cancer . . .'"

Still unseen by Job, Franny crawls up the slope on hands and knees. She gets to within a foot of the Sony TV then collapses, dizzy and exhausted. Meanwhile, Job sets down the newspaper and gestures in a manner that encompasses the entire heap.

JOB   So I'm back. The old neighbourhood: it looks mighty different. We didn't have electricity way back when. We didn't have major appliances. Ah, but the aura's still the same. Can you see the holiness rising from these egg shells? Good. Do you sense the godhead in these coffee grounds? Of course you do. I spent some of the most intense days of my life in this place, railing against the cosmos, demanding to know the reason for my suffering. (*raises eyes to heaven*)

. . . .

Listen, sir, I want the contest to continue. I'd like to see you once more — today, if you can make it. This is your servant Job speaking, and I'm asking, most humbly, for a rematch. (*protracted pause*) Silence. Utter quiet. He's been like that lately. So aloof, so distant, so . . . (*gags on the air*) Pfffooo, the smell hasn't changed, has it? A sea of hog vomit at low tide. (*recovers*) Still, I'm glad I'm not home now. Every day at this time, the maids tune in *One Man's Misery*. The damn thing echoes all over the mansion. Here, at least, I'm safe . . .

Franny flicks on the Sony. An organ theme bursts forth, the sort of nervous chords heard in 1940s radio dramas, but the screen remains blank. Job is startled by the sound – and equally startled to see Franny squatting in front of the TV.

JOB   Jesus!
DOCTOR'S VOICE (*from the Sony*)   That's right, Mrs Barnes. Your baby has no brain. You could use his head for a piggy bank, were you so inclined . . .
MOTHER'S VOICE (*from the Sony*)   Are you certain, physician?
DOCTOR'S VOICE (*from the Sony*)   That's not God's grace you see streaming from his little ear — it's the light of this candle.

Music: organ bridge.

FRANNY (*resignedly, as she lowers the volume*)   The Sony has sound but no picture. The Zenith has picture but no sound. Between the two of them, they make a reasonable home entertainment center. (*gestures toward the Zenith*) Would you mind?
JOB   I hate this show.
FRANNY   Please.
JOB   It feeds on pain.

FRANNY (*coughing*)   Do a poor sick woman a favor.

Job flicks on the Zenith: mid-shot of Jemima, married daughter of the hero of One Man's Misery, *dressed in the fashion of the fourth century B.C. She sits at a loom, weaving. As Franny raises the volume on the Sony, one of Jemima's handmaids, Lilia, rushes into the shot and throws herself on the floor.*

JEMIMA (*on television*)   What is it, Lilia?
LILIA (*on television*)   Mistress, a tragedy has occurred.
JEMIMA (*on television*)   Speak its name.
LILIA (*on television*)   I fear to.
JEMIMA (*on television*)   Obey me.
LILIA (*on television*)   There was a camel stampede.
JEMIMA (*on television*)   And?
LILIA (*on television*)   And your firstborn son. He's . . . dead.

Music: organ bridge.

NARRATOR (*voice-over, from the Sony*)   Will life get even more trying for Job and his family? Will Kezia come out of her coma? Will the village surgeons give Keren-happuch the lower jaw she so fervently desires? Will our hero continue to trust God? Tune in tomorrow for the next inspiring episode of *One Man's Misery.*

Job flicks off the Zenith. Franny flicks off the Sony.

FRANNY   Damn. I slept right through it. Just my luck.
JOB   Who the hell are you?
FRANNY   I live here. Franny Fenstermacher. (*assertive*) This dung is all mine.
JOB   Squatter's rights?
FRANNY   Exactly. (*friendly but cautious*) I'd be happy to help you find your *own* dung, but this heap's taken.

JOB (*pointing to cables*)   Are you responsible for all these wires and transformers and things?

FRANNY (*proud*)   Uh-huh. Ever visit Fenstermacher's House and Garden Supplies over on Central Avenue? I'm the co-owner. (*hand sweeps across the heap*) I expect I'll install some plumbing next. You know — get the toilet working, maybe put in a Jacuzzi. (*struggles to her feet, coughing*) Assuming I don't go blind first. Diabetes.

JOB   Oh, dear.

FRANNY   Not to mention the emphysema and the osteoporosis and the arthritis.

JOB   How horrible . . .

FRANNY   It's terrible, but it's not horrible. Horrible is what happened to my husband.

JOB   (*gulps*)   Oh?

FRANNY   He lost everything when our local savings and loan went under. The day Bill got the news, he walked straight into a McCormick reaper.

JOB   Killed?

FRANNY   Shredded . . .

JOB   I'm sorry.

FRANNY   Like a CIA document. I can talk about it now, but I nearly went mad at the time.

JOB   I can imagine.

FRANNY   Then there's my son. Do you know what a Bradley-Chambers child is?

JOB (*to audience*)   I don't want to hear about this.

FRANNY   A Bradley-Chambers child suffers from Bradley-Chambers syndrome. This means he has a cleft palate, a hare lip, too many fingers, kidneys pitted with lesions, and a defective heart. It means he lives in constant pain. My Bradley-Chambers child is named Andy.

JOB   Mercy.

FRANNY (*points to the Zenith*)   One of these days, Job

....

Barnes is going to get it all back — his possessions, his family, his health.

JOB (*retrieving newspaper*)   Not as long as the ratings hold out.

FRANNY   Are you being cynical? I don't like cynics. (*lifts eyes to heaven*) Listen, Lord, I want you to know I'm not bitter. You have your reasons. (*turns to Job, points skyward*) He has his reasons.

JOB (*reads*)   "School bus plunges off ravine." (*turns page*) "Bridge of San Luis Rey collapses." (*stares at Franny*) I wish I had your faith.

FRANNY (*pulls Job's book from apron pocket*)   This sustains me. *The Job Barnes Story: How I Suffered, Suppurated, and Survived.* It has a happy ending.

JOB (*reads*)   "Cholera death-toll reaches fifteen thousand in Iraq." (*turns page*) "Floods destroy Peruvian village."

FRANNY   Sooner or later, God will fix everything. He'll heal my child, take away my infirmities, find me a new husband . . .

JOB   And by coming here, you thought perhaps you could speed up the process?

FRANNY (*defensive*)   Is that so crazy? Isn't it reasonable to suppose he's more likely to notice me if I'm crawling around on Job's own dung heap? (*taps on book*) It all really happened, you know. *The Job Barnes Story* is one hundred percent true.

JOB (*nodding*)   Indeed. I wrote it.

FRANNY (*shocked*)   What?

JOB   I wrote that book.

As Franny consults the author photo on the back of the dust jacket, her jaw drops in astonishment.

FRANNY   Good gracious, that's you! You're Job Barnes! (*coughs*) I'm so ashamed. Here I am, droning on about my problems to the man who practically *invented* suffering. (*indicating Job's book*) It says here you lost your herdsmen, your camel drivers, your sheep . . .

JOB   My children.

FRANNY   Your oxen, your donkeys — and then you got all those awful boils.

JOB (*reminiscing*)   Scraping myself with a potsherd. Scratching myself to the bone.

FRANNY   The pus oozing out of you like sweat.

JOB   "Curse God and die," Sheila said.

FRANNY   But then you accepted the divine will. (*pulls ballpoint pen from apron*) You repented in dust and ashes. (*thrusts book and pen toward Job*) Hey, do me a favor, Mr Barnes?

Job takes book and pen from Franny, autographs the title page.

JOB   There. (*returns book*) A collector's item.

FRANNY   I understand what I'm doing here, but I don't understand what *you're* doing here.

JOB (*matter-of-factly*)   I want a rematch. I want the debate to continue.

FRANNY   Debate?

JOB   "Resolved: Job Barnes should never have withdrawn his case." (*to heaven*) Got that, sir? I hereby retract my repentance. I'm back on the old ash pile, and I'm as indignant as ever. (*opens vest-pocket Bible, reads*) "God destroyeth the perfect and the wicked. If the scourge slay suddenly, he will laugh at the trial of the innocent." Now *that's* a Job I can respect, keeping his creator on the hook. (*flips ahead*) "I was at ease, but God hath broken me asunder. He hath also taken me by my neck, and shaken me to pieces, and set me up for his mark. His archers compass me round about. He poureth out my gall upon the ground." That's the real me, Franny — bloodied but unbowed!

. . . .

FRANNY (*unimpressed*)   Okay, but ultimately he answered your accusations. He dazzled you with the majesty of the universe. (*coughs*) He awed you, he amazed you, he —

JOB   He pulled rank on me. (*reads in Godlike tone*) "Where wast thou when I laid the foundations of the earth?" (*snaps Bible closed*) In other words, "I'm God, and you're not." Is that an argument, Franny?

FRANNY   What're you so upset about? He rewarded your patience handsomely. New family, new house, new herds . . .

JOB   Stock options, trust funds, book royalties, TV residuals. Bribery, all of it. Hush money.

FRANNY (*struck by the idea*)   Hush money . . .

JOB   Hush donkeys, hush sheep, hush oxen: anything to keep me from telling the world how I really felt. He *used* me, Franny. He put me through hell on a dare, then passed it off as an inquiry into the problem of pain. I think he owes me an apology.

FRANNY   An apology? You're going to ask God for an *apology*?

JOB (*surprised by his own nerve*)   Yes. Not justice. Not mercy. An apology.

FRANNY   I'll tell you one thing — I'm not going to hang around when you do that.

JOB   You want to know the worst of it? The wager wasn't even Satan's idea. God instigated the whole sordid affair. (*opens Bible, reads in Godlike tone*) "Hast thou considered my servant Job?"

FRANNY   "That there is none like him in the earth, a perfect and upright man."

JOB   A perfect patsy. (*to heaven*) Look, God, we needn't start out with eschatology. A game of chess will do. I'll give you a bishop advantage and the first move. (*to Franny*) He's not talking. *Deus absconditus.* (*to heaven*) Backgammon, sir? Dominoes? (*reads from Bible*) "Who hath laid the measures thereof, if thou knowest, or who hath stretched the line upon

it? Whereupon are the foundations thereof fastened? Who
laid the cornerstone thereof?" (*sarcastic*) Cornerstone.
Earth's cornerstone. Okay, sure, that's fine for the fourth
century B.C., but now I want to hear from the *modern* God.
(*reads*) "Hast thou given the horse strength? Has thou
clothed his neck with thunder?" (*to heaven*) These old
metaphors won't do, sir. Not in the post-Darwinian era.

FRANNY   Sometimes, at noon, standing in the sun with the
heat leaping up from the ashes and the flies buzzing in my
ears, I'm overwhelmed by the utter sacredness of this place.

JOB (*selecting a dung nugget*)   Sinai, I'm told, was cleaner.

FRANNY   He's near. He's very near.

JOB   Have you ever considered the taxonomy of turds?

FRANNY   What? (*offended*) Certainly not.

JOB   At the very bottom: dogshit. The lowest of the low —
rag pickers, bag ladies, and those who hang out on dung
heaps. When you treat somebody like dogshit, your contempt
knows no bounds. (*tosses the nugget, selects another*) Next we
have chickenshit. Chickenshit allows for a certain humanity.
A chickenshit may be a contemptible coward, but at least
he's not dogshit. (*tosses the nugget, selects another*) Bullshit
comes after that — blatant and aggressive untruths. But at a
certain level, of course, we admire our liars, don't we?
Bullshitters get elected, chickenshits never. (*tosses the nugget,
selects another*) At the top of the hierarchy, at the summit of
the heap: horseshit. Horseshit is false too, but it's not
manifestly false. Horseshit is subtle. Horseshit is nuanced.
Horseshit plays to win. Horseshit fools some of the people
some of the time. Divine justice, for example, is horseshit,
not bullshit. Indeed, we hold horseshit in such esteem that we
decline to bestow the epithet on one another. A person can
be a bullshitter, but only a horse can be a horseshitter.

FRANNY   What a thoroughly depressing man you are. I wish
I'd never met you.

JOB   I'm thinking of writing a second book. Kind of a

....

natural history of bullshit. Henry Kissinger will get a whole chapter. So will Oliver North. Know what I'm going to call it?

FRANNY   I'm not the least bit interested.

JOB   *When Good Things Happen to Bad People.*

FRANNY   Shut up.

JOB (*points toward heaven*)   That's what *he* wants too. He wants me to shut up.

A wheelchair rolls into the scene, bearing a thin, pale, thirteen-year-old boy named Tucker, a contemporary equivalent of Tiny Tim. Intravenous feeding tubes lead from his arms to bottles of nutrients set on aluminum poles. Wincing and groaning, he rotates the tires with his gloved hands, gradually maneuvering himself to the base of the dung heap.

FRANNY   Hi, fella.

Tucker grunts, gasps, and eventually catches his breath.

FRANNY   You okay?

TUCKER (*brightly*)   Hi, I'm Tucker, and I've got AIDS!

JOB (*looking around*)   Where are we — Lourdes?

FRANNY (*to Tucker*)   Poor child. Poor, poor child. (*admonishing Job*) Lourdes was once a dung heap too.

TUCKER   A mislabeled batch of blood, and before I knew it —

FRANNY   You mean you're —

TUCKER   A hemophiliac, ma'am. My father's about ready to kill himself. My mother's been doing the talk shows. (*points to the Zenith*) Hey, does that work? I think Mom's on at five.

FRANNY   We get a picture on the Zenith, sound on the Sony.

TUCKER   Excellent. Ever watch *One Man's Misery*?

FRANNY   Faithfully.

JOB First hemophilia, then AIDS. (*to heaven*) My hat goes off to you. You've outdone yourself.

TUCKER Did I come to the right dung heap? Is this the place where God appears?

JOB Every twenty-four hundred years or so. I hope you brought your toothbrush.

FRANNY You came to *exactly* the right dung heap.

TUCKER Are *you* sick, ma'am?

FRANNY Diabetes.

TUCKER My aunt had that. Are your legs going to rot off?

FRANNY I hope not.

JOB (*pointing skyward*) Don't give him any ideas.

TUCKER (*indicating Job*) Is he sick too?

FRANNY Uh-huh. He's got *hubris*.

JOB Monopoly? Tic-tac-toe? Croquet?

FRANNY Don't listen to anything he says.

TUCKER You know what I really hate?

FRANNY What?

TUCKER Eggplant. Eggplant and being a virgin. I don't even know what it *looks* like.

FRANNY Eggplant?

TUCKER Screwing.

FRANNY (*bewildered*) Oh, dear. (*ponders*) It looks like dancing.

TUCKER Bullshit.

JOB Exactly.

TUCKER Do you suppose there're any trading cards around here?

FRANNY (*amiably*) I wouldn't be surprised. (*picks through trash*) Let's go hunting.

Tucker slips a stack of trading cards from his shirt pocket, fanning them out like a bridge hand.

TUCKER I'm collecting the series called *Operation Desert*

....

Storm. (*consults checklist card*) I need "Number 42: Patriot Missile Control Center" and "Number 17: General Colin Powell."

Franny retrieves a cardboard rectangle from the heap.

FRANNY (*reads*) "*What Pierre Saw Through the Keyhole*: Number 34 in a Series of Authentic French Post Cards."
TUCKER   Ooo — gimme.

Franny hands Tucker the post card, then resumes her search.

TUCKER   Golly.
FRANNY (*finding Desert Storm card*)   Hey, here's one. (*brings card to Tucker*) Have you got "Number 4: General Norman Schwarzkopf"?
TUCKER (*disappointed*)   Two of 'em.
FRANNY   My own little boy collects baseball cards. (*coughs*) That is, he *will* collect baseball cards, after he gets well.
TUCKER   What's his name?
FRANNY   Bradley Chambers. (*shudders*) I mean Andy.
JOB   Ping-pong, God? Tiddlywinks? (*to Franny and Tucker*) Looks like he's closed up shop. He's off visiting the fifth planet of Alpha Centauri, dropping brimstone on the aborigines.

Suddenly the door of the Whirlpool clothes dryer flies open and the barrel begins to turn furiously, spewing socks and underwear across the stage. A calm, soothing, resonant male voice booms out of the chamber.

VOICE FROM THE WHIRLPOOL (*slow, measured pace*)   Don't be so sure about that . . .

Job and Franny jump three feet into the air and hug each other.

JOB   Jeez!
FRANNY   Gracious!
TUCKER   Wow!
FRANNY   And the Whirlpool isn't even plugged in.

The barrel keeps spinning, generating a strong wind that blows pieces of refuse off the heap and into the audience.

VOICE FROM THE WHIRLPOOL   "Who is this that darkeneth counsel by words without knowledge?"
JOB (*stuttering with fear*)   Er, you d-don't remember me? Your s-servant Job?

As the Voice continues to speak, we feel as if we're in the presence of a bombastic Santa Claus or a lame-duck Southern senator. The Voice certainly doesn't seem malign.

VOICE FROM THE WHIRLPOOL   "Gird up now thy loins like a man." (*beat*) Of course I remember you. What's on your mind, son?
TUCKER (*points to Job*)   He called himself Job. (*turns to Franny*) Is he really *Job*?

Nodding, Franny guides Tucker away from Job.

FRANNY   Uh-huh. Stand over here. I'll explain later.
JOB   Are you the right God? The twentieth-century God?
VOICE FROM THE WHIRLPOOL   I am that I am.
TUCKER (*to Franny*)   He's Popeye the Sailor?
FRANNY   Sshhh.
VOICE FROM THE WHIRLPOOL (*mildly chiding*)   Come, come, servant, I haven't got all day.
JOB   I don't want you to think I intend any disrespect, but

....
119

... may I speak freely, sir?

VOICE FROM THE WHIRLPOOL   Of course.

JOB   I believe you owe me an apology.

VOICE FROM THE WHIRLPOOL   A *what*?

JOB   An apology.

VOICE FROM THE WHIRLPOOL   I don't do apologies.

JOB   It's like this, sir. The way I see it, you tortured me to win a bet, then proceeded to buy my silence. I guess I'm feeling a bit ...

VOICE FROM THE WHIRLPOOL   Used?

JOB   Exactly.

VOICE FROM THE WHIRLPOOL   Exploited?

JOB   Right.

VOICE FROM THE WHIRLPOOL   Duped?

JOB   Sheila calls me history's stooge.

VOICE FROM THE WHIRLPOOL   Phooey.

JOB   How's that?

VOICE FROM THE WHIRLPOOL   I said phooey. *History's* stooge? (*stifles a chuckle*) You really think the wager ended with you? Let's not be vain, son. The contest between God and the Adversary goes on forever — rather like that lousy soap opera you all watch. Remember the bubonic plague?

JOB   Who could forget?

VOICE FROM THE WHIRLPOOL   It was largely my way of testing the faith of Samuel Schechner, a singularly pious and highly successful Jewish rug merchant living in fourteenth-century London.

FRANNY (*confused*)   Huh? The whole plague?

VOICE FROM THE WHIRLPOOL   The whole plague.

TUCKER   Gosh.

VOICE FROM THE WHIRLPOOL   Then there was polio. Satan and I wanted to see if Franklin Delano Roosevelt would curse me to my face.

FRANNY (*perturbed*)   You created polio just for that?

VOICE FROM THE WHIRLPOOL   Uh-huh.

....

FRANNY   Goodness.

VOICE FROM THE WHIRLPOOL   The 1983 Colombian earthquake? I was testing the faith of Juan Delgado, a prosperous coffee merchant living in Bogota. As for diabetes and emphysema — yes, Franny, they exist for the sole and holy purpose of permitting you to demonstrate your devotion to me.

FRANNY   I'm trying my best.

VOICE FROM THE WHIRLPOOL   Finally, of course, there's AIDS. A major pestilence, sure, but no match for the grit and gumption of young Tucker over there.

TUCKER (*unconvinced*)   Er, you bet . . .

FRANNY (*coughs*)   He's only thirteen.

TUCKER   Thirteen and a half.

JOB   How many of these showdowns have there been so far?

VOICE FROM THE WHIRLPOOL   Enough to keep my job interesting.

FRANNY (*insistent*)   How many?

VOICE FROM THE WHIRLPOOL   Four thousand, seven hundred and fifty-eight.

FRANNY   And the score?

VOICE FROM THE WHIRLPOOL   Let me show you.

The number 4758 suddenly materializes on the Zenith TV, the numeral 0 on the Sony.

VOICE FROM THE WHIRLPOOL   God: four thousand, seven hundred and fifty-eight. Satan: zero.

TUCKER   That old Devil's a glutton for punishment.

VOICE FROM THE WHIRLPOOL (*agreeing*) He never learns.

FRANNY (*apprehensive*)   And in every case, you restored the victim to health, wealth, and happiness?

VOICE FROM THE WHIRLPOOL   Maybe not in *every* case.

FRANNY   Do you know ahead of time you're going to win?

VOICE FROM THE WHIRLPOOL   Of course I do. I'm God, for Christ's sake.

....

FRANNY (*to Tucker*) I think he owes all those people an apology.

VOICE FROM THE WHIRLPOOL What was that, Franny?

FRANNY (*to clothes dryer*) I said . . . I think you owe all those people an apology. (*coughs*) And while I'm at it, I never thought the Plagues of Egypt were particularly fair either.

VOICE FROM THE WHIRLPOOL I'll make you a deal, Franny. I won't tell you how to run your hardware store, and you won't tell me how to run the universe. "Who hath laid the measures thereof? Who hath stretched the line upon it? Whereupon are the foundations thereof fastened?"

JOB (*contemptuous*) *Foundations*. Don't give us your flat-earth theory. (*brandishing a turd*) Don't give us your geocentric solar system, your pre-Darwinian evolution, or any of that crap.

FRANNY (*correcting Job*) That horseshit.

JOB Right. We're way ahead of you on that stuff.

VOICE FROM THE WHIRLPOOL (*condescending but not vicious*) Hey, you made some progress while I was gone. Great. I'm proud of you. But maybe *I've* been busy too. Haven't you been keeping up with the history of religion? A couple of millennia ago, I added an afterlife — a pretty good one, too. Follow what I'm saying? In one corner we have you people, diddling around with your science, and meanwhile here's the creator, solving death itself. So don't come whining to me about diabetes and AIDS when I'm doling out immortality okay?

JOB We don't want justice in *heaven*.

FRANNY We want it here.

JOB And now.

TUCKER He's not a very *nice* clothes dryer.

FRANNY He's putting us through the wringer.

JOB (*fully the accuser now*) Does the name Naomi Barnes mean anything to you?

VOICE FROM THE WHIRLPOOL Who?

JOB   Naomi Barnes.

VOICE FROM THE WHIRLPOOL (*slightly chagrined*)   I've created so many people . . .

JOB   She was one of those seven sons and three daughters I had in the beginning. Chapter One, Verse Nineteen. (*quavering*) She had a name. She had a face.

FRANNY   Freckles?

JOB   No freckles.

FRANNY   Andy has freckles.

VOICE FROM THE WHIRLPOOL   Ah, so you want to quote scripture, eh, bigshot? Let's move on up to Chapter Forty-two. Suddenly you've got seven brand new sons and three brand new daughters, just as good as the previous ones. Better in fact. "And in all the land were no women found so fair as the daughters of Job."

FRANNY   He's never going to apologize, is he?

JOB   It's not in his nature.

Franny sits down on the dung heap, thoroughly discouraged.

VOICE FROM THE WHIRLPOOL   You know what I like about you folks? You're so *innocent*. And around here innocence gets rewarded. Go ahead, name your price. You want a house in the country?

JOB   My herdsmen were innocent too. You arranged for their slaughter.

VOICE FROM THE WHIRLPOOL   A Lear jet? Superbowl tickets?

FRANNY (*rising*)   And his shepherds were also innocent. (*coughs and shakes fist*) You incinerated them!

VOICE FROM THE WHIRLPOOL   A table at Sardi's? A castle in Spain?

FRANNY (*coughing*)   Give this man his self-respect back! Give this boy his future back! Give my child a life!

VOICE FROM THE WHIRLPOOL (*slightly paranoid*)   "Where wast thou when I laid the foundations of the earth?"

JOB (*rolling his eyes*)   Here we go again.
FRANNY   A one-track mind.

Franny hobbles toward the Sony TV and slaps a white rag over the screen, obscuring the numeral 0.

JOB   That's the idea!
TUCKER   Go for it!

Rooting around in the junk, Franny draws out a can of red paint and an artist's brush.

VOICE FROM THE WHIRLPOOL   "Who shut up the sea with doors, when it brake forth, as if it had issued out of the womb? Hast thou commanded the morning since thy days?"

Slowly, methodically, Franny paints a red 3 on the Sony screen: Satan's half of the scoreboard. Job and Tucker applaud.

VOICE FROM THE WHIRLPOOL (*furious*)   "Hast thou entered into the springs of the sea? Hast thou seen the doors of the shadow of earth? Out of whose womb came ice? And the hoary frost of heaven: who hath engendered it?"

The clothes dryer barrel spins madly, generating a fearsome tornado that begins tearing the dung heap apart.

VOICE FROM THE WHIRLPOOL (*raging*)   "Canst thou bind the sweet influences of Pleiades, or loose the bands of Orion? Knowest thou the ordinances of heaven? Canst thou send lightnings, that they may go, and say unto thee, 'Here we are'?"
JOB   And now it's time . . .
FRANNY   To curse God . . .
JOB   And live.

The lights go out. The stage is dark but for the glowing scoreboard. God: 4755. Satan: 3.

JOB   Go to hell, clothes dryer!
FRANNY   Eat worms, clothes dryer!
TUCKER   Your mother's ugly, clothes dryer!

The three mortals continue hurling out curses, voices blending in a cacophony of rage.

JOB   Go to hell!
FRANNY   Eat worms!
TUCKER   Your mother's ugly!
JOB   Hell!
FRANNY   Worms!
TUCKER   Ugly!

The storm grows quiet. The lights come up. Job and Franny are nearly nude now, their garments torn off by the wind. Wads of trash cling to their flesh. The clothes dryer is still and empty.

TUCKER   Hey, you guys are *naked*!
JOB (*shaken by his own blasphemy*)   "Naked came I out of my mother's womb . . ."
FRANNY   "And naked shall I return thither . . ."
TUCKER   Will you show me what sex looks like?
FRANNY   Sure, Tucker. As soon as we get out of here.
TUCKER   Where are we going?
JOB   I don't know. East. We're looking for something.
TUCKER   What?
JOB   Better major appliances.
FRANNY (*agreeing*)   A clothes dryer without an ego problem.
JOB   A non-abusive washing machine.
FRANNY (*coughs*)   A loving refrigerator.
TUCKER   Anything else?

FRANNY   "Number 42: Patriot Missile Control Center."
JOB   "Number 17: General Colin Powell."
FRANNY   I hear Frigidaire has a good product line.
JOB   I'm told you can't go wrong with a Maytag.

Tucker pulls his trading cards from his shirt. Job and Franny join hands and together they start to wheel Tucker away.

TUCKER (*studying checklist card*)   How about "Number 15: Ready for Takeoff"?
JOB   We'll find one.
TUCKER   And "Number 6: Secretary of Defense Dick Cheney"?
JOB   Sure, Tucker.
TUCKER   It's pretty rare.
FRANNY   So are you, kid.

Job, Franny, and Tucker disappear off stage. Their voices drift across the ruins of the dung heap.

TUCKER   "Number 23: Mid-Air Refueling"?
JOB   Of course.
TUCKER   "Number 35: Bombs Over Baghdad"?
FRANNY   Naturally.
TUCKER   "Number 58: Burning Oil Wells"?
JOB   Right.
TUCKER   "Number 65: Mission Accomplished"?
FRANNY   Yeah . . .

Lights fade out.

Curtain.

The Last Priestess

MAUREEN DUFFY

"I am the last priestess," she said into the night as the gleaming half moon of the second manacle snapped into its fellow to form the perfect unbroken, unbreakable since she'd thrown away the keys, circle. Now there were only her wrists to do and she would be pinioned like that god she didn't believe in and in adoration of that goddess whom she worshipped. She looked down at her ankles with satisfaction.

Above her the moon, Her moon, rode between the clouds, her light putting out the pinpricks of the stars. The heavens should be rewritten, the priestess decided, with nothing but female constellations. Tomorrow, in the morning light when the city woke and all the commuters began to pour out of their carriages, through the cathedral stations into the streets heading for their stacked offices with their computer screens that were the missals of Mammon, the handbooks for his order of worship, she would be found hanging there. A crowd would gather, the police would be sent for, the fire brigade with cutting equipment, the television cameras to record it all.

They would ask why she had done it. She would tell them this had been the shrine of the goddess long before a church had been consecrated to the hanging man. It still kept her fiery name although they had made Her subservient to him, an adoring vessel instead of the source of power and light; the bulb rather than the generator, she thought. It was time to attach her wrists to the church railings. How empty the city was at night; the brooding cliffs of buildings that rose all around her were quite dark, apart from an occasional lit basement where an elderly caretaker no doubt huddled brewing tea with one eye on the video monitor that watched the empty corridors above his head.

Through a slash of street slung with lights between two blocks she could see the mirror panes of a skyraker where the reflected moon was swimming in and out among the cloud-banks. She would still be able to watch that progress in the tall looking glass once her wrists were pinioned and she could no longer turn round to study it behind the church spire.

The first would be easy. The manacles were already dangling in place looped where a horizontal bar conveniently met the uprights. Should she do the right hand or the left first, the dextrous or the sinister? Left was magical. If you stirred or danced anti clockwise, widdershins, against the norm laid down through patriarchal centuries of time keeping, you unleashed powers, people had once believed, that were beyond reason. She would do the left first but then how could the right be managed with no free hand to snap the bracelet shut? It was a problem she hadn't envisaged. All that careful preparation and she was stumped at the last minute. Her sacrifice must be incomplete; her symbol inadequate. Spreadeagled she would have felt triumphant, exalted. With one hand free to scratch, light a cigarette, lift a glass if she had one, she could only feel foolish. There was no point to the half gesture. She might as well abandon it and go home.

But that too was now impossible. She looked down at the pinioned ankles with distaste. If only she hadn't been so hasty with the keys. Both arms were still free and suddenly she was tired; her back was beginning to ache. If she'd been slung up as she'd imagined, dangling from the high cross bar, she would actually have been able to rest a little in her chains. The goddess herself was mocked by her failure.

She had planned it all so carefully with her map of archaeological sites, her dictionaries of mythology and Celtic etymology, reaching back into the past to drag the goddess out of obscurity, from the peat bog she had been tipped into, seeking her behind the colonising Latin names of Juno and Diana, and then all at once it had come with a flash of revelation. (A Damascus Road enlightenment perhaps. But there was none in the London A–Z, only a Dames Road and what might that conceal?). Beside water, the river, it would have to be, in an old place, preferably raised up. And there at last it was winking off the map at her. Llugh the god of light looked across at Breid the goddess of fire: Ludgate Hill led to St Bride's.

It was only one of her names and which name didn't really matter; it was the essence, the power that invested whatever combination of syllables in whatever tongue: Aphrodite who took the prettiest toyboys for her lovers or the deathly Morgan herself or Rhiannon of the singing birds.

Thinking of the names and faces of the goddess calmed her. She stretched up her hands and grasped the bar, swinging her feet off the ground and letting her back straighten. Traction, she remembered, that was good for the spine. She felt herself all bone, strung only on wire as she might have been one day if she hadn't left instructions in her will that she was to be consumed by fire and her ashes scattered on water, preferably that of the Thames opposite the church.

She had bought the handcuffs by mail order from an advertisement in the paper that had also offered aids to flagellation and vivid black and scarlet underwear. Once or twice, before she had found the ad, she had hovered near a sex shop without the courage to go in. All the times she had watched, nervously window shopping, at different vantage points, she had never seen a woman enter but the other advertisements she had pondered on in the windows of newsagents for services delivered by a variety of nannies, head girls, whiphanders, commandants of female prisons, had made her realize that somewhere a woman must be able to buy what she needed. It was only after the discreet box had arrived that she had seen identical shining bracelets in a joke shop among the rubber spiders, plastic dog turds and devil masks. Yet to buy them in such a place would have been unthinkable, a mockery, a heresy. There was a certain rightness in the anonymous brown wrapping paper and the straw coloured box. She felt herself part of an underground, an underworld where the goddess had often been worshipped, a secret society, a mystery. After all, fecundity, passion, sex was still part of her worship, though divorced from cycladic rhythms and dressed up in dirty macs and G-strings. It was wrong to deny its importance as the followers of the Hanging Man had done bringing sadness and death in place of fecundity, the cross instead of the cornucopia.

She remembered the childhood misery of Easter, the darkening of Black Friday, with its stripped altar, torture, the death that was called a passion, the spear thrust letting out blood and water. Then the entombment of Saturday when it was wrong to laugh or run because of the swaddled figure lying inside the rock with the flies buzzing at the stony door in spite of the sweet oils and unguents, and the exhaustion of Sunday when she was trailed from service to service feeling nothing and having to pretend to gorge on fatty roast lamb.

It was at university that she had first met the goddess. The reading of classical myths even as retold for children had never been encouraged at home. She had come across some of them in her "A" level Latin set books but taken them simply as the fictions of poets, men certainly, to clothe stories of war and adultery. This was different; a reference in Bede; a Christian monk admitting that the goddess had once been so powerful that her name, her festival, still named the Spring rising from the winter of death: Eostre. She was so excited by this revelation that she had pursued it through the labyrinths of reference books, works on matriarchy, the Willendorf Venus, Cycladic figurines, back through those classical meanderings she had dismissed before, stitching it all together into a seamless gown to throw over the image of the goddess in her head.

Behind her the church clock struck two. Some progress must be made. She felt in her pockets to see if there was a key she hadn't thrown away. Her own front door keys were both too large but she came up with a nail file whose hooked end might do. She began to jiggle it in the right hand lock and after a long few moments of hooking this way and that felt the point suddenly engage and something give. The manacle dropped tinnily to the ground. She picked it up and put it in her pocket, faced with the even more complex problem of what to do now.

If she simply reengaged it beside the other she would be able to snap both shut but then she would be slung at a ludicrous and uncomfortable diagonal across the railings. Using the nail file she unpicked the other lock and repositioned both handcuffs directly overhead. Then she returned the nail file to her pocket and without any further hesitation snapped first one then, with some strained manoeuvring, the other fetter into place. As soon as she'd done this she began to laugh as the name of the nearby street surfaced suddenly into her consciousness. What a pity she hadn't been able to do it in Fetter Lane.

"Oh well you can't have everything." She gazed down the lamp lit cutting to where the moon was about to sail out of the last top right hand pane of the tower block and felt a seep of desolation as she watched it go, leaving her alone with a sky empty except for the mirrored clouds.

The sharp edges of the metal soon began to cut into her wrists as the sack of her body hung from them, except when she rested by drawing herself upright with her hands hooked over the rail. She felt a little breeze chilling her that she hadn't noticed before and her stomach complained gustily into the silence. Her back ached and the constriction of her chest made it hard to breathe.

As the clock struck again she first saw the cat picking its delicate way towards her. She realized at once that it must be a messenger come to comfort and strengthen her. It stalked on purposefully, charcoal against the grey reaches of pavement under the translunary, translucent sky until it stood in front of her.

Hello, she said.

The cat came forward to brush its warmth against her legs expecting her to bend down and stroke it. When it got no answer it flung itself down on the stones and rolled, curling its head enticingly and pouring itself with arched back legs from side to side showing a pure white belly. Then it began to wash between the toes of a front paw, clenching and unclenching the soft pads over the retracted thorns. It seemed a shorter time until the clock struck again but her breathing had become very shallow and her own ribs seemed to be crushing in on her heart and lungs. Gradually she drifted into a half conscious doze.

It was in the very first pearling of dawn when a blackbird began to sing behind her in the churchyard somewhere, to be answered antiphonally from some distant peak of branch or roof through the backing group of sparrow cheep, that she sensed that the goddess was near. How would she come? Riding down from Cheapside on a white horse or striding across the water to bend over her and take her up as the Lady of the Lake had taken Launcelot to sink with him into the water or as great Astarte drawing back the setting moon to hold up the sun.

WPC Amen Johnson's 300cc roared past the tall silent blocks silencing the birds and putting a tabby cat to flight. Her promotion should be through this week and if it didn't come she was going to complain of discrimination but she hadn't decided yet whether to go for race or sex. She'd just check the church on her way. These days they'd take anything: fireplaces, pews, even the paving stones. Anything could end up as a garden ornament: fonts filled with wallflowers, statuary, water stoups for bird baths. The slumped figure was at first too far away to make out clearly through her visor. Someone had hung some old clothes on the railings or a sack. Suspicious bundles or packages had to be sussed out. She began to gear down.

The white moon of the helmet with its silvery eyepiece floated swollen imploding in front of her eyes. The police radio cracked and fizzed.

"Get an ambulance over here fast. Looks like we've got some sex maniac on the loose. Strung a woman up to the railings. I'm going to try to get her down. Come on now honey don't you snuff on me. We'll get that bastard."

WPC Amen Johnson took a bunch of keys from her pocket and began to try each in turn until she heard the liberating click that freed first one then the other ankle. When she had undone one wrist she put her shoulder under the limp bundle to support it as she undid the last toy shackle. She felt herself stagger a little as she took the full dead weight.

Leaving By Plane, Swimming Back Underwater

LAWRENCE SCOTT

God gave me a love at the end of autumn
when the trees last fruits taste of the worm.
God (or the Devil) brought me this harvest,
and I thank both givers for the love I gain.

Field of Flowers
Carlos Drummond de Andrade

1

The afternoon was hot.

I had set my heart upon this journey so far back, that there was no turning away now. The very first enthusiasm had faded into a kind of fate. This was what was to happen and there was no changing it. I kept the growing doubt beating in my heart and fluttering in my stomach, hidden from those, who, if they themselves had any doubts, did not show them, but only encouraged and aided me in my choice to leave, as the gospels put it: *mother and father, brother and sister and country and go follow Him.*

I was giving my life to God.

I was leaving by plane that afternoon for England.

The previous weeks had been a round of farewells to family and friends, and with each event, my fate was clearer and I could do nothing about it. I was toasted and feted as if fatted for the sacrifice, my mother's Benjamin, but now Abraham's Isaac. Would an angel descend from heaven to stay his hand?

I choked at the sight of my packed, open suitcase on the bed. There was not much to take, I would be given everything I needed when I entered the monastery. *If you have a bag in the house do not go back to get it.* There were a couple of shirts and most particularly long woollens, my mother's obsession with the cold I would have to suffer.

It was winter in England. It was 1963.

It was a hot afternoon. I wore a warm suit. We waited in the departure lounge for the flight to be announced. I was carrying a large bouquet of pink anthurium lilies, my Aunt Lucy's gift to her sister Claire in London. Their large fleshy hearts and erect yellow stamens pressed against the cellophane which was to save their tropical beauty against the hazards of the journey and death of the cold to come. Under my other arm a shiny black Bible, the Old and New Testaments in the Douai version, a gift from another uncle and aunt. The flight was announced and I held myself against every inclination to do the opposite thing. There was a sense that I did not know what I was doing. Very young at nineteen. After kisses and hugs I walked away without turning round till I got to the top of the steps into the plane. Then I turned and waved.

I watched the island become a flat distance: the mountains, the plains, the archipelago between Trinidad and Venezuela. All that I loved disappeared.

It is the theology of this that I am now swimming back to retrieve and examine. Theology? Words about God. Emotions about God.

It feels like swimming under water. Breathing is limited. I need to come to the surface for air.

I used to soar. Now, I dive.

2

A moon hangs in the window.

When I wake again the night is stretched so thin that behind

....

the darkness is a fast growing light, the sun, before it burns and before it is so strong that I cannot look at it. Now, still, the insects are breathing. Later, a cacophony of birds asking questions, Qu'est ce qu'il dit?

This is an ascetic's time.

I look out from the back bedroom window straining my eyes to see the outline of the Barackpore hills. A cool breeze comes off the shore of the night, the palms move their black fronds, their colour and the night's are the same. But I know them and I can distinguish their difference. Day is rousing, dew is like a cold sweat. The grass is drenched. I breathe in the damp, longing for the heat.

The darkness is thicker as I look out from my lit room. I turn off the light and the night is stretched so thin on the horizon that I can see the humps of the Barackpore hills drawn with a soft grey pencil. I can forget the loneliness of the electric light bulb.

I know those hills now as having an Indian name, but then as an adolescent ascetic, it was a name without a history, then I read theology and devotional treatises, not history: Thomas Merton's *Elected Silence*, his *Seven Storey Mountain*; and below my window, beyond the hibiscus hedge, were the barrack rooms circling the estate manager's house like ring-worm indentured to my skin.

My pain is invented. It is a theory concocted, and called sin, the devil's work, his temptation in my childhood Eden. I must punish it, purge it, confess it, resist it. I pray here at this bedside altar with a relic, a piece of a young Italian girl's flesh, a martyr for purity, an adolescent like myself. Maria Goretti. I kiss that dead flesh to protect my own, to enable me to say farewell to my flesh. This is my carnival. An adolescent's chastity is a fever. My pain is not the hunger of a distended stomach which wakes the small child in the barrack room early, so early that the cane cutters have not as yet moved to process to the fields wrapped against the dew, relieved that they are still alive, or dreading the day. I know nothing of this, yet, this is not a ceremony of innocence. This is a knowing which has wrecked paradise. This is a knowing which must be guarded against with rosary beads, the kissing of relics and crucifixes, the whispering of miraculous ejaculations:

> Tower of Ivory
> Pray for us.
> House of Gold
> Pray for us.
> Ark of the Covenant
> Pray for us.

There is the Roman Catholic chapel of The Holy Innocents among the canefields.

This is my waking for the early morning mass in San Fernando and I am seventeen. I am a seminarian on vacation and must not let my term-time horarium slide. I wake even before my parents, before my father's effervescence of Andrew's Liver Salts, his daily purge, tinkles with a silver spoon in a glass as he returns down the cream corridor to his room, and my mother's cups of hot tea, for him and her on a tray on her dressing table, and even before the night watchman leaves his post, the green bench beneath the pantry window where he sleeps and pretends to watch over us against the thief from the barrack rooms and board house villages along the road into San Fernando, now enslaved to my memory. Our trust is in God and the black man against the treachery of the coolie.

What do I hear in the whispering casuarinas?

This was how we spoke. This was what I heard. This is what I must say, what I must write down. It does not explain everything.

It is the metaphysics of memory which I develop here.

A theology of the plantocracy, the catechuminate of the colonial Church.

I wake before the servants come up.

The house is untouched from the night before, the house with *The Second Heart* enthroned, and last year's Palm Sunday palms twisted and dried stuck behind the frame, scraping against the cream concrete wall in the breeze.

It is that in-between time of day which begins the day, as there is that short in-between time as afternoon slides to the edge of the gulf and the blue mountains of Venezuela and a green flash inaugurates the night. Now, still, there is a morning star and the moon as the light behind the scrim of sky surges with the strength of the sun which blinds you at dawn on the Mayaro beach, with ocean breakers and sand all light, St Peter's church transfigured as are the fishing pirogues *Dou Dou* and *God Is Love*, and you feel you are the first person in the world to be touched, to be blinded. And if you pull seine you will catch fish.

The tendency is towards narrative, but the texture is torn from a tropical poetics.

3

But it was not yet light enough: still dark enough, for the beam from the headlights of the Princes Town bus to come over the cusp of the hill like a pantomine moon directed by an erratic child. As the racatang box of a bus freewheeled into the sugarcane gully after its grinding climb up from Monkey Town, already exhausted with its journey from Barackpore, and still the hill to climb from the bottom by the railway line and the cane loading derrick, where the road takes a right to Debe. When it starts its climb in the bend where the Roman Catholic chapel used to be in a barrack room, and then changes down into first for the steep climb past the Methodist school, I kiss my mother's cheek and say I am gone, leaving my father to understand my leaving. "Your father is not a demonstrative person," she said. It meant that I yearned for his love and could not feel it. It was an exercise in absolute faith, a belief in the invisible, and when it was given I was so enraptured that I could not hold it. It shattered like a crystal glass falling on the pantry floor: dramatic, incandescent, dangerous.

I went out into the dawn night without his touch.

As an adolescent ascetic I feel that my love for my mother crucified me to a higher ideal, to be a saint. It was her approval more than the invisible God and his son Jesus or his mother Mary, or the third person, the Holy Ghost. These were her pantheon, but my love was her and I carried my lips on her cheek pressed between my lips, between my gold-edged missal, marked with an image of Dominic Savio, another teenage saint of purity to counter the gyrating pelvis of Elvis Presley and the teenage culture of the nineteen-fifties, *Shaking All Over*, at the Rivoli Theatre. My lips opened at the confessional grid with words I had even once told her of the fever of my sin and then made pure for communion. My kiss on her cheek came with me out into the yard and down the gravel gap past the whispering casuarinas and the moonlight shadows of the tamarind tree, till I came to stand by the pitch road near the *Chiney* shop for the bus driver to pick me out in his beam, and stop.

Then as I entered the brown racatang box of a bus with wooden shutters against the dew and fresh colds, I entered another music far from the Roman Catholic hymns of the parish, or the Gregorian chant of the monks who taught me in the mountains of the north. I entered the night of black skin turbaned in clouds of white cotton, trembling with drums silenced by the dawn, made hesitant by history, their percussion silenced, the music of a singing which conjured *Shango* inside Saint John the Baptist. The gods of one place inhabit the saints of another, that is the belief of the people, if not of our priests.

See the circle, hear the bell, Baptists by Library Corner. This was their mourning ground.

....

These are my travels. The beginnings of that journey to give my life to God.

"These people," my mother said.

I know now that I felt safe among the black people of the bus and they protected my fear from *pujahs*, the mantra of the pundit, the Koranic verses of the Imman, Hindi, and *tassa* drum music which tore up the night and the black galvanized barrack rooms encircling my cream bungalow home on the hill, the estate manager's house, behind the wild tangle of bougain-villaea and the strictures of the hibiscus hedge. I feared the cutlass. I feared the desperate chopping, their desperate poverty, bush rum, love and *tabanca*, the passion of their unrequited loves which delivered them to death upon the branches of a mango tree. On hot Sunday afternoons when the siestas of Sundays were strewn with newspapers, and I still held the memory of the black parish priest smoothing out my mother's damask linen table cloth with his large black hands, like he did at the altar still smelling of altar wine and communion wafers; black hands with yellow palms and wiping his red lips on her large linen napkins, his voice modulated like his sermon. Hindi blared from loudspeakers on top of crimson taxis heralding the wedding procession of cars driven wildly across the canefields, tearing the sunshine and the gravel roads into ribbons announcing the wedding car like a *hosay* with bamboo and crêpe paper and Christmas-time tinsel housing bride and groom and page in satins and net and jewels, yellow gold from Patel's in San Fernando. Daisy, my nurse, used to lift me up to look down inside the car: "See the little boy, he sleeps between them to make sure they don't *jook* in the night," wise Daisy said, coming not from their world but living in an Indian village up Diamond way and knowing what she thought Indians did. And their faces were delivered beyond their childhoods, boy and girl and baby boy, and I tried hard to imagine them ribboned to the little boy, themselves children in the night of the galvanized barrack room that wedding night. *Jook she, jook she!*

Now I recited the villages like my rosary beads: Diamond, Esperance, Palmiste, Cocorite, Union Hall where I was conceived in the overseer's house, over the fields Golconda, then here we were at the Cross-Crossing down by the Cipero River before it reach Embarcadier. I slumbered, jostled against the warm shoulders of a market woman going into Mucurapo market with crocus bags of ground provision, a hand of green fig stored under the seat. As we went in and came out of the potholes she cradled me with my prayer books on my knee. "You is the madam child from Picton?" I nodded, glad to be recognised and given an identity in this night of a bus. My mother's fame spread far into the foothills of Monkey Town and Barackpore: school children walked miles barefoot to learn catechism at my mother's knee under the cream bungalow, black children, not Indians. They went to the Canadian Mission Methodists and Presbyterians to get their Christian God and education. What black children got was more, my mother, Coca-Cola, the Pope's infallibility and the transubstantiation of bread and wine into the body and blood of Christ. If they could learn the little blue penny catechism by heart, the black parish priest would let them make their first communion, and the Irish archbishop would come all the way from Port-of-Spain into the country to confirm them in their faith with a slap on the cheek.

"You grow into a fine boy, say a prayers for me," the market woman said as she let herself down into Mucurapo Street letting in the light and the smell of freshly cut oranges.

The pandemonium of the early morning coming into market banged around us in the box of a racatang bus grinding up Mucurapo to where it crosses with Lord and Coffee Streets. The cocks were crowing a new morning, echoing betrayal in my ears; a cacophony of car horn, cart wheel, newspaper boys, "*Gazette*", "*Guardian*", and the poor Princes Town bus straining up the hill to the Library Corner. It was part of my adolescent asceticism to travel by the bus rather than take a taxi from out of Diamond village: the hard wooden seats. What was my asceticism was life for others. And I remember my mother saying that after the war when my father didn't have a car, money was short and she had seven children; saving her cents she travelled into San Fernando and to market in Princes Town by the bus, much to the consternation of the wishes of the overseers and the English women out from England with their husbands who worked as engineers and chemists at the Usine Sainte Madeleine Sugar Company factory. She said she told them: "When I enter the bus I am Hélène Scott and when I come out of the bus I am still Hélène Scott." Whenever she told the story, and she found time to tell it often, I smiled with a pride in my chest and at the same time with a sadness in my heart and lump in my throat. Our lives were confused, something as simple as that — and the market woman had no other way to travel and she too was not changed by the bus.

It changed me utterly, for I am not a white child who has not travelled on the bus sleeping against the market woman who brings in the light and the smell of freshly cut oranges cut into two halves of the sun.

This journey changed me.

I came out into the hot sunshine and the blinding light to climb up from Library Corner to Harris Promenade past the Presbyterian church to the Roman Catholic church of Notre Dame de Bon Secours, Our Lady of Perpetual Help. Down the road, past the Town Hall, was the Anglican church, the two thieves on either side of Christ on Calvary, that is how I was taught to see the three churches of the promenade.

This was an age when the talk was still of heretics, pagans and Jews, their conversion prayed for at the mass of the pre-sanctified on Good Friday afternoon, hot boiling sun, three o'clock, fire sermons.

The promenade is opposite my old primary school, "Boys

School". It is the boys' RC school, smelling of coconut oil and the memory of Indian children, smart at sums. They are my *pardners*: Espinet, Hutchison, Redhead and Ramnarine. On the promenade are statues of Mahatma Gandhi and Uriah Butler, the Oil Field Workers' Trade Union's leader. There is a bandstand. Race and politics, politics is race. History is not simple and the meaning of freedom is different; bread of freedom broken is a different bread, some eat cassava, some flour.

The freedom I walked into was the freedom and theatre of the high vaulted church built by my uncle. The drama was the Catholic liturgy in Latin —

Introibo ad altare Dei —

Ad Deum qui latificat juventutem meum —

Indeed, the joy of my youth was this. I knew no other, except sin, the sin of impurity; that blinding, delicious passion, masturbation, which locked out all fear until twilight, and then out of that darkness, fear of death and hell, kept at bay with fingers chained to rosary beads.

For I also knew this journey in the afternoons or evenings, sometimes forgetting my asceticism, to enter the palaces of Hollywood, Satan's church: the Empire on Penitence Hill, the Globe, Radio City, Gaiety and the New Theatre, which gave me bad thoughts to fight against, having to make my act of contrition. Then, sleep, like balm.

Morning brought the hope of confession and starting all over again.

Purity, sin, impurity, confession.

I rest here, genuflect, enter my pew. I rest here, and there in front, my Aunt Lucy kneels where her family name is in a brass plaque at the front of the church with the names of the other families, French creoles — Lange, Farfan, de Verteuil, Agostini, de Pompignon, d'Abadie — religion and privilege, the church of the plantocracy.

I rest here, to return, keeping my eye on my aunt, in her fine

....

neat cotton frock, with a small brooch which is a butterfly on the lapel, and she smelling of vetivier and cus cus grass from Dominica.

I will return to her and another journey, one through art, without which there would not be this one now told.

4

This is my mourning ground. I surface to breathe. I dive for my visions.

I am travelling another way.

My first vision was when I was six and a half years old. The wings of the Archangel Gabriel in the church of Mary Magdalen. They turned out to be the shadow of the canopy above the high altar, an optical illusion misunderstood by a small child. Faith then was young and innocent and could deal with disappointment. The desire for visions was not dashed. Faith was learnt in the little blue penny catechism.

The company school bus of white children mostly, put me down at the gate of the little red brick Catholic church in Sainte Madeleine for catechism classes with Miss Vivvy and her class of black village children and her green parrot. And so it was that we learnt our penny catechism by heart and by parrot under the sapodilla tree, the questions asked and answered by us and the green parrot.

"Who made you?" Miss Vivvy.

"Who made you?" The green parrot by the sapodilla tree.

"God made me." The first communion class.

"God made me." The green parrot by the sapodilla tree.

"Why did God make you?" Miss Vivvy.

"Why did God make you?" The green parrot by the sapodilla tree.

And so on and on, at the age of seven, the age of reason, my vocabulary and metaphysical reflection expanded beyond all recognition as I learnt the theory of transubstantiation, infall-ibility, the immortality of the soul and what I should take most care of, my body or my soul. My soul. Somewhere inside of me, hidden, and I always imagined it was in the middle of my chest and the same shape as my heart. It was stained but capable of being made clean by confession and I embarked on a long list of sins over my first seven years. Mostly these were venial sins. The mortal ones were to come later and terrify me almost unto death and the brink of hell. These venial ones did not terrorise me, though if the truth was the truth, they added to the horrific pain of that man on the cross. I was responsible for his pain. At seven. Guilt was something so tangible to carry when everything else was so ethereal. I chose guilt and worked on it. The sweetness of the cleansing formed a habit I still find very difficult to kick: sin, confess, get clean, be forgiven, and you can do it all over again. There is only that night of real agony in case you died and might go to hell before you made confession the next morning before Mass. If you had a real nerve you could sleep having made an act of contrition with the intention of going to confession at the earliest possible opportunity. That might just save you if you died. Phew! An adolescence of sheer hell once those wet dreams started and I learnt the delicious activity of *jocking*, our colonial name for masturbation. 'Wanking' was a term I learnt much later. The name never carried the same marvellous connotations of energy and pleasure. We don't use the derogatory *jocker* like the English use 'wanker', a real term of derision when everyone is trying to salvage its meaning secretly. To call it masturbation felt like metaphysics and long words like transubstantiation. From a very early age religion and sex were inextricably entwined, the pleasure of each and the guilt of each. There is no more potent mix with which to be driven to sainthood, my real ideal.

My second vision was at eleven just prior to my confirmation, which was earlier than usual because I was so keen. I remember my new shoes which gave me blisters, wanting to walk up the aisle with the Lebanese girl from the convent school. Many forbiddens there. The fact that she was Lebanese, *Syrian*, and almost because she was a girl. I was already destined for the priesthood. That desire for the Elias girl foundered like my love written in messages at the back of holy pictures and delivered by a go-between to a Portuguese girl whom I later discovered never got my messages: my go-between, herself disappointed by unrequited love, pretended the cards were sent to her by her love-throb and scratched off my name and the girl's name to whom they had been sent, and inserted her own from her dearest fantasy. I discovered that flicking through her school books and finding my card. I kept silent about it, deeply shocked, angry, disappointed that my wooing had never really occurred, but even then, saddened and learning something about the nature of love. It is oneself that one loves, the eyes, the mirror, the pool. Sweet reflection of oneself.

But I digress, what of my vision?

I woke with a start, lying on the bottom bunk in the bedroom I shared with my older brother. Though now I think of it, reconstruct that memory, the bunk had been moved out and the twin beds put in, and it was the August holidays when my obsession with death and my dying was at its height: and as that brief twilight of evening held the canefields and the avenue of casuarinas and the large tamarinds with awful shade in relief, in vivid relief, I watched for the encroaching darkness from the ledge of the verandah, my fear increasing with each shadow until the lights went on in the barrack rooms and the board house villages obliterating that cruelty, that injustice and the guilt of it, so that now, like flickering fireflies their ugliness could seem beautiful, thus teaching a lesson with its own parable; but with that darkness my fear of death, with that guilt that other guilt, my sexual sin, and so two guilts, two sins, and death was the punishment which only my mother's comfort and the whispering of the rosary could soothe as she left her husband's bed to sleep with me each night, and I had by an awful trickery won my first prize, her love, taken away from him. It was there on that bed, she by now snoring, that I awoke to Our Lady of Perpetual Help transfigured in a halo of bright light against the creamy wall of my bedroom. And as I raised myself up in bed to focus, she vanished in a flash streaking down the long corridor to my parents' bedroom where my father was asleep on his own. Our Lady was exactly as she was in the parish church of Notre Dame de Bon Secours where I had learnt to make my visits to the Blessed Sacrament since the age of seven.

Guilt was so pervasive and death had not slain me for my sin, that the absolute fear faded and I continued in my sexual sin, forgiven and cleansed repeatedly by confession.

God was not to be offended. He had become a man and died for me and I by my sin continued to crucify him. I never questioned this retrospective logic, but bowed to its terror.

5

By now, I was at a boys' Benedictine boarding school in the mountains and seeming quite a different world from sugarcane, barrack rooms, board house villages, visions and my mother's love. This was a man's world. But, also, a world of angels and desired visions. My inherited, or learnt, piety continued, and I learnt to serve mass, and from that very first morning that I heard the Gregorian chant of the monks in choir, my resolve to be one of them was set upon, and my yearning for the love of another like myself, my complicated sexual desires, confirmed me in my resolve, which eventually led me to hate the school and seek admission to the junior seminary where I had a good friend.

Complicated sexual desires. They were as powerful as my visions, my desire to be a monk and a saint.

This was theology too.

....

I became a builder of shrines, grottoes in the mountains, imitating Lourdes and Fatima and my intense wish was that if I knelt long enough at these shrines alone in the forest, another vision would come, something more lasting which would become more public and I would be like Bernadette of Lourdes or one of the children of Fatima with a message for the Pope on the conversion of Russia and the end of communism in China. In these wild places, my aspirations went beyond the ordinary, and I sought to emulate the mystics, the true ascetics, with flagellations, attempting it and drawing back with a fear from somewhere else.

The monks in their abbey were never far from my thoughts and fantasies of my future. In their dark library I sought out books on monasticism and came upon those huge picture books published from American and French abbeys. My favourite pictures were the portraits of monks at prayer, at work, walking in the country, standing by a lake in contemplative mood. The focus was on the tonsured head, the hands at the pottery wheel, the profile of a face enlivened by the light and shadow of candle light, *film noir*, the folds of the cowl, the sweep of the scapular, the silence of their hoods, their sandalled feet. By a strange alchemy, my sexual sin found a shape in this aestheticism, this asceticism, and what were the playful antics of small boys discovering the meaning of their bodies, re-formed itself and came now with the rush of crushes and first love and admiration for boys and men older than myself. Then followed the admonitions against particular friendships and *never in twos, always in threes*, killing goodness and suggesting sin.

On Friday nights, the bell after compline, and then the sound of the monks flogging themselves. Did Father Chris hit the pillow instead? We giggled.

Celibacy was hard, no affection with boys, and no girls. Fleeting memories: the first French kiss, the touch of a warm breast, that nest of hair, even a clumsy attempt to enter that forbidden and secret place, that wet flower.

These desires mixed with the desire for the other, the other like myself, other boys, with similar bodies, forbidden, sinful. Much, much more sinful. "Michael de Freitas has the biggest cock" scratched on the walls of the Scout's den.

A melancholic youth. What to do with these affections? Never discussed, never explained, only called sin.

6

The afternoon was hot . . . I was giving my life to God . . . I was leaving by plane for England . . . It was winter in England . . .

I clutched my bouquet of pink anthuriums. The yellow stamens drooped, the petals folded.

Drifts of snow like on Christmas cards.

Day was dark like night.

The corridors between the parlour and the refectory and the cloister smelt of boiled cabbage. I ate leeks for the first time. I was sick. Homesick. I sat in my cell and cried. I wept over my mother's letters.

Then I fell in love. Suddenly. Yes, in the midst of everything new and strict and silent, the meeting of eyes, the brush of an arm. A hooded smile. The ecstatic meeting of souls in chant, in the eucharist. He became my mentor, my ideal. I would become him. A pure love on the brink of hell, but desiring heaven.

I learnt that I was different. I was dark. I was other. I spoke differently. They said I sounded Welsh. I stared at myself in the mottled wash-room mirror. Homesickness left me.

One night we kissed, and then, no, no further. The kiss forbidden and confessed.

This great welling up romantic ideal to which I fated myself began to shatter once I was in my English Benedictine monastery. What was somewhere a colonial rejection of the local, despising the monastery of my island as not the proper thing, not strict enough, not the primitive life according to the

....

right interpretation of the Rule of St Benedict, fell away. Not at once, but gradually, these destinies fell away. How long could I feed just on feelings and guilt? Sin and punishment? Romance and sentimentality?

Two things happened to change me. I fell in love, yes that. And, I began to read, to study. I discovered the library, not always revealing to the novice master what I was embarking on. I discovered that I had a mind and it was exciting to use it. I discovered Saint Aelred of Rievaulx, his struggle with Satan and his affection for young men, his theology of friendship.

But the really important things were against the grain of the routine, the system, the official theology, the older monks, the authority of the abbot and the novice master. What developed was a kind of adolescent rebellion mixed with the turmoil of the whole Church in the throes of Pope John XXIII's Second Vatican Council, opening the windows and letting in a great wind of change. I was coming of age with the Church in the modern world.

My fingers ran along the spines on the shelves in the literature section of the library, and as the four seasons changed in the park outside, I turned the leaves of books, mixing novelists with philosophers, poets with painters, words with pictures of paintings and sculpture. Renoir and Rodin. New theologies were growing in my mind. Nature and Form. Words. I was guided by my love and mentor. We met there and our friends became the authors we pulled off the shelves and which I tucked under my scapular as I returned along the corridors to my cell discreetly hooded and walking close to the wall. I pillaged most of D.H. Lawrence in this way. Also, François Mauriac and Graham Greene. Catholic angst.

This was not the approved *lectio divina* for a novice, but it became the reading which began a new way of looking at the divine. While the scriptorium offered Aristotle and Aquinas, creeping onto the shelves were the "Brown" and "Blue" Books, and the *Tractatus* of Wittgenstein. The ones which bulged

....

under the scapular were Sartre's *Being and Nothingness* and Heidigger's *Being and Time*. Heady days those salad days.

The mould of my narrow colonial white French creole Catholic religion began to crack. I needed a bigger and freer space for all of this. My mind grew and opened. I read Freud and Jung. It was a kind of university education in art, literature and philosophy, the new theology. It happened in a haphazard way. I should have had more guidance. The older monks could not cope, the young monks were eager.

And I was still in love, a forbidden love with a senior monk, and we brought our desires in line with the ideals of Saint Aelred of Rievaulx. A dangerous chastity. We used our eyes, a stolen kiss, the press of a hand, our minds, our journals kept with a passion, our letters in keeping with a venerable twelfth-century monastic tradition, our meditations on the Song of Songs: *Let him kiss me with the kisses of his mouth*. Sublimated desires.

A new and original Christian ideal was being searched for, the corporate church, the church of the poor. This was stripping off the medievalism, the devotional romanticism, the sentimentality.

Christianity became socialism.

An intellectual and psychological revolution went on inside of me. Neither my spirit nor my body could cope and I broke down. Then everything fell apart and I began the task of re-forming my self. Psychoanalysis helped, but then got rejected for its own dogmatisms. Only after I examined my early religiosity, my love for my mother and the absence of my father's love, or me not feeling loved by him. "Your father is not a demonstrative person." Excusing him like the invisible Father is excused. Not then a theological metaphor or analogy which can work for me now, a fathering God.

I held on to some threads, but slowly I developed a kind of agnosticism.

The world had been beckoning through blind Brother

....

Gabriel's radio in the pantry where his fingers weaved mats for missionary nuns and the company of the radio was a compensation for his handicap. I lingered over collecting tins of tomatoes and sliced peaches and heard "Lucy in the Sky with Diamonds". One of the monks was allowed to develop playing the guitar and we sang "We Shall Overcome"; my heart full of rebellion against the abbot's autocratic ways. Another student monk returning from Germany arranged for us to have permission to listen to *Sergeant Pepper's Lonely Hearts Club Band*. We sat in a circle in the common room and listened and I was changed. Whispers ran through the refectory when David Madalla came to lunch at the high table barefooted and dressed as a flower child. I remember pressing my face against the library window to see Allen Ginsberg out by the fish pond. Later reading *Howl*. Then another afternoon putting my ear to the door of the senior common room to listen to John Cage's noises. Both these boundary breakers had come to visit one of our monks who was a leading exponent of concrete poetry.

The decision to leave the monastery came, fired by the desire for more education, the practice of socialism, understanding and embracing my bi-sexuality. Or, so I see it now, then a bonfire in my mind.

7

It is here that I return, where I left my early morning journey, where my aunt sits in her pew in the high vaulted church. After Mass I returned with her to her beautiful stone house overlooking the sea, and there, after having a gentle breakfast with her, talk of writing her nativity plays and the tending of her dead husband's orchids which she liked to paint in water-colour; it is here that I dive for an early understanding, that I later developed, that to make sense of my world I had to interpret it myself, and I had to pay attention to interpretations other than the dogmas of Catholicism or the Gospels of Christianity. I had to take a hard look at the full nature of things. Nature and Form. It was the interpretation through art, her intense desire to capture the changing skies with her watercolours, realising that she could not represent them but had to interpret them, to her dying day, more and more abstract, when she was ill with Parkinson's Disease, and her attempts became blots, splodges, molecules, elemental explosions, that I found an early faith for my present way.

GOD, DOG, anagrams, mere phonics, a monosyllable, theology, words about god, this business is now tackled through art: poetry most importantly, the metaphorical way (analogy, that ancient way, paradox), prose: the assessment, re-assessment, imaginative entry into place, life and character. Theatre, that secular liturgy. Painting, sculpture, when words alone fail. Space, form, kinesis. Music, dance. All these expressions of the spirit. These and the form and pattern you discover in nature: the waterfall, the stone, the piece of driftwood, the immensity of the sea, light. These are my sacraments. Seven times seven and more.

In this business of "God" I find no sense in absolutes. Being is becoming.

"God", that which is other, that impetus to "becoming", is in art and in socialism; a being with people which holds friendship as a sacrament and the joining with people for justice against the great systems failing us in our care of people and our planet.

I marvel at the becoming of myself, the becoming of the world. The questions for me remain in this area, not in the evangelisms, the fundamentalisms of institutional religions which I see as profoundly limiting the human spirit, colonising that space for "awe", waging in it a polarised battle between good and evil. I see us engaged in a much more various embrace, forming and re-forming like my aunt's last atoms and

....

molecules, her last dots in her search for form and order, eluding her. Ironically, I return to the Jesuit poet, Gerard Manley Hopkins's *Pied Beauty*: "Glory be to God for dappled things — . . . / All things counter, original, spare, strange;/ Whatever is fickle, freckled (who knows how?)". I find the last two lines of the poem: "He fathers-forth whose beauty is past change: Praise him" difficult to say as prayer, but I am open to them as poetry. If there is a father who can father-forth such a world and love it, *then*, there is an analogy to look at. It is not a concept of father I have come across with its accustomed authoritarianism and paternalism.

Does this father have to punish? Can this "God" embrace Satan? (Words we carry like baggage.)

Can we embrace our sin and not be banished from the garden of Eden? (I hang in there, now no Catholic or Christian, but the poetry and the metaphor still there.)

Meeting my older sister recently and talking about belief in "God", I explained my adolescent religion and what took me to the monastery. She stopped me to say that she had not heard me mention God. Her conclusion was that the Church had come between me and God. I thought that was perceptive at the time, and yes, my emotional religiosity had come between me and good thinking. But ironically it is "the church", the coming together of people, whatever people and whenever, but not with those aspects where priests or leaders seek to have power over people, to which I am still drawn.

I feel each different culture, each different geography and history has something to add to the concept of illumination and "becoming", depending on the quite different experiences and perceptions of light.

8

I begin again today at Diwali, the Hindu festival of lights. I,

....

French-Creole Trinidadian, once Catholic, and my wife, English and agnostic, with my *pardner* and his wife; he is Trinidadian Indian, eclectic, she is Scottish and Presbyterian. He had an eclectic religious upbringing, at least culturally, if not theologically: we go together to a Hindu friend's house for a Diwali *pujah*. We celebrate this with his family. The friend is not a pundit, but training, can take prayers. The group of friends is mixed and there are some African Trinidadians there as well. We take our shoes off in the house, some of us, what we feel comfortable with. I remember as a child the taking off of shoes before entering Hindu temples. I remember my mother's stories of her taking off her shoes. I had been curious to see their gods: Hanuman who leapt from the balustrade, Shiva, and Mother Latchmi, and this was her festival. Some of us sit on the floor cross legged. Gyan, my *pardner*'s friend and our host, is dressed traditionally, and he draws his small children around him on the floor where a cloth is laid with flowers and there is a fire for incense and sandalwood. He explains in English after saying the traditional words in Hindi and Sanskrit according to the Vedic tradition of Hinduism.

The point of this for me is not the belief in God. The story which lies behind the festival is one of return from exile. For me it is a return from the exile of being estranged from people by colonialism (the colonial Christian Church) and racism. The lighted *deyas*, wicks placed in earthen bowls of oil placed along the paths and the edges of the house, lead me back, lead us all back from our exiles to each other for the "becoming". We share a meal together afterwards.

It is as other festivals in Trinidad, which were foreign for me, part of what was the other in the colonial era, part of a kind of racism, that is what Indians do, what black people do, the Shango, the orishas, the Spiritual Baptists. They were part of my fear of the other, those drums.

We (I come with friends) climb into the red dirt hills above Port-of-Spain. I carry some of that fear mixed with safety I felt

....

when I travelled in the Princes Town bus among the women of the Shango. I am with friends and we are travelling into the district of Trumacac, one of those congregations in the hills above the city, here for work. We are going to attend an Orisha feast. A place of manifestations.

There are the drums once outlawed by state and church, but now a legitimate church of the poor, growing. The drums and the conch call people here, call to ancestors to look and see themselves remembered.

A candle burns in its saucer of molten wax on the top step of the Palais. I rinse my hands in a bucket of water mixed with oil. I enter the congregation of chanting, clapping women dressed in blue, red and white. Their heads are tied in cloths of those colours. The drumming and the chant connect me with people who connect themselves to Africa.

It is a ceremony of natural things: water, fire, earth, oil, flowers. These are offered, used in blessings, in the ritual manifestations of spirits and gods.

We are embraced and made to feel at home in this congregation.

Ritual dances and movements show the different spirits inhabiting individuals in the congregation. They are cared for and led to the shrines.

The drums cease.

We dip into Catholic prayers: Our Father . . . Hail Mary . . . Hail Holy Queen . . . My soul does magnify the Lord.

Drumming begins again, chants fill the rough red brick chapel covered with a roof of galvanize.

Before we leave, we enter the inner room where a feast of cakes and flowers is laid out on a table with a red cloth. We are given candles to light at the shrines of Ogun and Legba. Images of Hindu gods adorn the walls. The theology of Africa and India mix in the New World. Some choose to light their candles. I take mine away with me. We are blessed with oil and water sprayed from the mouth of one of the possessed.

We say our farewells and leave.

It is now a coming together of people at points like this: Diwali, or Pagwa, or the Muslim Eid or Hosein, a Spiritual Baptist Meeting. It is at these points of *enchantment*, the Catholic Corpus Christi, or the Siparia Mai when Hindus make pilgrimage to a Catholic madonna, La Divina Pastora, and garland her with gold and adorn her with flowers. Catholics do the same thing on the feast of La Divina Pastora; there is the syncretic way African religions have survived: Da Lua in "The Sacred Heart", Damballa/Saint Dominic, and Legba, believed to be the devil, not demonic but mischievous, a guard and a protector. For me this is not some fixed absolute belief in "God", it is rather a "becoming" of peoples in the ex-colonial world, an ex-empire world. I note Santa Ria in socialist Cuba and Condomble in Brazil, mass religions, both syncretic religions.

I want to be open to that "becoming". But this is "against" the evangelisms, and fundamentalisms, which are in themselves against the "becoming", and are fixed in absolutes, with power concentrated in the hands of priests over people.

9

These days I return to the Benedictine monastery of my childhood, which has incidentally always has been a place of pilgrimage of all people, and a favourite with Hindu people. I am looking for the paths I knew then, trying to see if I still remember them, see where they lead. And when I am not on my island, each time leaving by plane, and having to swim back underwater, I visit a Cistercian monastery in the Midlands of England.

Why don't I stay there in the desert? Because I must return to the city, the world, where the struggle for justice against the failing systems must be embraced. Then again to the desert. In both places there is a harvest to be reaped and I give thanks to "both givers for the love I gain" in each.

My Stigmata

CHRISTOPHER HOPE

I remember the morning I found that I had the wounds. I got up and went downstairs to the bathroom, holding my side, the pain was that bad. On my way I met my landlady, Doris Clench. "I think I've got the stigmata, Mrs Clench," I said.

"Garn," she said.

"No, really." Nodding vigorously, I pushed past her to the bathroom, the better to examine the extent of the damage.

My left side was pierced by a red raw wound about the size of a shilling. My hands and feet carried the traditional marks. They looked like bullet holes, dead centre through each palm and neat, with no ragged edges, covered by a transparent membrane through which the red flesh gleamed. Anxiously I explored my hairline in the mirror for signs of the crown of thorns, but it seemed that I was spared that at least. On second thoughts, it didn't cheer me up much because I remembered that exterior stigmatisation may be preceded by invisible stigmata, as happened with the celebrated Padre Pio. But then Pio had been a natural candidate for the honour, and honour it is among mystics. What with his levitation during the consecration of the mass and his almost supernatural percipience in the confessional, you could have said that he was asking for it. But not me. It was only because I was a lapsed Catholic that I had recognized the symptoms, but for the rest I was barely a Christian, and I certainly wasn't religious. Something was very wrong, somewhere.

As I made my careful way up the stairs to my room, I met my

CHRISTOPHER HOPE

neighbour, Mr Patel. We did not get on too well. He had a
succession of icy blondes coming to his room most nights and
the bumps and groans and shrieks in the small hours kept me
awake. I hadn't had a decent night's sleep in weeks. Mr Patel
made the point of apologizing to me on every possible occasion
for the exuberance of his lovers. They became too excited, he
explained. I did not want to speak to him, but one look at his
face showed me that there was no escaping. His smooth hand
rested on my sleeve. "Courage, my friend."

"I suppose Mrs Clench told you?"

He nodded and patted me on the shoulder gingerly. He kept
glancing at my hands which were sunk in the pockets of my
dressing gown.

"It is a holy affliction."

"It's a bloody tragedy." As I fumbled at the door of my room
with my key, I noticed that he had not moved and was gazing up
the stairwell at me, his eyes liquid with concern.

"The love of God can hurt a man," he called.

I managed to get my door open. "Yes," I said, "especially
when he gets too excited."

I went into my room and sat on my bed for what must have
been at least an hour, maybe more. It was some while later,
anyway, that I snapped out of it. There was no point sitting
there like a dummy. I had to get out and about. I put on gloves
and carpet slippers and went downstairs.

Outside the sun was shining and the sky was a blank and
lovely blue. The sun lit up the vacant little park across the way,
the "gardens" from which the neighbourhood took its name,
with its locked gates to which only the oldest in the Victorian
boarding houses flanking the road had keys and there were
fewer of those each year.

Obviously there was no question of my going to work,
wearing gloves and carpet slippers, my body a dull ache. I could
not go back to my desk at the Imperial Insurance Company and
continue writing all risks policies covering the jewels of rich

women. I could not give up my mind to anything at that moment but to the control of the pain that bent me double, dogged my footsteps and held my hands tightly.

There was nothing for it but to see the doctor. I sat in the waiting room, leaning up against the frosted glass, reading an article in *Life* about outer space and the universe and how if one imagined the sun as an orange then the earth was no bigger than a pea, or something, a hundred miles away. At last the light went on above one of the brown-painted doors and the nurse called my name and showed me in to the doctor.

He was very kind. I removed my left glove and he made a thorough examination of the wound. "A nasty business," he said.

"I have another on my right hand," I told him.

"Gracious me!" he snorted, "you've really been in the wars, haven't you? We'd better have your shirt off."

"Actually, I have two identical holes in my feet," I said, as casually as I could, struggling with my shirt buttons. I took off all my clothes then and lay down on the bed.

He drew in his breath sharply when he saw me. "Who has injured you like this?" he demanded.

"I think it was an accident," I said.

"Well," he said, after examining me closely, "the least I can do is to dress them. Though, I'll hand it to you, you've kept them remarkably clean without the use of bandages and antiseptic. How you managed it, I don't know. Anyway, I'll give you something for them and then, remember please, a clean dressing every morning." He bent to examine the wounds again. They fascinated him, I could see that. Clearly, he didn't want me to put on my clothes yet. "Remarkable symmetry about them," he said. "Of course, if you had come to me earlier, I'd have stitched them for you. It's too late now. They're healing."

I walked home. Mrs Clench and her daughters awaited me in

....

the hallway. Mrs Clench's daughters attended a convent school. All looked at me with earnest eyes.

"So we're off to work, are we?" Mrs Clench asked, not unkindly.

Her daughters eyed me hopefully. What did they expect me to do? I smiled as best I could and went upstairs to my room. The pain was no worse. No better, but no worse. The dressings the doctor had used were comfortable and maybe he was right about the wounds healing. Voices were raised in the hallway below. I lay down on my bed and closed my eyes. Clearly, the news was getting around.

In the morning I dressed the wounds. I could detect no change in their glassy surface although they seemed to throb less painfully. I put on my gloves and carpet slippers and went down for a walk. A small crowd had gathered outside the door. Mrs Clench was addressing interested neighbours. They stopped talking when they saw me and looked embarrassed. Two mild men in grey raincoats pressed forward.

"Hansome, of *The Times*," said the taller of the two, holding out his hand.

"How do you do." I kept my hands firmly in my pockets.

"My photographer, Pounder, Rutland Pounder." His companion nodded cheerily. "I wonder if you would mind if we spoke to you briefly about the rather strange situation in which you find yourself?"

The neighbours smiled encouragingly. They knew, their smiles assured me, that perhaps this wasn't a proper occasion for the press, but it was after all *The Times*.

"Come inside," I said, "we can talk in my room."

The pictures the next morning were very good and the story beside them was concise and lucid, not at all sensational. I found myself reading it with interest. Although now a stigmatic, I was very far from being an expert on the subject. I wondered if the doctor who had treated me took *The Times*.

As I neared home with the newspaper I saw the neighbours

....

gathered in what was now a regular knot on the steps before Mrs Clench's front door. I saw, too, a bus parked by the kerb, a school bus. Ranged next to it was a long, orderly, crocodile of convent girls. I recognised the uniform as being the same as that worn by the young Clench girls. I stopped dead and then, of course, just as I realised I should get away quickly, they saw me. A fat, brisk nun with silver hair and rosy cheeks trotted up to me and bobbed a knee. She and her girls were there, she explained frankly, in the hopes of meeting me. The young Clench girls had talked at school about their mother's lodger who had been blessed with Christ's five glorious wounds. Nobody had paid very much attention to them until the report appeared in *The Times*. She and her girls had not come to stare, but to look and to marvel at the works of God.

"It's a very wonder the marks the good Jesus puts upon a man." Her Irish lisp conveyed her sentiment and I was reminded of my schooldays, when it was always an Irish voice that led the general prayers in the parish church after confessions each Friday. Mind you, it was a Jewish boy who'd led the prayers in the classroom when the bell rang on the hour and the class rose to recite the Hail Mary as they did again at twelve o'clock for the Angelus. From then on all prayers for me were prayed in Irish or Jewish voices and even the tones of those voices in banal conversation took on a sacral quality recalling the giant Christ who swung in agony upon his cross above the high altar in the cool gloom of the parish church when we prayed our communal prayers on those Friday mornings after confession. Outside one could hear the doves calling in the fir trees. It was very peaceful and miles from school and almost worth praying for. Often I was tempted to sneak out of the side door as we left the church to straggle back to the classroom and to hide myself behind the hedge that flanked the garden and orchards and sit there in the sun. Just sit there, quietly, untouched by anything but my own thoughts as the sun moved higher in the sky, warming my bones.

....

"I'm sorry," I said, looking into her blue eyes, "but what can I say? I have all the wounds, but this is not the place . . ."

"Except the crown," she said.

"Except the crown," I agreed. "I've been spared that."

"It takes some differently, my dear," she said. "Now, Maria Razzi of Chio, why, she had the thorny crown alone."

"You've made a study of it, Sister?"

She beamed. "We're doing a project in class."

She took her girls away, with some giggling and downcast looks in the rear files of the crocodile. She seemed moved. I walked inside without a glance at the little groups of people who stood on either side of the street before the rows of silent houses, talking and staring.

That tour of the convent girls and their sweet-cheeked teacher was the start of a wave of publicity that hit that afternoon and continued for a week. In that time I was assailed by people wherever I went, wanting to know how I felt, the extent of my pain, the shape of my wounds, the health of my soul, the heat of my faith, my plans for the future. Worst were those who made joking allusions to Doubting Thomas and licked their lips, not daring to ask me out loud to let them see and touch my stigmata.

The day after the visit of the convent girls, a great scarlet coachload of bishops drew up outside Mrs Clench's house, and a deputation of their lordships entered to greet me. They had come, I was assured, not to gape, but to congratulate me. They had learnt that I was an unwilling stigmatic and so they hoped that I would not take it amiss and feel even more put upon were they to offer me their warmest greetings and prayerful good wishes. They were immensely grateful for this wonder that had been worked in me, and however vicarious their satisfaction might appear to me to be, I was respectfully asked to bear with them in their joy at the greatest fillip Christianity had received in England for decades. Stigmata had become more common in comparatively recent times, perhaps through devotion to the

Sacred Heart, but that was hardly an English practice. Indeed my stigmata seemed to fill the bishops with much the same confidence and enthusiasm as my role at the Imperial Insurance Company did for rich women by making certain that their jewels, even if by some horrid catastrophe reduced to their natural elements, would retain their value in our books at least.

I saw the bishops off, talking happily, all smiles and waves, and turned inside. I was moving a little more easily. The pain was still there. But it was no worse. It seemed hard now to imagine a time when I had not had this dull ache in hands, feet and side. Perhaps I was getting used to it.

Mr Patel stood in the entrance hall holding the public telephone which served us all in the house.

"It's the *Psychic News* on the line," he whispered, covering the mouthpiece. "They want to talk to you."

I looked at him. I could think of nothing to say.

"I shall tell them that you are indisposed."

I went upstairs to bed. I washed my wounds and applied the antiseptic and dressings the doctor had given me but I did so more out of habit than conviction. The wounds seemed unaffected by the treatment. They seemed to have a being of their own, affixed to myself, but independent of me. Then I settled into a long, dreamless sleep.

In the morning I awoke almost refreshed and reflected that, perhaps, my strangeness was being made too much of, by myself as well as by others. Men had fragile, paper-thin skins, which wrinkled and tore easily. My tears were coincidentally localised, that was all. Altogether, I decided, there was too much fuss being made. My stigmata had become too much of a good thing.

It was early yet and the house was asleep. I decided to take a walk, donned my carpet slippers and gloves, and went quietly downstairs. But I had no sooner opened the door and taken a breath of the morning freshness when windows and doors opened all around me. There were faces at panes. Dogs barked,

....

the milkman arrived and housewives appeared on the doorsteps with their dogs and children and husbands and gazed at me. I lost my nerve and closed the door. Perhaps I would venture out later.

Mrs Clench faced me in the dark hallway. She smiled encouragingly. In her hands she held a copy of *The Times*. I took it. She had opened it at the centre page which carried the editorials. Her eyes were shining. I followed her trembling finger and understood the cause of her excitement: I was the subject of the third editorial.

What can be said of this young man? He has been visited by a strange and novel experience. One which is perhaps even more shocking since it comes to him without either his knowledge or his encouragement. His behaviour in this matter has been exemplary. So much more so than that of those people who have taken an interest in his religious experience. We salute him. It might be thought by some in these Islands that the phenomenon which he has experienced is confined to those who embrace the Church of Rome. This extraordinary, some will say miraculous, event, has given proof, if proof were needed, that the division of faith is the failure of our times – and nonsense, to boot. Besides, there is no room, surely, as recent and bloody events not far removed from us have shown, for this sort of sectarian prejudice.

"Well . . . yes," I thought.

Sometime later I slipped outside by the back door. I could not stand being cooped up any longer. I put on my gloves and slippers and, after a moment's thought, a black woollen balaclava helmet. No one recognized me as I walked swiftly through the morning sunshine. I came to a pond, spanned by a narrow little bridge, where people stopped and gathered to talk.

"They say that he has holes, gaping holes, nail marks in his hands and feet, Doris says, though she's never seen them," a little old lady, well wrapped in green coat and muffler, was saying to another in a red trench coat and wellingtons.

"Ever so painful they must be, too," the other agreed. "I saw the pictures in *The Times*. And him not even the least bit religious."

"I know," said the little lady, "it's not nice, is it?"

"Of course you can't believe everything you read in the papers, now can you? I mean, Doris didn't actually *see* these wounds, did she? I mean, she saw the photos in *The Times*, same as we did. That's all. And she says that he doesn't go to work any longer."

"You've got a point there," her friend nodded.

"And you know, sometimes I think these people bring these things on themselves. Besides, we all have our problems, don't we?"

But she had lost the attention of her companion who had turned and was looking straight at me.

"Didn't you say that he dressed in gloves and carpet slippers?"

"So Doris said."

Then they were both looking at me. I put my head down and walked away entering my boarding house by the back door. I had hoped to avoid meeting anybody. But once again Mrs Clench accosted me at the foot of the stairs. I eyed her defiantly through my balaclava helmet. In the silence I became aware of my heavy breathing.

She eyed me with faint curiosity. "No change?"

I shook my head and went up to my room, undressed and got into bed. By seven o'clock that evening, I was still awake. Several bumps, a groan and a giggle behind the wall told me that Mr Patel's lovers were once again becoming too excited.

God, an Untitled Story

JUDITH KAZANTZIS

The birds sobbed for joy in the bushes, the mice, the frogs and the woodlice showed emotion, the Master was coming through the trees of the wood. His great white feet trod on twig and dry leaf, with no crackle. Down at the bottom of the oak-tree's bole crouched the little pointy-eared leprechaun, brown-skinned and warty, hiding itself because it was ugly. Then, "The Master is nigh!" Not daring to look up. But the great white feet, upon which there were no corns, paused. Light fell on the poor ugly little leprechaun and a young man's voice, a musical tenor, said, Little pointy-ears, I love you too, be clean. And the white feet moved off steadily like two white liners. The ugly little leprechaun felt its ears round, its skin peel off; underneath it was pink and white all over. Then its body hair shrivelled off and the hair of its head brushed out easily into a red-golden cloud. She was beautiful. "Thank you." She sobbed for joy in the bushes.

Bored as usual, she was studying the head of the man in front of her: he had tried to espalier his one remaining hank across a naked white pate, but the hank dangled back under its own unwashed weight — Also the smart hair-do of his wife beside him: how she had forgotten the crown, where a bald coin shone surrounded by darker roots — how mortified the woman would be. Guilty of malevolence, Elsa prayed, but Jesus had long passed on back to Heaven. Though Father Seymour-Jones was even now preparing to lift Him right up in his hands and show him for adoration to the congregation. Josh, on Elsa's left, was running a Dinky rubbish vehicle surreptitiously along the ledge at the back of the bald folks' pew. He led it considerately up and down the blue and red hymnals. Beyond Josh knelt Helen their mother and then Jake their father; they were hiding their eyes in their hands. Father Seymour-Jones bent over the silver-gilt salver: it was his moment of intimacy with the little round wafer before he Transubstantiated it to the Son of God and Man and held Him aloft with two clean hairy hands for the full church to adore. Saints prepared to adore, angels folded up their pink and lilac wings and knelt down, leaning down from the blue and gold painted and pillared dome of the sky, above them all Himself: He smiled, immensely, quietly and very slowly as Father said quietly, and all over the globe other Fathers said quietly: This Is My Body, This Is My Blood.

The bell tinkled, the packed adults raised their eyes, blinded them again in their hands. Josh's Waste-Care Vehicle made a squeak. Elsa stared at the raised Host, all but she had hidden their eyes in their palms, what she was doing was irreverent, a cat may look at the King, all of a sudden it came to her as the little white disc stood up and bowed in the white straining hands: this isn't Jesus God the Son, this is a wafer. This is what it looks like, in short this is what it is: a wafer. Moreover she realised with a bound of her heart that she had known it for years. She was fifteen. Lightness filled her. Mystery and sadness dropped onto the floor around her like a metal cloak off a snapped clasp and chain. Josh's truck ran forward; crouching, he fingered a wheel and whizzed it. Their parents prayed.

Elsa, kneeling quietly, smiled, couldn't stop smiling, for like lightning she had realised her great cause for joy: if there was no Consecration, there was no God, no Redemption, no need for Salvation, there was, finally, no Hell. She began to rise, to turn happily to the others, take them by the arm, listen, I have brought you wonderful news, news that will make us all happy now, we can stop praying and repenting and being miserable

....

sinners for there is NO HELL, no Hell, nowhere to fear, nothing at all to make us cringe, we can stand up, be ourselves, put our faith in ourselves and in our own rightfulness, we are good after all, virtuous — listen, be proud of yourselves, stop burying your faces in your hands, I will pull your hands away, stop cringing and adoring — we are human beings!

They went up to take Communion. Elsa sat on the wooden seat with astonishment and watched a hundred serious and perceptive adults line up to eat what they still believed was the Body and Blood of God Made Man. The more she watched the more she was dumbfounded with amazement. How could these well-turned hairstyles and collars and ties, and more, these Levis and fun sweatshirts, not know they were lining up for a big joke. But the Pope must know! Jake, her father knew! They were laughing behind their hands! She glanced at him coming back, his well cut pearly grey suit, his ginger hair brushed and turned to silver in front of the neat white ears handsomely curved to the bear head. He carried his clasped hands before him, ginger freckled hands slung before his slim lower belly under the stylish jacket; he was not winking, his large eyelids drooped in prayer, he clambered along the kneeler and knelt two beyond Josh, lowering his bulk swiftly. Silently, rapidly, without opening his lips, he swallowed and then buried his eyes in one big hand, his heavy elbow supported by the pew in front. The couple in front returned, and once again displayed their hair problems to Elsa before they disappeared into such forward crouches that their heads were swallowed by their smart coats. Josh's truck squeaked. Elsa sat stiffly, the flood of love flowed out of her like waste water, she was shut out from Communion, from her family. Her mother's surprised glance fell on her as she too returned; it said, why didn't you go, are you feeling ill? She couldn't speak for she too, like a cat carrying a mouse, carried a wafer tucked in her mouth. Elsa hunched. Her mother raised her eyebrows, two black wings, and clambered past, silently snatching the truck out of Josh's hand as she did so, and whispered "Shh!" to his "Yee-ow!"

It was only on the way out, as they passed the Pietà, a scarred life-size copy of the Michelangelo, that stood at the back of the church next-door to the Victorian font, and beyond it the stone Holy Water stoup, it was only as her mother took a dip of her hand and her diamond ring took a dip and swam shining in the blessed water, that Elsa saw that there was no Heaven either, no white country, shining refuge or endless haven beyond cloud and wave. How dully she saw that freedom was a trick, after all no freedom. How does one cope with this? I still don't know. Who does? Tell me please. To put it more poetically, a second metal chasuble more terrible than the one Elsa lost clenches me so that I am still from time to time on the point of a scream, except that there is no point. Going, going. Winter is here. Going. Me and you. But as I said, who copes with this — tell me! They say the old begin to ache for oblivion. Some powerful old stoic? Let me talk to him.

Yet no collapse when Dad died. It's true; and my failure to die too came as a bonus and some relief, though never again have I felt the bounding lightness of Elsa when she soared out and up from religious faith. Never again have I felt that light spirit and mind, never quite like that, like a cloud of pigeons out of the top towers of the Bastille; not even at the beauty of my kids, the sweetness of their father. They say you fall from faith. In my experience you fly up from it. It is only death, extinction, that stings in the tail; the little teaser, the delayed action cyanide in the Margarita, the bullet after the fiesta.

It distressed Elsa, for her bedroom lay midway between her parents' bedroom on the one hand and the lavatory on the other hand, one flight of stairs below. So that on the one upper hand came her father's snores stopping and starting from the double bedroom and on the other she would often wake in the morning to the patter of his feet hastily running past her door, down the stairs, and then his gassy retorts and squelches in the lavatory. It was in that lavatory too that Elsa caught sight of a bloodstain on her pants, but her mother was entertaining a guest so that she could not tell her she felt she must be injured, how she didn't know, somewhere horrible inside; she must have swallowed a cutting edge but how? At the same time Elsa knew that this was her first period.

And in her bedroom in between these two other rooms, papered with a rose trellis interlocked with blue ribbons, it was for hours there that, nauseated and sometimes crying, she suffered excruciating pains, the Curse, as her mother still called it calmly and made hot water bottles and gave her aspirin and went downstairs.

But in the double bedroom Elsa's mother sat before the oval gilt framed mirror set on the fake marble dressing table, kidney-shaped and gilt handled, and at night creamed her beautiful creased white skin and quickly brushed her black hair back into short unmoving waves.

Sometimes, yet earlier, when she was eight or nine, Elsa was the first one up and she would knock on their door. Can I come in? Come on in, her father would sing out loud in his nasal voice, and she would first go round to kiss her mother, and then him, and one foot before the other set off to school with her brown satchel, late as usual. Resentfully she would leave the two of them lying there. Why should they lie nesting in a swather of pink silk-edged blankets and laundry starched sheets and reading the papers and pouring the tea out of the silver teapot set on the big tray with a wicker edge, and toast, marmalade, butter, and two rashers of bacon each and fried tomato? The au pair, Antoinette, brought all this up the stairs; she and Elsa had cornflakes in the kitchen, and bacon and tomato, so they weren't physically deprived. But neither the au pair girl nor Elsa were welcome on the peach silk eiderdown, each to her bowl of sugared cornflakes, each spilling the milk and staining the silk and squashing someone's foot. So they sat silently crunching cornflakes in their teeth. The au pair, Antoinette, a student, had her first smoke and read *Bonjour Tristesse* propped against the milk bottle. Oh la la, she said with indifference as Elsa knocked over the cornflakes and they ran away in all directions over the kitchen floor as if trying to escape, as if they were all fragments of some gingerbread boy leaping off the biscuit rack and fleeing the parental embrace.

There came a day when Helen went away to hospital with complications. Later she was to come home with Elsa's new baby. It was at that time that without knocking one morning, for she was late, Antoinette was still asleep and she had got her own breakfast — and besides with her mother away what need was there to knock on the door — that Elsa burst into her father's bedroom so that he could kiss her good morning before she plodded off to school. But as she opened the door Antoinette's pale eyes stared at her upside down from under her father's white breast. At the other end of the eiderdown his bare soles protruded like dried white cod.

"Get-out-of-here!" he shouted at her, his eyes bulging, his voice metallic and urgent. Elsa ran down the stairs, her satchel bumping. A blush ran with a life of its own down her face. Like an intruder she bundled out of the quiet house. She dared not look up at the drawn curtains on the first floor.

Her mother brought her little baby brother home and everyone was thrilled, Antoinette had to wash the terry towelling nappies and the fine cotton nappies with their little yellow-brown staining; yellow because Joshua was drinking breast milk, so her mother explained to Elsa one day briefly.

"Pooh, what a pong," said Elsa rudely.

"Don't be silly," laughed her mother, tossing the dirty nappy in a bucket for Antoinette, "he's only a little baby boy. My baby boy! My baby boy! Are you, oojums boojums bunny-rabbit." — With her flattened palms she grasped Josh hard on his tummy and rubbed and tickled and he convulsed with fat laughter, staring up at her, lips pulled back over an irresistible red-gummy smile.

"Well, I think it's a pong," Elsa said.

When Elsa was sent to boarding school, Our Lord came gliding across the water, more dexterous than a waterskier for he had his feet only, bare white, like two small boats, to walk the lake with; stepping forward irresistibly to Elsa hushed on the green lawn shore beyond the tennis courts. Morning mist flushed with sun rose up around his feet, his long white advancing dress. Motes danced in the air, the birds began to wake up in the beeches and the willows. The grave and gentle young man, Our Lord Jesus, came nearer and nearer, bouncing softly through the lake mist until he was only twenty feet offshore and now Elsa opened up her arms to Him in joy and homecoming.

As evening fell she was praying in the wood of wind anemones and aconites while the Nature crocodile went on ahead. She knelt down, last year's leaves cracked and rustled, the aconites thrust up, she pulled her peasant head scarf tighter, tied the knot tighter, and she opened her arms to Our Lord in contrition and joy, two tears slowly filled her eyes and one even ran down her cheek. When she had finished and he had gone away back to Heaven to sit at the Father's right hand, she licked the tear off with her tongue poking round her right cheek, taking the salt on it as when a baby she must have licked salt from the priest's big warm finger at baptism.

Her sight of Our Lady was different however, for there was, so a senior girl told her, the Blue Virgin who roamed the upper landing at two a.m. Elsa avoided the upper floor after dusk, though she was wrong to feel so, she knew, for the Blue Virgin could appear only at two and by nature would certainly be loving and friendly, indeed the life size statue of Our Lady of Lourdes in the hall before which they clustered at eight to say night prayers . . . this Mary smiled down at them so sweetly, their mother forgiving them, the stars sang in an electric ring round her mild head.

There were many devotions to Our Lady. But Elsa could not quite feel that competitive enthusiasm to become a Child of Mary, to fasten the blue cloth ribbon across the new breasts whose softness stole into her hands in bed at night. Give me two plain Lourdes, you can have my 3D golden Fatima. It worried Elsa, her lack of love for the Blessed Virgin when others exchanged gilt-edged prayer cards, little tokens of Mary's love, so eagerly. Because Nicki, her friend, said all that was stupid, babyish, Elsa could not share the problem with her. On the contrary, she longed to open her arms to Mary, as she did so often for Mary's Son, Elsa's brother and in a pure way her husband, beautiful clever brown-ringletted Jesus. To come forth then one day from an effulgent shine which was all Mary's, some blue and silver shine in which she had been Mary's little child, meek, gathered to Mary's hand, drawn under her silver starred veil, so that they walked together wrapped in Mary's perfect goodness, to emerge from this was both delight and great relief . . .

Yet the communion with Our Lady had been a formal one. In some fashion Elsa had remained the polite child. Though filled with grateful love she hadn't enjoyed that trustful, glissading delight she had come to know with the young man, in short Mary was slightly dull. Still she was happy to have walked with her in Heaven; for a while it made everything all right.

Parents are such fair game, is it fair — my father was crude, my mother over-elegant: I know it. Easy-peasy, as we said at school. Easy-peasy to mock Mother St Declan the Prefect nun for her beak, her reddened eyes, her icy control, her expulsion to hell of Nicola Crosthwaite-Ayre for flicking a rubber at the back of the nun who was writing out adjectives on the blackboard. One should forget such stupidities, theirs and one's own banal grudges. "Abandon Hope evil Nicola

Crosthwaite-Ayre", her reddened nose turns up when she is angry, down for happiness, today it is right up and pinched white at the nostrils. Humming red at the beak tip. Nicki was taken home but gave me a V sign on the school steps. I wanted to giggle, and I was afraid. I forget what adjectives, what language, maybe it was antonyms, synonyms, homonyms, wonderful mannequins of words bowing on the green glass board. Elsa, teacher's pet, wiped them off with a duster at the end. Good, evil, white, filthy, stinking, dirty, pure, disgusting. Indelible. They wave their hands from behind the glass, bowing from the waist, synonyms, antonyms, homonyms, mannequins. Later, Elsa took her hairy cunt along to confession.

Father I have sinned, a man came up to me in the wood and I lagged behind and he took me from behind. I was like a brown maned pony, the man cantered me through the wood. The birds sang and a hare ran out before us and we hunted it with silver horns and the hare leapt into our arms and we tore it bloodily limb from limb as if we were dogs, hounds, and ate it rejoicing, and the birds sang to us in tongues which we could understand. Father, I was so happy, was it a sin or was it a sacrifice?

Say three Hail Marys my child for committing the sins of disobedience, perverted lust, cruelty, blasphemy and gluttony, the blessed Virgin your Mother bleeds, her heart bleeds. When you hurt her Son His side bleeds, His hands bleed. Look at the life-size Pietà in the marble-floored passage between school and chapel, turn His palms up or the other way, they bleed, the lips of the piercing holes are ragged and the blood wells up drop by drop through swollen furrows, between cracked and pussy ridges of flesh. Look down, place your finger in the pus and make an Act of Faith, believe, my dear child. I forgot the feet, they bleed very badly, there's also His flayed scourged back running badly, black caked, come down and turn round, Lord, show Elsa: isn't blood beauty? For greater love hath — Perhaps almost too boldly to sum up by venturing if I might a small play on words, it's all crowned by thorns. Thorns. Have you meditated on thorns, digging into your naughty little brown head of hair. Well I have. Jolly painful! You may well say, Yuk. *In Nomine Patris et Filii et Spiritui Sancti* Amen. Go in peace my little trembling brown hare.

Last year in the Pyrenees it was wonderful. I taught the kids the wild flowers in English and French. We learnt them together, while he, my love, lay near lazily. I recreated the time my beautiful black-haired mother Helen taught me wild flowers on holiday in Brittany, my tall red-haired father Jake taught us wild flowers, trees, stones, rocks, in Tuscany, Apulia, Egypt, Peru. I know the names of things all over the world. My father Jake was a polymath, he was a charmer, he knew the world, he had power, a Department, he made things work, as a student I found myself, terrified, obliged to meet people at their dinner-table, to make conversation to the famous. I admired him enormously from a distance, he died slowly of a cerebral disease and when he died, Atlas left the world to its fate. Even now when I think of his decline — so many sad for him, for he impressed so many people — I'm stabbed still. Seedy and sad, in and out of nursing homes . . . my mother gone before him . . . he was incontinent, querulous, asked for my mother, called for his official car to take him to the office immediately, became enraged when he saw me: "Who the hell are you," he shouted, "Nurse! Intruder!" He had forgotten who I was, but I fed him another spoonful of semolina. He pursed his lips and spat. Then he grinned at me. "Darling," he remarked tenderly. You had to admire the old boy. I cried angrily, and I smiled. Finally the old man, his big chin covered with a greasy silver beard growth, quavering, his balls hanging between his white shanks like those of a sick old bull as the male nurse led him down the passage to the toilet — I remember meeting them like that, he was wearing only a vest and a cheap hospital bathrobe without a girdle — he was forever a-dying, finally he shambled round the corner.

I teach my children rocks in his memory: granite, flint, basalt, black strata, auburn strata, volcanic glass, lodes of irilium, uranium, diamonds, emeralds. He gave his all to his public so he wasn't great on the individual, but it *was* there, the gold. In the end I was glad to be his minder, to ask nothing but to fight with him over semolina.

An imperturbable man in his fifties. His seeing eye was in operation 24 hours. He knew all Elsa's thoughts, his finger in every cranny. Before Elsa's meddling grubby fingers got there, he was there, a finger raised: Saw you! And yet he was as big as a zeppelin, as Planet Earth, a refulgent splodge as wide as the universe, as big as big. He sat on Elsa like a supreme toad, like Sauron out of Mordor, but he was out of Heaven, which was Himself. A thin gas, a plasma that could stretch through you, a virus shape shifty to all receptors. Turn round but too late by far, He was not behind you, He was hiding inside you, He was you. Alien.

But Nicki and I could ignore Him, we could simply take no notice of Him either in Heaven or in our pores. We could demote Him to him: easy-peasy. We could untitle the enormous old man. Then was he hurt! Then was he sad! Then did he grow angry! His bosom grew angry with us, his nose turned up as the waves of the sea churn up to grow enraged in a storm. Rage, ye waves!

Why should I not take my revenge?

A furry Husky dog presses on top of Elsa, curled up dozing, lead heavy, warm dead weight pressing her down; there is just this thin coat between them, hiding her. She knows with fearful horror that the dog's hide mustn't touch her, yet its furry auburn tail slides in by the side of the thin coat and begins to wag against her gently . . . She's in a pit in the earth. On top of her a tarpaulin. Round the rim of the trap paces a half mad man, laughing, his eyes rolling like dolls' eyes. A gentle man argues with the mad man, let her go, but the keeper won't . . .

....

Later a fat, placid man with absent-minded curly hair appears and quite quickly and calmly persuades the half mad one to let Elsa go . . .

After the wild flowers my husband wants to make tender love to me. I ask him, blushing, to do interesting things to me, curious things with straps and this and that and at first he won't, he doesn't want to, he just wants to love me. I am ashamed too, but obsessed, he knows, he's beginning to see what a ritualist I am beneath my tough line. Later in the evening he gets into it, into me, as I murmur, "I'm nothing, I'm nothing, I'm your thing . . ." We come valiantly, exuberantly together, heart to heart, cock to cunt, we lie luxuriously, we fall to sleep in the damp sheets while an owl pierces the dusk in the Pyrenees.

Next door my little girl cries in her sleep, "No! No!"

I go creeping along to her, silky with juices under my gown, white and lean as a hound. I lie down and cuddle her and sooner or later she sleeps curled up behind my back like a little brown rabbit.

"Do you think I'm wanting to control you too much?" I ask my husband earnestly, hesitantly. But he looks right through me . . . He's helping our little girl press the flowers they picked, tree mallow, pink and emollient, and ladies' bedstraw, delicate gold, and rest-harrow, hairy rose-lipped, and toadflax with its merry yellow beard. And when we return to the north he is still more silent, working hard, the sky closes in, the woods close off, what can be done? Time passes like a train with empty wagons. It keeps rattling away into the night. What goods to put in the wagons? I'm afraid I will die before I know. I feel the bullet pressing on my temple.

The Temple is in tremendous activity, black and white, rich and poor, what a democratic feasting! Five hundred are singing with all the doors and windows open, in beautiful hair styles. I smile on the dark pavement below, benevolently and contemptuously. It's a warm night, the city seems perfumed for a while even under the utilitarian and diseased plane trees. So I sing along with them: Blood Of The Lamb, Blood Of The Lamb . . . which isn't much fun, but then I'm in. The young Black girl next to me, her hair beautifully curled, takes my hand and we rock politely, in plea, in yearning, and sway and sing, "Blood . . . Blood . . ." I drop my hand and edge away to leave but over the heads of the congregation the Minister catches my eye.

"God wants you today to talk to him in a brand new language, that you've never used before," he cries in the most unctuous manner imaginable into his hand-held mike, ducking his scanty eyelashes, wriggling his seedy grey-suited abdomen, tiptoeing, placing his other hand under his left breast as if to damp down his own bile which is rising up disgusted at his own rubbish. And this linguist of the Divine, an Australian guest minister, speaks gleefully into his hand-held mike as he sidles up and down in front of everybody. And led by him they burst into tongues, which goes on for ten minutes; the linguist leads off: Quaggimultipotococorissolelulu shashina paparipassuponto pong bidaluphrugelejz."

I enjoy it immensely: Sunb grupazlyzklophonisej. The five hundred strong congregation enjoys it like mad; everyone can babble whatever he or she feels like and the roof of the Temple resounds and re-echoes until the Minister who, though a guest from Down-under, is very much up to it and has some brilliant ideas for getting in touch with the Lord and yourself, stops; and then everyone stops except one baby.

Outside in the cheerful goodbyes, a woman dressed in magenta satin, rouged and sparkly with eye-shadow, congratulates the guest Minister, shaking his firm hand up and down, up and down, her buttocks and breasts jumping to match, up down, so that the vivid rosy dress twinkles among the trees. I know she must be that old best friend of mine, the sinner Nicola Crosthwaite-Ayre, whom I lost, and she will wink at me behind the linguist's back while continuing to imprison and pump his hand satirically and then she will merrily rub him out with her rubber.

But the magenta woman doesn't wink and the rubber lies in my pocket stuck together with a drawing pin and a boiled sweet and dust and chewing gum. So I walk away down the street and look up straight through the gracious, infected trees and through a tangerine cloud wafting high and semi-transparent in the city night. And there sitting on it are the two rounds of Jesus's ass, tight and brown-skinned, covered with shining brown ringlets. Between his shapely thighs there peep his hairy balls and there too peeps the round pink tip of his plump cock.

Elsa smiles up and opens her arms to the orange city sky and she opens her pink mouth to Jesus. But who's there? It doesn't matter for long ago she invented him: Papiprodi hindimuzzi blinkablonkabalalaika doggiJesupoopooyootoo.

The Space Around God

DAVID PLANTE

When, during Easter Holy week in Athens she said she wanted to go to all the church services, which she had never gone to before, he should have known that a shift had occurred in her that was greater and meant something entirely other than what he could have imagined in her. He imagined that she, a Greek, had just become aware of being Greek, and going to the Orthodox services was a part of that awareness. He, living with her in Athens, from time to time became aware of being an American. Clarence, who himself never went to church, never even went back to his native town in New England where the church of his youth was, went with her to church. He went with her so that she wouldn't be alone. He felt Phyllis, though born and brought up in Athens, mustn't be alone. But, in the end, she was alone —

On Holy Friday, the church bells tolled, and they went from church to church to see the Epitaphios, the flower-decorated bier draped with a shroud of stiffened silk velvet embroidered with gold and pearls. Some of the devout, after crossing themselves and kissing the shroud, crouched low and passed under the bier and out the other side.

And in the evening, they went to a church in Plaka, the old part of Athens under the Acropolis, to watch the Holy Friday ceremony. Sweating in the inside heat of the church, filled with the smell of melting candle wax and incense, Clarence stood by the open door, but Phyllis penetrated into the crowd so he couldn't see her. Over the heads of the solemn congregation he saw flower petals thrown up, and perfumes sprayed from silver phials. He moved to the side to let the bearers of the Epitaphios out, and got a glimpse of it, held by young men as on a wooden stretcher, covered with petals and wet with splashes of perfume. The church was as filled with chanting as incense. Clarence waited until he saw Phyllis at the end of a procession of people carrying candles and he joined her. She had a candle for him. They followed the Epitaphios out and around the church, through a garden of flowering lemon trees where an old woman was pulling ropes to toll the bells in the belfry. It started to rain.

For the Resurrection service the next night, they went to a small Byzantine church near a football stadium. There were fragments of broken marble from ancient buildings lying about the churchyard, where, the church being so small, most of the congregation stood, Clarence next to Phyllis, both holding unlit candles. The small church was lit up inside with candles, and, from time to time, someone stuck his head out of a low doorway, and it was as if Clarence were looking at one of those Byzantine mosaics in which gigantic people lean out of the doorways or windows of tiny buildings. At midnight, just at the moment when Holy Saturday became Easter Sunday, the priest in bright red robes came out of the church into the churchyard and called out, "*Christos anesti!*" and everyone shouted, "*Alithos anesti!*", which meant Christ had risen indeed from the dead, and people lit their candles, those near the paschal candle of the priest lighting theirs first and then passing the flame onto the rest of the congregation, so the flame spread out from a centre through the crowd and people's faces were lit in the darkness and the light shone between fingers held about lit candles, and bells were rung and firecrackers exploded out in the street. Tears rose into Clarence's eyes. Smiling at him, Phyllis gave him a tissue from her small shoulder bag. He looked at her eyes, dark within dark circles.

He thought: her God wasn't his God. This thought had never before occurred to him.

....

When, walking to their apartment through night-time Athens, where some people in groups walked with lighted candles to try to get them home and mark in the smoke of the flame crosses on the lintels of their doorways, Clarence asked Phyllis if she really believed, she answered quietly that this was not a question she ever asked herself. She found it to be an uninteresting, because unanswerable question, as all such ultimate questions were.

"Uninteresting?" he asked.

"Yes," she said.

He asked, But did she rely on her God? Did she pray to Him to help her in her despair?

"Stop it," she said in a heavy, deep-throated tone. "Stop it."

He did. He didn't understand.

They were standing on a street corner, waiting for the light to change. A trolley passed, and a lit cigarette butt was thrown out of the back window of the trolley and hit the asphalt and exploded in sparks.

Her God and his God, he thought. He could not believe in her God because he hadn't been born and brought up with Him. And what was the God he had been born and brought up with? He was a North American God, and He was surrounded by dark. His darkness was the darkness of eternity.

Looking at Clarence, she touched him on his cheek.

He didn't believe in God, but he sometimes, in his own deepening despair about her, prayed to Him for her, pleaded for His saving grace to be sent to her.

Perhaps he should have prayed to her God, who might have, in His love of the temporal, His love of rose petals and pearl and gold stitched vestments and vials of sweet-smelling scent, been less constrained by eternity than his and dispensed more freely His grace. Perhaps the Greek God was surrounded by light. But Clarence could not change his God, not the God he had been born and brought up with in his small Canuck Catholic parish in New England. One could not change Him, not only because one could not change one's past, but because nothing made a life more what it was than the God who had given that life. And his, Clarence's, God had no more choice in being what He was than Clarence had in being what he was. His God might have loved the temporal, as Clarence himself did; his God may have wanted to dispense grace to everyone, everywhere, unconditionally; and his God may have longed, above all, to be a God of light. But He could only be what He was and had been for all eternity, an eternity, as if it existed beyond God, that made grace impossible, that condemned us all. God suffered His inability to do anything for us. He bled, and His scourged and thorn-entangled and spear-lanced body hung on the cross, all in the agony of what He could not do for us, of what was impossible. His agony was that impossibility was our condition. And we accepted that, because we had to. He was our God, and He was a God of darkness. He wept for us.

How, how to explain to anyone that the very contemplation of this God, who did not exist except in eternal darkness, inspired love in us, as if hopelessness and love were, in Him, one? How explain that in our hopeless love for Him, we wept for one another?

How could he have told Phyllis this? She had her own God, and threw herself, by throwing herself off the high balcony of the apartment in Athens where they lived, upon the mercy of her God.

Pressing his forehead against a wall of the large white room in the house on the Greek island where he and Phyllis would have been together if she were alive, Clarence closed his eyes.

Then he stepped away from the white wall and looked at the marks of the trowel and the fine cracks and the dried strokes of the whitewash brush. She had had her history, she had had her God, and these had been so present to her she had not questioned them. He, on his part, had questioned his American history and his American God, and he had left them behind, he'd thought, by leaving his America and his God and marrying a non-American and living far away.

He sensed the presence of someone behind him, and for a frightening moment he thought Phyllis had come back, and if he turned he'd see her standing, as still as he was, in the slanting planes of sunlight. He turned quickly. The room was empty. A lightness, perhaps of relief and perhaps of something more, rose in him.

(From a novel-in-progress, *The Centre*)

Work-in-Progress

JOYCE CAROL OATES

Michael O'Meara's secret, the engine, as he thought of it, that drove him, and that probably accounted for his professional success, was his sense of guilt.

An obscure guilt, a seemingly sourceless guilt.

More than that, a sense of having done wrong in some specific way; and of being unable to remember what the wrong had been, or upon whom it had been perpetrated.

Guilt lay like a shallow pool of dark, rancid water at the base of his skull. So long as he kept himself occupied he scarcely knew it was there but of course, yes it *was* there. It hadn't been possible for Michael to make such inquiries of his father, but he'd tried several times to ask his mother, had anything happened in his childhood, had he done something for which he'd been severely punished, or, perhaps, insufficiently punished? — had anything upsetting or mysterious happened that had never been explained? Michael's mother was a sociable woman, with many friends; a shrewd bridge-player; but easily wounded, and quick to take offense if it seemed to her that she was being criticized in the most oblique of ways. She'd laughed nervously, and, Michael thought, a bit angrily, at his earnest questions, denying any bad memories of the past — "Up until your father's death we were all *so* happy." Michael's father had been a very successful retail furrier who had died of stomach cancer when Michael was a sophomore at Williams College.

Nor had Michael's sister Janet, five years his junior, been any more helpful. Janet now lived in Manhattan and worked for

CBS-TV in a sub-subordinate managerial position, as she called it, and she'd acquired a cheery, brassy, fast-talking manner in which all personal history, including remote family history, was best served by being translated into rowdy capsule-anecdotes of the kind one might hear on television talk shows. She spoke of Michael in rounded generic terms, saying he'd been the ideal older brother when they were growing up, sweetly protective of her, smart, helpful, even, in his own idiosyncratic way, good-looking, so he'd become a model for the other boys and men in her life — "Unfortunately, since set beside Michael, most men today are bastards, or gay, or *both*!" And Michael's young sister would throw back her head and laugh with crackling-canny laughter, of a kind he'd never heard before in her.

Michael's boyhood in Darien, Connecticut certainly seemed to him, from an adult perspective, both very American and uneventful. He could recall no memorable traumas, hurts, disappointments; he'd never been snubbed in high school; in fact he'd been a popular guy, a football player of slightly above average ability, an officer in student government, a very good but not exceptional student. His anxiety about being guilty of something obscure and unnameable surfaced from time to time, but was readily banished. And then he went off to college, aged eighteen, and entered a new world — not that, in the late 1960s and early 1970s, Michael O'Meara was radicalized, like many of his contemporaries, by anti-Vietnam War agitation, but, being an idealistic and sympathetic young man as he was, he'd been profoundly moved, spiritually engaged, by the example of an activist clergyman, a "renegade Christian" as the man called himself, who had been publicly censored by his church for his politics. So, after college, Michael intended to become a clergyman too: it scarcely mattered which denomination, in that era of ecumenical feeling.

The O'Mearas, two brothers, had emigrated from Dublin, Ireland, early — in the 1840s. Apparently, with surprising alacrity, they'd cast off their Roman Catholicism and became assimilated into New England; they and their children married where love, or perhaps business interests, guided them. Michael's mother's family was Protestant, but not very decisively — to Michael's mother, such subjects as God, redemption, "soul" were as embarrassing to speak of as physical intimacies and maladies. Michael's father had no formal religion at all but referred vaguely to himself as Christian, as if to set himself apart from Jews, his fierce rivals in the fur trade.

Though it wasn't the Word of God so much as the Spirit of God Michael O'Meara hungered for, he'd enrolled in a distinguished, indeed very famous, seminary in New York City, with the intention of becoming a Protestant minister who was also (about this, Michael was vague) a teacher. Immediately, however, he was overwhelmed by the seminary's requirements and expectations of its students, in such contrast to the amiable Bachelor of Arts curriculum he'd taken as an undergraduate: ancient Greek? Latin? Hebrew? His introductory courses forced upon the twenty-one-year-old the paralyzing fact that he had no idea what "religion" meant, let alone what "God" meant — these were mere words, word-symbols, concepts, political/historical/sociological/geographical phenomena, ever-shifting and evolving — or devolving. (Michael had been certain he'd known who Jesus Christ was, but, exposed to a critique of the New Testament, he quickly came to see that the Jesus Christ of His time was not the Jesus Christ of subsequent times; nor was the Jesus Christ of His time altogether consistent in His teachings or His behavior.) The Bible, subjected to dissection, turned out to be not the Word of God — hardly! — but a ragtag anthology by diverse hands, compiled, not altogether fastidiously, over a period of centuries; in short, a work of fictions, some very weird indeed, containing competing ideologies and even religions. The Lord God Yahweh, so jealous, threatening, and unpredictable, was traced back to humble sources — he'd begun as a volcano god somewhere in the ancient world! Like a mediocre local politician who ascends to extraordinary heights not by merit but virtually by chance, this volcano god somehow ascended to the highest throne of all, *and now cannot be dislodged*.

Of course, Michael O'Meara's teachers at the seminary did not say such things directly, nor even simply. It is not the intention of scholarship to say things directly or simply; for then, and very quickly, the game might be up.

Michael was also forced to consider what he'd only vaguely realized in the past — that Christianity, in fact the Judaeo-Christian tradition as it was called, was but one tradition among many; and by no means the most enduring. The world was layered with religions extinct, near-extinct, living, flourishing, freshly seeded, like the very Earth itself, layered geologically in time. Each religion was divinely chartered, and each religion had its saviour, though more usually saviours; there were holy books, and holy men; miracles, mysteries, authorities; rites and rituals; sacrifices; sacraments; demons; heavens and hells and points in between; every variety of punishment, every variety of childish wish given form. As in a budget-conscious stage production in which a few actors played many roles, the gods of one sect were the devils of another. If love for one's neighbour was preached, hatred for one's enemies was practiced. The most pacific-minded people could be galvanized into becoming the most bloody warriors, once their god bade them act, and their priests blessed their swords.

None of these revelations was new. But all were new, to Michael O'Meara.

Dazed and demoralized but unwilling to give up, for, after all, there was the example of the activist-clergyman who had been a very intelligent and reasonable man, but had nonetheless believed in Jesus Christ, as there were similar, numberless examples, through history, of men who had managed somehow to accommodate both intelligence and faith, Michael had saturated himself in a purely intellectual study of philosophy and theology. Some of it was course-work, some of it his own meandering research, amid the millions of volumes (most, unfortunately — or was it fortunately? — in languages Michael did not know) in the seminary library. Xenophanes, Descartes, Voltaire, Plato, Pascal, St Augustine, Martin Luther, Nietzsche, St Thomas Aquinas and many others, in a jumbled chronology; Tillich on God-symbolism, Eliade on myth, Kierkegaard on fear and trembling, Tolstoy on Christ's teachings, Dostoyevsky's Grand Inquisitor; the significance of the Dead Sea Scrolls; Barth, Buber, Maritain, Schweitzer, Weil; papal encyclicals — Pius IX, Leo XIII, Pius XII, John XXIII. There was the flashing, glamorous weapon of structuralism, there was the laser-ray of semiotics, there was the audacity of Freudian psycho-analysis, there was the ray of hope of Jungian "individuation". There was of course anthropology, pitiless as a surgeon's scalpel, laying bare brains, blood vessels, nerves. There was even an interlude of Ingmar Bergman films, austere, chill, beautiful, which Michael and some of his new-made friends at the seminary saw frequently, obsessively. Near the end of his third viewing of *Through a Glass Darkly* Michael O'Meara broke down and began to cry, and stumbled out of the movie theater into the sulphurous haze of early evening on Bleecker Street. For some frightening seconds he truly didn't know where he was, still less why.

Where had it gone, he wondered, that quicksilver leap of certitude he'd had only a year or so before, that almost rowdy happiness pulsing in his veins, that conviction in his heart that drove out all absurd shadows of guilt, that there *was* a living God, a communal spirit to be experienced, if not understood?

"Too late have I loved thee, thou beauty of ancient days" — these words of St Augustine's, disembodied as the lyrics of a popular song lyric, ran through his head.

Was it too late?

Unshaven, underweight, hoarse with a bad cold, in a visibly

desperate state, Michael made an appointment to confer with his advisor at the seminary, a man who had studied with Tillich in the 1940s and who was highly respected in his own right as a New Testament scholar. Michael asked bluntly, "I just want to know — *is* there a God? And if so, what are we supposed to do?"

It was determined, during the course of the conference, that Michael O'Meara was perhaps not suited for seminary studies; nor for scholarly pursuits in general.

Following that disaster, Michael became a student again, in order to prepare for medical school. He was all afire with the idea that, to do good, whether God exists or not, is after all the aim of men (and women) of good will: but in order to do good, one must be trained to do a specific *good*. He reasoned, and in this he was very like many of the pre-med students he befriended, that there was no other more direct opportunity for helping others than being a doctor.

Michael was admitted to a less-than-prestigious medical school in upstate New York, at the mature age, as he thought it, of twenty-four. Here, he was to last even a shorter period of time than he'd lasted at the seminary, where at least he had been able to finish out the year.

It was not to be the numbing rote memorization that defeated him — Michael had always been the kind of eager student, unburdened with an excessive imagination, cooperative rather than rebellious, to whom the memorization of even dull unrelated facts came easily. Nor would it be the protracted hours of sleep-deprivation, for which medical school was notorious — Michael was the bearer of that sort of metabolism, common in muscular endomorphs, that allowed him to remain awake for long hours but granted him too, virtually at will, the ability to take quick, wonderfully refreshing cat-naps, sometimes as short as a single minute, anywhere he found himself. What defeated him was gross anatomy: his first cadaver.

Michael O'Meara, even as he'd made out application forms for medical school, had known, but had not wanted to think about it, that he would be required to dissect a cadaver at some point in medical school. He had known, but had not wanted to think about it, that this task might give him trouble. (In her carelessly entertaining anecdotes for her model older brother, Janet O'Meara often spoke of Michael's excessive sensitivity and empathy — "He's the kind of person who wouldn't hurt a flea, and I mean an actual *flea*.") He had not quite understood that he would be confronted with a cadaver on the very first day of classes, however. "Are they serious?" he asked a second-year student, and was told, "Are *you* serious?"

Upperclassmen at the school were amused by first-year students and condescending in their advice, which was, regarding the inevitable cadaver, not to get stuck with one that had been dead too many years.

The dreaded dissection lab was preceded, early Monday morning, by an introductory lecture; after approximately half an hour a cadaver was wheeled into the amphitheater, with no ceremony, no theatrical flair, as the professor of anatomy continued his lecture, and everyone continued, or tried to continue, taking rapid notes. Michael, seated in the fourth row of the steeply rising seats, close to one side, fumbled with his pen, dropped it and snatched it up again, his eyes blurred with tears and his nostrils assailed by a sudden acrid odor. The body on the gurney was discreetly draped in white; a human body in outline only; when the professor's assistant pulled aside the white cloth, at the professor's bidding, there was childlike relief in the amphitheater — the cadaver was covered with an opaque plastic sheet. And beneath this sheet, as it turned out, was another protective layer, wrapped in gauze; beneath the gauze, yet more gauze that protected the hands and the head. By this time, Michael had relaxed slightly, like most of the others around him. The cadaver's face — his identity — would not be revealed. Not in the lecture.

....
193

Still, Michael stared entranced at the mummy-like form, so utterly motionless. The anatomy professor was an energetic gray-haired little man, speaking in measured cadences, pausing to allow the taking of notes, his eyes moving quickly yet mechanically about the large room: how alive *he* was, as unlike the dead body on the gurney as he was, in his aliveness, unlike the gurney itself. Michael was thinking how uncanny a thing, to be in the presence of a . . . corpse; a being like ourselves, once possessed of a personality, an identity, a soul; but no longer. A guilty sensation washed over him, a taste as of bile at the back of his mouth. How evil you are, Michael O'Meara. How evil, and never to escape it.

He swallowed, he roused himself to full wakefulness. The anatomy lecture was concluding; the cadaver, now harmless, a mere object, was being covered up again, wheeled out of the amphitheater. Michael thought, This is nonsense. I'm strong. I'm motivated. I know what I'm doing, and why.

Since his disillusion with formal religion, and with the galaxy of ludicrous competing gods, he wasn't even certain he believed in "evil".

Immediately following the lecture was the anatomy lab, a two-hour ordeal, into which a powerful surge of adrenalin carried Michael, determined not only to get through the first dissection experience but to excel in it. He was smiling vacuously, and noticed that some others were smiling too, though their eyes were somber, scared. Michael O'Meara's characteristic response to situations of crisis — a response he was to retain all his life — was that of a quarterback of limited ability but visionary dreams: there was a heavy-footed grace about his stocky, affable body, an air of control, and enthusiasm in control. Since the age of thirteen, since summer camp in the Adirondacks, he'd discovered himself looked to by others as a natural leader; the kind who does not seek leadership, may in fact be embarrassed by it, but accepts it, at least some of the time, because others so wish. So, in the dissection lab on that

Monday morning in September 1975, in that nightmare of a room, stinking of phenol, in which, on twenty-five tables were twenty-five cadavers, each covered with an opaque plastic sheet, Michael assumed an air of equanimity, and smiled and nodded as one of the graduate instructors spoke, and, as the class divided into groups, each assigned to a table and to a cadaver, he smiled too, encouragingly, at his team-mates — three very sallow-skinned young men who were clearly waiting for Michael to position himself at the head of the table, and to be the one to uncover the cadaver.

The table to which Michael's group had been assigned was near a tall window, thank God, and the cadaver to which they'd been assigned did not somehow look full size. (Several of the cadavers in the lab looked enormous.) Was this good, or was this bad? Even as he was smiling at the others, as if he'd done this sort of thing many times before, Michael was gripped with a sudden sensation of horror: what if their cadaver was not an adult, but a young person? — a child?

The instructor was still lecturing, and, as they were bid, the students opened their dissection kits, examined scalpels, scissors, a hacksaw. (A hacksaw? — for sawing through the skull?) Dissection was a technique one learned as one learned any technique. The human body was a body, a model of anatomy. Michael nodded, as if in absolute agreement. The instructor had already noticed him, seemed to be speaking to him, as teachers frequently did. Michael O'Meara the intelligent, capable-looking young man with the strong face, the alert unwavering eyes, the fair red-burnished hair that, on his head and thinly and fuzzily covering his bared arms, gave him a faintly singed look, as if he'd been forged of some material sturdier and more reliable than that of the others who surrounded him.

At last the lecture ended, and it was time for the cadavers to be undraped.

Michael stared down at the form directly before him. His

three team-mates did not look at the form at all, but were watching Michael, intently. Beneath the plastic sheet there would be gauze — wouldn't there? Head and hands, at least, wrapped mummy-like in protective layers of gauze?

The instructor repeated his command, since no one in the room had moved. Michael, his senses blurred, was but dimly aware of the nightmare of tables, draped forms, students uncomfortably crowded together, breathing in the vile-smelling preservative that would become, from this day onward, a routine fact of their lives. The surge of adrenalin had ebbed, he felt now without strength, defenseless. Yet he must move, he must take command, others were looking at him expectantly, he had no choice. *How evil you are, to have done this. And never to escape.*

Elsewhere in the room sheets were being lifted, timidly. Michael O'Meara lifted the plastic sheet covering the cadaver before him — in a daze pulled it aside — one of his team-mates murmured, "Oh!" and another clenched his fists — and Michael blinked and stared seeing, before him, *a naked corpse.* Only the hands and feet were wrapped in gauze, the rest was exposed, *naked.*

Somewhere distant the instructor's voice rang out assuringly, they were being told to pick up a scalpel, to begin, to begin with a leg, two people on each side of the body, yes now it's time to begin, to begin, no going back you must make the first cut, you must utilize each second of lab time, it's precious time, you'll learn how precious since you must keep on schedule through the semeseter you must be finished with your dissection in twelve weeks, elsewhere in the lab tentative movements were being made, scalpels lifted, Michael too had a scalpel in his badly trembling hand but he had little awareness of it, little awareness of anything save the corpse stretched out before him, a young male, Caucasian, very pale in death, skin the sickly hue of bleached mustard, bruised eyes shut but seemingly about to open showing a thin crescent of bluish-white beneath the lids, nose somewhat bumpy at the bridge as if it had been broken, fair red-brown hair, thick on the head and sprouting like wires on the well-developed chest, belly, pubic area, arms and legs, Michael O'Meara was staring in horror seeing a cousin, a brother, a twin battered and disfigured and even discoloured in death, no mistaking it, the dissection lab had been so arranged as to bring him to this, this unspeakable horror, everyone was watching covertly as he, Michael, stood trembling above his victim, who was Michael too, the one still living, with a deadly weapon in his hand, his eyes rapidly blinking, a mottled flush in his face and his skin covered in icy sweat, unmistakable symptoms of guilt, here's the guilty man, here's the guilty boy, this time we see you, this time you can't escape, and now the cadaver's lips drew back tightly from his stained teeth in a supercilious sneering accusing expression as he peeked beneath his eyelids at Michael, *How evil, how evil, you, you're the one, did you think you could escape it?*

Someone spoke. Someone, the lab instructor perhaps, called out. Michael had stepped backward, or had he slipped, or been pushed, and the floor had opened up behind him, a pit, a sheer drop into utter blackness, into which, no longer conscious, and not at all resisting, he fell.

Following this disaster, after a six-month recovery period, Michael O'Meara went to law school, in Philadelphia, and did exceptionally well. His mother was vastly relieved, and many times told him so. Law school, with a specialization in corporate law, was exactly what his father had wanted for him, after all.

Sherry at the Rectory

JOHN WAKEMAN

Tim White was an enlightened solicitor in the pretty and therefore Tory town of Hampton, a few miles from Cambridge. He did what all country lawyers do — divorces and conveyancing and wills and writing to other lawyers about moral and physical boundaries. In addition, he campaigned — against American bombers in Britain and for humanity to chickens and against sexism in the legal profession and much else. He worked his heart out for young offenders, though there weren't many of those in Hampton.

He stuck to his principles even at home, for example sending his three children to the town's comprehensive, even though one of them was offered a scholarship to a choir school. His wife Lesley, who was getting steadily more beautiful as she hurried through her thirties, shared all of his convictions except his ferocious atheism.

At best, Lesley could go no further than agnosticism, and one day she confessed to him that she could no longer manage even that. She had slid back to being a Christian and had already taken Communion at the parish church, the bread and the wine, the flesh and the blood. Tim was a vegetarian as well as an atheist and he had a vision of his wife gnawing raw human meat, blood dribbling down her chin.

He described to Lesley his physical revulsion at her behaviour. There were wantonly destructive arguments, in which each said things they had thought for years. The children sobbed and their ten-year-old marriage often almost ended. They hung on somehow, out of inertia and love and a shared dislike of failure.

Tim hung on even when all three children were voluntarily and simultaneously baptised, standing giggling around the font at the parish church. He was a fair-minded man and could detect no pressure from Lesley in this choice, which was of course theirs to make. In fact they soon became bored with this new spiritual toy and turned to the *I Ching*. Tim reserved the right to make blasphemous jokes to Lesley, who smiled at them and sometimes laughed, and to their many friends, all of whom had stuck by them. The years passed and the crisis, unresolved, faded into the background of their lives.

It returned to the fore when Lesley admitted on her fortieth birthday that she felt a vocation to the priesthood. "This has to be addressed," Tim said, so they took pizzas out of the freezer for the two children still at home and themselves drove through watery sun to Dunwich, on the crumbling Suffolk coast.

Slouching along the shingle beside the brown and silver sea, Tim reminded Lesley with renewed urgency that priests had been responsible for the Crusades and the Inquisition, and had blessed the slaughter of the Great War, and had always stood with the rich and powerful against the poor. They were the treacherous clerks, the scum of the earth. Not all of them, Lesley insisted. There had been Archbishop Romero and Woodbine Willie and Bishop Tutu and George Herbert in some ways and the Reverend Martin Luther King, and that was the sort of priest she wished she could be.

They had baked potatoes and Adnam's at the pub in the village, and afterwards walked on the dangerous cliffs, listening in vain for the bells of the church that had gone into the sea. It had stopped being sunny by then and begun to drizzle. They came upon a circle of about twenty people, mostly young, singing a hymn together in the rain, and Tim asked Lesley if this was what she sought, this pathetic madness. She said it was not pathetic but no, that wasn't the sort of religion she felt at home with. She just wanted to serve people through God. If they'd let

JOHN WAKEMAN

her, that is, because of course the best she could hope for at
present was to join the diaconate.

Lesley explained that deacons were sort of apprentice priests.
They could preach sermons and christen people and marry and
bury them. They could even conduct most of the communion
service, but they couldn't consecrate the bread and the wine and
they couldn't forgive people their sins. After a year of being a
deacon, a man could expect to become a priest, able to do the
lot, but as things were a woman had to stay a deacon forever.
The General Synod was debating the ordination of women, but
many clergymen were opposed to it and threatened to walk out
and split the Church in twain, or twain-ish.

Tim already knew some of this from reading the *Guardian*,
but had managed not to take it on board. Now he had to and,
picking his way through nettles and thistles and briars, rusty
gorse and crippled hawthorns, he experienced conflict between
his atheism on the one hand, and his feminism, which won, on
the other. He told Lesley that if she wanted the grotesque job,
he would do all he could to help her get it.

Lesley was able to receive her theological and pastoral
training at home, without having to unload many domestic
chores onto Tim. There were occasional study weekends, but
mostly she read books and wrote essays for a tutor. After three
years of part-time study, Lesley was ordained a deacon in Ely
Cathedral. The whole family attended the ceremony and the
children, though of course not Tim, took communion from the
hands of the Bishop and Lesley. When the kids sipped the wine
from a silver chalice offered with great love and grace by their
mother, it reminded Tim of when they were small and Lesley
held their cocoa mugs for them. It moved him to tears.

The Rector of Hampton had a little empire of four churches.
One of them, St Mary Magdalen, was in the dozy village of
Dryford, a few miles from Hampton, and it was run under
supervision by a young curate with so elevated an accent that
only the commuters in the congregation could follow his

sermons. Lesley was allowed to be his assistant, handing him things at the altar, preaching an occasional humanistic sermon, organising rotas for the flowers and the laundry and the cleaning.

Three years after she started at St Mary's, Lesley understood the curate to say that he was moving on to a second curacy in some inner city. And perhaps martyrdom, she thought. She began to pray that she might get his job, if God at all willed it. Her Bishop was reasonably progressive, and the diocese already had two woman deacons in charge of parishes. Dryford was rich in old retired clergymen who could be propped up to mumble the magic bits of the service taboo to the unclean sex.

The only obstacle was the Rector of Hampton. He had been as nice as pie to Lesley when she was drudging at St Mary's. They'd had a Christmas card from him, thanking Lesley for doing so much to hold up one small pillar of the Church and blessing Tim for his "unstinting support of Lesley's Work". But he wouldn't have her as deacon in charge of St Mary's, and the Bishop couldn't make him.

Lesley would fight harder than Tim himself for a principle, but she wouldn't fight for herself. When she found out that the Rector had quietly blackballed her, she cried a bit and said that was that then. Tim said he really understood now why Nietzsche had despised Christians, and that Lesley had no right in this instance to turn the other cheek — that the issue was not a personal but a feminist issue. He used all of his formidable forensic skills on Lesley, bullying her skilfully until she at last agreed that they should have, *not* a confrontation, but all right a talk with the Rector.

Without giving a reason, they made an appointment to visit him at eleven o'clock on a Saturday morning in November. Their children had all grown up and moved away, but their daughter Julia was home again, having dropped out of Keele after an agonised affair with her supervisor. Julia wished them luck, and they left their old white house and walked through the

Saturday market, waving to or joking with people they knew, and up the hill, past the beautiful stone church like a small cathedral, to the tall red brick walls of the Rectory garden. It was a blustery day, with streaky clouds like stretch marks spreading across a grey flannel sky.

Lesley had put on a rust-coloured woollen two-piece and a light raincoat and a cheap Indian scarf. She wore no make-up because she never did and didn't need to. Tim couldn't remember whether or not the Rector smoked but thought he probably didn't and stopped to light a last cigarette as they started up the drive. It had rained earlier and the old beeches dripped on them.

It was that sort of Rectory — not a protean modern box but a small Victorian mansion, its bare-faced ugliness moderated by blood-coloured Virginia creeper. The Rector's wife was rumoured to have money of her own. Tim grinned rakishly at Lesley, flicked his cigarette into the wet rhododendrons and pressed the shining bell. Wind moaned through the clustered chimneys. The Rector flung open the door.

The Reverend Bill Manners was fifty-five. He was tall like Tim, but different in everything else. He didn't have a beard like Tim, who had a neat black one, and his grey hair was cut very short all over. He wasn't thin like Tim, but heavy shouldered and barrel-chested and barrel-bellied in his old black cardigan. He had once played rugby for the Navy, whereas Tim had played badminton for London University. Bill had pale blue eyes under eyebrows like furry caterpillars, and he twinkled the former at Tim and Lesley. Tim was relieved to see that he had left off his dog collar and further was smoking a small curved pipe.

Bill snatched the pipe from his mouth. "Come in my dears," he bayed in his Class A voice, just a touch of Midlands for comfort. "Come you in out of the cold." He slammed the door and, waving both arms, drove them over polished boards into a big drawing room with beige sacking on the walls and wet french windows and a small smoky fire in a white marble vault of a fireplace.

"Take a pew," he belled. "Just wherever you fancy." They chose a flowery sofa beside the fireplace.

"I've got us a fire going, of sorts, but it's never been my strong point. Any advice Tim? Any tips?"

"I always leave it to Lesley, myself. She's a dab hand at conflagrations, aren't you?"

"Only by comparison with you," Lesley said, rudely for her. "I'd just put a bit more coal on, Bill. It needs something to chew on."

"You're the boss, Lesley." Bill flung himself on his knees in front of the fire and, thrusting his right hand into a filthy left-handed gardening glove, began to build a great cairn of coals. Thick white smoke gushed up the chimney, veering out into the room when someone opened the door.

"Shut the damn door," Bill shouted over his shoulder, and she quietly did, Virginia Manners, long sensitive face with prominent cheekbones like a kangaroo, but with silvery-gold hair coiled on top of her head and a splendid tweed coat. Tweaking on gloves, she murmured the names of Tim and Lesley with an anxious smile, told her husband that she was stepping down to the shops and had left a coffee tray ready in the kitchen if they would like . . . "What on earth are you doing with that fire, Bill? There'll be a holocaust."

"Don't you worry, Virgo. I'm not ready for the flames yet. It's all part of Lesley's greater plan." She nodded vaguely, opened the door a crack, and evaporated away around it.

Bill stood up, groaning and grinning, and wiped his hands on his bottom. "I'm going to be a bit naughty," he announced. "While the cat's away. You'll tell me the sun's not quite over the yardarm, Tim, but I'm going to award myself a small glass of sherry. What for you two?"

They all had sherry and Tim lit a cigarette. Bill stared at it greedily. "Sheep as a lamb," he said. "May I have one of those things?" He jammed himself into an armchair facing their sofa and, puffing vigorously on his cigarette, leaned eagerly forward.

"You're wanting to have a go at me about St Mary's. That's what it is, isn't it?"

"Yes it is," Tim said.

"Of course it is. Come on then. Let fly. Rake me stem to stern."

Tim looked sternly at Lesley and she sighed and said, "Well. I've been there for three years, and I know the work. Also I had one or two ideas about, you know, possible improvements. And the congregation seem to like me . . ."

"They love you. Be fools if they didn't."

Lesley smiled gratefully and explained that she'd had a word at Diocesan Synod with the Bishop's chaplain. He'd given her the impression that the Bishop wouldn't mind her taking charge at St Mary's, but that Bill would.

"Indeed. Yes. That's exactly it."

"Can you say why?"

"I *must* say why, my love. I'm going to hurt and deprive you, and I must try — not to make you think as I do, because I shan't be able to do that — but to explain to you, *and* to myself, my starting point."

Levering himself out of the armchair, Bill stamped over to the little table between the french windows where the drinks were and came back with the sherry bottle. Lesley didn't want any but Tim did. The noonday sky was darkening and so was the fire, only one small flame flickering in the heart of it. Bill switched on a tall lamp beside his chair, and then the flame was no longer visible.

Bill stared into the writhing smoke and then earnestly into Lesley's eyes. "Putting you in charge of St Mary Magdalen wouldn't make you a priest, but it would be a step towards that, a *stride* towards that. Some people would *see* you as that. And

Lesley, my dearest Lesley, that idea fills me with dread and — I must say this — with revulsion."

"That is a shocking thing . . .," Tim started, but Lesley asked him to shut up.

"This has nothing whatever to do with the person you are, Lesley — that *wonderful* person. It's beyond personalities, yours *or* mine. I've prayed about this, of course, and it's as clear to me as it can be that this gut feeling of mine — pardon my French — is a physical expression of the Revealed Truth. I don't know any way to depart from it."

"*I* want to be a priest and *I've* prayed about it and it feels right to me. That's *my* gut feeling, and I wouldn't be able to depart from it either."

"Of course. I understand that. And I respect it. But we have an impasse my dear. That's what we have and there's no help for it . . . Irresistible force, immovable object."

"*Is* it immovable," Tim asked quietly, "or just very powerful? Aren't we really looking at an entrenched male hierarchy that wants things to stay just the way they are?"

"You're entitled to your opinion, Tim. But I know it's very much more than that, and I would guess that Lesley knows that too."

"Do you Lesley?"

"I know it's not as simple as you'd like it to be."

"Explain it to me then."

"I don't want to, Tim. Not now, because something has . . . We can talk about it at home."

A tongue of flame poked out of the middle of the fire and, with a small jolt of an explosion, the fire caught, smoky flames fighting their way through the shifting coals.

"Hoorah," cried Bill. "Well done, Lesley! I really think we should drink to that. And to us, if you will — that we can agree to disagree." He fetched the sherry, and now the flames made flickering spectra in the sticky cut-glass *copitas*. "It feels like evening," Lesley said.

Tim drained his glass and glanced intelligently from Bill to Lesley and back again. "You know, I *would* like to understand all this a bit better. I genuinely would."

"Your own profession isn't exactly overloaded with women in high places," Lesley said glumly.

"My own profession is *shamefully* sexist. But some of us are trying to do something about that, and there's been a little progress and there'll be more. At least the legal profession doesn't officially and publicly prohibit a woman from becoming a solicitor or a barrister or even a judge. The Church does have such a prohibition and to an outsider it seems, well, medieval."

"Oh it's much older than that, Tim," Bill said firmly. "It goes back two thousand years. When the priest at the altar consecrates the blood and the wine, he stands as the icon of Christ, recreating for the billionth time what Jesus did in that upper room at the Last Supper. He re-*presents* Jesus. And Jesus was a chap. He cannot be represented by a woman."

"He was also a Jew. And a carpenter. I don't think *you* are."

"*Tim!*"

"It's all right Lesley. Better out than in. It's a familiar point but an interesting one. All the same, Tim, a person's gender is rather more central to his, um, being than his trade or his race."

"Is it? You might not think so if you had a blazing car tyre round your neck in Soweto."

The door opened and the enormous fire jumped in the draught. Virginia Manners came in and switched on the wrought iron chandelier and blinked at them.

"Oh goodie, you *are* still here. When I saw that no one had had coffee . . . Oh Bill, that fire is like a furnace. And look, it's spitting all over the carpet." She hurried over and took up a folded brass fireguard and opened it in the hearth.

"That's better. Would anyone like some coffee now?"

"We're all guzzling sherry, Virgo. Won't you have a smidgen?"

"No, I've got a small headache, actually. I think there's a

storm coming. The sky is so dark and the wind is ferocious. It's the strangest day."

"*Götterdämmerung*," Tim muttered, but everyone ignored him.

"We ought to leave," Lesley said. "Before it starts."

"Oh stay a moment more. I never see you. Look, I'll risk a tiny sherry, if you'll stay."

No one spoke until Virginia had a glass and sherry in it. The fire roared and the wind howled in the chimney. A leaf like a wet yellow hand slapped flat against the french window. Virginia jumped.

"Goodness. It's quite exciting, isn't it? And what have you three been gossiping about?"

That renewed the silence, until Lesley said: "Bill has been explaining why he doesn't feel able to put me in charge of St Mary's."

"Oh my dear," Virginia said, her pale face suddenly flushed. "Of course. He did tell me but I forgot again. I'm so brutally clumsy and should never have married him, a clergyman I mean. I'm not fit for the task. He can't change his principles, of course, but everyone knows you were perfect for St Mary's. It must be dreadful for you, a bereavement."

"It is a bit like that, Virginia, yes. But as you say, Bill can't abandon his principles. I do see that."

"If they *are* principles," Tim said slowly, "and not prejudices."

"Don't start again, Tim. There's no point in talking about it now."

"Religion, sex and politics — they're what we're not supposed to talk about, aren't they? I wonder why. Unfortunately, they're what we *are* talking about. Sexual politics in the context of religion. I was just suggesting, Virginia, that if priests must be male because Christ was, they ought really to be Jews and carpenters as well."

Virginia giggled. "That does seem logical, Tim, yes. But how confusing. You wouldn't be able to be Rector, would you Bill? He's actually jolly good at carpentry, but not a bit Jewish, are you?"

Bill laughed uneasily and got up and rammed his chair back from the fire, which was giving out great heat and seemed to be vibrating. "That's a devil of a fire you've created there, Lesley. Anyone for more sherry while I'm up?"

"I'll have a little more," Virginia said. "It's making me feel better." Weighing the bottle in his big hand, Bill explained to Tim that the theology of Christ's maleness was a bit knotty. "It has to do with something we call 'the scandal of particularity'. Unless you've read quite a bit of theology, which perhaps you haven't . . ."

Lesley looked puzzled. "But that's Kierkegaard, isn't it? I mean, it's a relatively recent argument. I thought your position was more . . ."

"Indeed. Indeed. And also I'm not the first to point out that every one of the Apostles was a man."

"He's got you there, Tim," said Virginia. "And what a recruitment problem it would be, finding all those Jewish carpenters. And anyway, Jews don't even recognise Our Lord as the Messiah. They *are* funny. I expect things were different in biblical times."

"Exactly," said Tim. "It was a shamelessly patriarchal society, and that's obviously why the Apostles, if they were to be listened to, had to be men. Perhaps we're not much better now, but you really can't organise a major institution in late industrial Britain on the mores of a virtually prehistoric pastoral culture in the Middle East."

Bill said that cultures came and went, but the Church was unchanging. Lesley remarked mildly that this wasn't entirely true, because for example the Church used to endorse slavery and didn't any more. Bill quoted St Paul as saying "let women keep quiet in church." Lesley retorted quite angrily that St Paul had also said that in Christ, "there is neither slave nor free, man nor woman." Tim said it was well known that the Church Fathers were misogynists to a man, terrified of their own sexuality, and which of them was it who called woman "a temple built on a sewer"? Bill said the past was not the issue. Virginia had another sherry and said it was lovely to see Lesley and her curate serving the Eucharist together, like the church having a father *and* a mother, a proper family and not a broken one, and how were Lesley's children, oh, and apropos, Bill himself had said that quite a lot of men had joined the congregation of St Mary's after Lesley started there. Bill asked with a smile whose side Virginia was on, and he certainly hadn't meant to imply anything, um, sexual in that context. Tim said that he couldn't see why not, since women traditionally went to church in the pious hope of seeing up the skirts of male priests. Bill said it was a pity that the discussion had sunk to such a level, and the fire thundered in the chimney.

Lesley stood up, close to tears, and said she was sorry. The children were fine, except that Julia was a bit low and they'd better go home and give her some lunch.

"Julia can give herself some lunch," Tim said. "This is important, Lesley. What about your so-called vocation?"

Lesley thought for a while and then said that she'd written to the Bishop of Newark, New Jersey, and he'd told her that she could go there and be ordained a priest of the Episcopal Church and that's what she thought she'd better do. Bill said after a pause that he would be terribly sorry to lose her, but he respected her right to . . .

"Who's going to look after the house?" Tim asked. "What about Julia?"

"It would only be for a year Tim. Julia could come with me. It might be just what . . ."

"It might be just what? Your bloody mumbo-jumbo has always been more important to you than your children. Or me of course. Well, I'll tell you one thing, you needn't expect me to

....

pay your fare to America. Or keep you there. That's not what marriage is about."

"I've only just heard, Tim. We can talk about this at home. But the Bishop says there's some sort of fund that would cover most of the cost."

"I have some money, Lesley," Virginia said, her eyes shining with excitement. "If you would let me, I'd be so gratified . . . You *are* a priest. I felt that the first time I saw you at the altar."

Tim said, "It's really not your business, Virginia."

"That's not your money to give away." Bill said.

"Yes it is my money, Bill. My father gave it to me and there's quite a lot of it and I can do what I like with it. I want to do this."

Lesley went over to Virginia and kissed her, and Virginia kissed her back. An enormous clump of burning soot fell down the chimney and flattened the fireguard and exploded on the carpet.

"Look what you've done, you silly woman," Bill shouted at Lesley. He hurled himself into a pall of smoke and began scooping the soot into the hearth with a small brass shovel.

"You do that," Tim shouted, "and I'll phone the Fire Brigade. Have you got any kitchen salt, Virginia?"

"Oh dear. I think so."

"You find that and bung it on the fire. All you've got." A great bolt of lightning lit the garden, turning green to white, then another, on its heels a clap of thunder that shook the house. Rain pattered, then hammered, on the french windows.

"*Not* so pathetic, the pathetic fallacy," cried Virginia through the smoke. "Just as I've always thought."

Another lump of burning soot burst in the hearth.

"Kitchen salt," Bill shouted. "In the kitchen." Virginia ran out of the room. Lesley found another small shovel beside the coal scuttle and knelt beside Bill.

The fire in the hearth was like a wet slag heap, smothered by soot and drenched by rain sizzling down the burning chimney.

Clots of smouldering soot still flopped onto the steaming embers. Like a mixed double of tennis players, Bill and Lesley fended back with their shovels any that tumbled towards the scorched and filthy carpet.

Bill grinned at Lesley, his teeth luminous white in his black face. "The worst is over. Rain saved the day."

"Yes."

"On our knees together, eh? You'll ruin your skirt."

"It'll be all right."

"What about you and Tim? Will *you* be all right?"

"I expect so. We always are in the end."

"Will you write to me from New Jersey?"

"If you like."

"You know how fond of you I am."

"Mm."

"It's such a battle you know. Against evil. One's own as well. And when those forces are drawn against you, and everyone is looking to you for leadership, you want the decks cleared and the women below out of harm's way. *Afterwards* you need them, their support and healing. You feel you've earned it. Their task is crucial then, very important indeed. But you don't want them up on the firing line beside you, confusing . . . confusing things." He glanced sideways at Lesley, and pushed a lump of soot neatly out of sight under the firebasket.

Virginia hurried into the room, shaking her head in despair. "I'm so sorry but I can't find the salt."

"I thought you'd turned into a pillar of the stuff."

Tim strode into the room. "They're on their way," he said. "Everything's under control. Christ, Lesley, you'll ruin your skirt."

In a moment they heard the excited bells of the fire engines, but by the time they arrived, the rain had put out the fire in the chimney.

....

Breaking It Up

BAPSI SIDHWA

A brief but fierce deluge that had followed the dust storm the night before had brought respite from the June heat. As it was, holding the letter in her inert fingers — the obscene photograph having already fluttered to the bedroom floor — Zareen found it hard to breathe.

After a while she became conscious of the servants chattering in the kitchen, the cook laying the table for lunch, and as the initial slam of shock wore off slightly, the news, with its tumult of ramification, sank deeper into her sinking heart. With shaking fingers Zareen dialed the number of her husband's office, and, relieved at the thought of transmitting her anguish, began to cry at the sound of his voice.

"What is it . . . What's the matter?" Cyrus's panicked voice rang in her ears.

Drawing comfort from his concern Zareen blew her nose, and, with a supreme effort of will, choking on her tears, managed to say: "I got a letter from Feroza. She wants to marry a 'non'."

Cyrus found his wife huddled on their bed beneath the slowly rotating and creaking blades of the ceiling fan, her attractive eyes swollen, her elegant nose red.

Cyrus scanned the letter silently. His eyes automatically focused on the significant sentences: Feroza had met a wonderful boy . . . Like her, he was also very shy . . . She had agreed to marry him. She knew they would be very upset — particularly her grandmother — at the thought of her marrying a non-

Parsee . . . His parents were Jews . . . The religious differences did not matter so much in America . . . They had decided to resolve the issue by becoming Unitarians. "Please, please, don't be angry, and please try to make grandmother understand . . . I love you all so much — I won't be able to bear it if you don't accept David."

David had blue eyes and frivolous gold-streaked longish hair. His image in the photograph struck them as actorishly handsome; phony and insincere — if not sinister. But what upset them both most were the pair of over-developed and hairy thighs — which to their fearful eyes appeared to bulge obscenely as a goat's — as they burst from a pair of frayed and patched denim shorts.

"You'd better go at once," Cyrus said. "He can't even afford a decent pair of pants! The bounder's a fortune-hunter. God knows what he's been up to . . ."

The last was an allusion to the imagined assault by those hairy thighs on the citadel of their daughter's virtue.

Thus it was that ten days later, after praying one thousand Yathas and five hundred Ashem Vahoos, jet-lagged and duty-bound Zareen landed at Denver airport.

Zareen emerged from the customs, groggily steering her luggage, and right away spotted Feroza. Conspicuous in the thick fence of pink faces Feroza's dusky face glowed with affection and delight at sighting her mother. A little knot of love and happiness formed round Zareen's heart.

Feroza was wearing a light brown tank-top, and, as Zareen had expected, no make-up. Feroza's plump well-formed shoulders and arms were chocolate dark with suntan and her body radiated a buxom brown female vitality. But her most striking feature — even at that distance — were her eyes: a luminous yellow-brown, lighter than her skin or the straight hair falling about her shoulders. Zareen held her breath: her daughter was lovely.

And then Feroza was hugging her and taking her traveling

bag from her hand. A nondescript young man in long pants and shirt, crowned by an unsparing short hair-cut and wearing rimless glasses, smiled awkwardly and picked up her suitcases.

Feroza said, "Mum, this is David."

The little radiation of happiness and love in her heart was nudged aside as Zareen assessed her adversary. The photograph had been misleading. David bore little resemblance to the confident, actorishly handsome image. His shy blue eyes blinked with anxiety to be liked behind the unadorned squares of glass.

"How are you, David?" Zareen said, coolly holding out her hand with the three diamond rings. David, divesting himself of the two heavy suitcases, and hastily wiping his hands on his pants, shook it formally. "Welcome to America," he said, and then mumbled something neither of them could decipher.

As they followed David to the little Chevette in the parking lot, Feroza whispered, "He's had his hair cut; he's all dressed up in long pants for your sake." She gave her mother a hug. Zareen decided to postpone any thinking on the issue till after she'd had a cup of tea. She glanced at the straight-backed, muscular young man walking ahead with a self-conscious spring to his step, and turning to Feroza only said: "You've become very dark — your grandmother won't like it. You'd better bleach your face before you come home."

Throughout the drive Zareen talked about family members and addressed herself exclusively to Feroza. David sat quietly in the back with bits of left-over luggage that could not be crammed into the trunk.

When Zareen stopped talking to gape at the massive skyscrapers that had looked so toy-like from the airplane, David started doggedly pointing out landmarks:

"That's City Hall. That's the Denver Philharmonic Center. Can you see where all the glass is? Right there . . . that's the best shopping mall around here. That's the Museum of Contemporary Arts — it has a good show right now . . ."

But once they were past the awesome masonry and glass down-town, Zareen continued directing her remarks at Feroza; and subconsciously registered the orderly passage of the wide paved streets, the tidy row of houses, and the glossy leaves on thickly spreading trees.

Feroza turned into a gravel drive, announcing: "Here's where we live." And Zareen realized that "we" included David. She cast a startled glance at her daughter, and Feroza quickly added: "Four of us share the house, mum; David stays in the converted garage. Two other girls, Laura and Shirley, share a room. They didn't want to be in the way when you came . . . You'll see them tomorrow."

Zareen regarded the house with raised eyebrows. Coming from a part of the world where houses have 13-inch thick brick walls and reinforced concrete roofs, her daughter's dwelling looked like an oblong shack of painted wood, set up to be blown away by the puffing nursery-rhyme wolf.

But once she stepped inside Zareen was pleasantly surprised by the thickly carpeted interior, and fell in love with the large green fridge and matching dish-washer in the spacious kitchen. She touched the shining surface of things with delight, appreciating the materials that could be kept so easily clean without the help of servants. She was quite civil to David, but with an inflection that left him a bit breathless and fumbling as both he and Feroza showed off the house.

Feroza made a pot of tea and after a decent interval David left them to talk. Almost at once Feroza asked: "Mum, what do you think of him?" And she was a little crestfallen when her mother said, "It's too early to tell. We'll talk about it tomorrow."

The next day, refreshed by her sleep, Zareen launched what she believed was a mild offensive. She lauded the virtues and earning capacities of the three marriageable Parsee boys in Lahore. Their worthy mothers had expressed ardent desires to make Feroza their daughter-in-law.

. . . .

Feroza kissed her mother fondly and teased: "I think I'm too young to settle down with mothers-in-law. Besides," she said, indicating with a shift in her tone that she was serious, "David's mother is really quite sweet. His parents live in Boulder, near Denver. His father is a bookkeeper at Con Edison, the electric company. They are not rich but they are respectable people."

This gave Zareen the opening she was looking for. "You are too precious. We are not going to throw you away on the first piece of riffraff that comes your way."

Feroza's shining eyes lost a part of their lustre.

"You know what we do when a proposal is received," Zareen continued, ignoring the change in her daughter's regard; aware though, she must be more guarded in her choice of words. "We investigate: What is his background? His standard of living? His family connections?"

A well-connected family conferred advantages that smoothed one's path through life. What did she know of David's family connections? His antecedents?

"What do you mean: antecedents?"

"His ancestry, his *Khandan*."

"Don't be absurd, Mum," Feroza said. "If you go about talking of people's pedigrees the Americans will laugh at you."

Cut to the quick Zareen plucked a tissue from the box on the kitchen table. "It's no laughing matter. You'll be thrown out of the community! You know what happens to Parsee girls who marry out?" And then, like a magician conjuring up the inevitable rabbit, proclaimed: "They become ten times more religious! Take Perin Powri: Like most of you girls she never wore her *sudra* or *kusti*. You should see her now that she's married to a 'non'. She drapes her sari in the Parsee way with her *sudra* showing, and her *kusti* dangles at the back! She misses her connection with community matters . . . she'd give anything to be allowed into the Fire Temple."

"We're having a civil marriage; a magistrate will marry us," Feroza said. "That way I can keep my religion if it matters so much to you . . . of course, you know, David and I are Unitarians."

"Unitarians!" Zareen said, wrinkling her nose disparagingly. "You talk of it as if it were a religion! My dear, your magistrate's marriage will make no difference to the priests. They won't allow you into the Temple." Zareen moved her coffee mug to one side and placing her arms on the table, said: "Do you know how hurt and worried we all were when we got your letter? Your father and I couldn't sleep. Your poor grandmother actually fainted! She told me to beg you on her knees not to marry this boy. You know she adores you; she'll be heart-broken. You won't be allowed to attend her funeral rites, or mine, or your father's!" She picked out the last tissue and wiped her eyes. "Do you know how selfish you are . . . thinking only of yourself?"

Zareen blew her nose, and addressed herself to what, next to the thought of her daughter's outcast status, caused her the most agony. "It is not just the case of your marrying a boy; the entire family is involved — all our relationships matter." She tried to describe how much added prestige, influence and pleasure their interaction with a new bunch of Parsee in-laws would bring. "You are robbing us of a dimension of joy we have a right to expect. What will you bring to the family if you marry this David? But that doesn't matter so much . . . What matters is your life: it will be so dry. Just husband, wife, and maybe a child — rattling like loose stones in America!"

"You'll have to look at things in a different way, mum. It's a different culture."

"And you'll have to look at it our way: You can't just toss your heritage aside like that: It's in your bones!"

Feroza stared at her mother. Her face had become set in a way that recalled to Zareen the determination and hauteur with which her daughter had once slammed doors and shut herself up in her room.

"You've always been so stubborn!" Zareen said angrily.

"You've made up your mind to put us through this thing . . . You will disgrace the family!"

"I'm only getting married . . . If the family wants to feel disgraced, let it!"

Zareen checked herself: she recalled her husband's sage advice: she must not push her daughter to rebellion.

"Darling," she pleaded, "I can't bear to see you unhappy." She buried her face in her arms and began to sob.

Feroza brushed her lips against her mother's short, sleek hair, and putting her arms round her cried: "I don't know what to do . . . Please don't cry like this . . . It's just that I love him . . ."

Zareen reared up as if an exposed nerve had been touched in her tooth. "Love? Love? Love comes after marriage! And only if you marry the right man! Don't think you can be happy by making us all unhappy."

"I think I've had about all I can take!" Feroza said, pushing her chair back noisily.

Zareen suddenly felt so wretchedly alone in this far-away country. "I should have listened . . . I should never have let you go so far away. Look what it's done to you . . . You've become an American brat!"

David, who had entered the kitchen at this point to get some cookies, silently withdrew to brood in his book-lined garage.

"I don't know how I'll face the family," Zareen cried. "I don't know what my friends will think!"

"I don't give a fuck what they think!"

Zareen glared at her daughter open-mouthed, visibly shaken by the crude violence of the language. "I never thought that I'd live to hear you speak like this!" she said, wagging her head. With affronted dignity she stood up, and walked from the kitchen with the bearing of a much taller woman.

After a while Feroza followed her into the room they shared and hugged her mother. Zareen's pillow was soaked with tears.

"I'm sorry . . . I didn't mean that . . ." Feroza said, herself weeping. "I don't know what came over me."

Chastened by the storm of emotion they had generated, and the unexpected violence of the words exchanged, each called a frightened, silent truce. Neither brought up the subject for the rest of the evening. David had wisely elected to stay out of their way and had left the house. Feroza, though made wretched by his absence, appreciated it: it was best that she be alone with her mother. They talked late into the night of family matters, of Feroza's progress in her studies, and, carefully circling the subject of marriage, each ventured, gingerly, to mention David. Feroza casually threw in something about David when the opportunity presented itself, and Zareen just as casually tossed up a question or two to show she bore him no ill will and was prepared to be objective.

"David has wonderful road sense," Feroza said at one point. "In fact, he'd love to show you around . . . he can explain things much better than any guide."

"That would be nice," Zareen said carefully, and on a note so tentative that Feroza expected her to continue. She looked at her mother with a touch of surprise when she didn't, and quickly Zareen said, "But will he be able to find the time?"

"Of course he will. He's planned the weekend for you."

Feroza had already mentioned how hard David worked. Besides devoting every moment he could spare to his studies, he held two part-time jobs. "His father can pay his fees, but he won't," Feroza said, stretching the point somewhat, aware that David's father would have paid the fees if he could. "He feels David must earn his way through university."

"Quite right," Zareen said, approving the parental decision. "It will teach him to stand on his own two feet." It was an attitude Parsee fathers would approve and encourage. If Zareen were to believe all the allusions slipped in by Feroza, David was a genius, a saint, and had a brilliant future in computers.

"He seems like a nice boy," Zareen said graciously, and Feroza, delighted by this quantum leap in his favor, hummed as she brushed her teeth. She heard Laura and Shirley move unobtrusively in their room. She saw the light, that had come on in David's garage, go out. Hugging her mother goodnight saying, "And *do* let the bugs bite!" she laughed so raucously at her own old joke that it infected the small frame house with her joy, and Shirley and Laura, talking softly in their room, suddenly found themselves giggling about the least little thing. David, who was inclined to bouts of gloom and self-doubt, found the thunderous cloud that had descended on him after his encounter with Zareen — convinced he had made the worst impression possible — lift somewhat. He smiled in the dark and longed to be with Feroza. He hoped she would slip into his room later. But hugging her pillow in the narrow camp cot next to her mother's bed, Feroza blew him an invisible kiss and fell peacefully to sleep.

Zareen, who had to cope with a twelve-hour time difference, was wide awake at two o'clock in the morning. She found the quiet in her strange surroundings eerie: and the opaque glow behind the curtains as the night sky reflected the tireless city lights, disorienting. In Lahore, at this hour, the pitch night would be alive with a cacophony of insect and mammal noises: with the thump of the watchman's stick or the shrill note of his whistle. And, the population explosion in Pakistan having extended itself also to the bird community, some bird disturbed by a sudden light, or by an animal prowling in the trees, was bound to be twittering, some insomniac rooster crowing.

Covering her eyes and her ears in an old silk sari she kept for the purpose, Zareen summoned the imagined presence of her husband, her caring kinsfolk, and filled the emptiness of her second night in America with their resolute and reassuring chatter. Their voices, trapped in the sari, rustled in her ears: "Our prayers are with you. Be firm. We must not lose our child."

By the time she drifted off to sleep at about five in the morning Zareen had glimpsed the rudiments of an idea that had the potential to succeed.

Feroza awoke her mother with a cup of tea. "It's ten o'clock, Mum. We've planned a lovely Saturday for you."

Zareen was at once wide awake. Refreshed by her sleep, and subconsciously aware of having spent the night in fruitful endeavor, she was in a happier and more adventurous frame of mind. After all she was in America! The New World beckoned.

They breakfasted at McDonalds and lunched at Benihanna, where the Japanese chef performed a fierce ballet with his sharp knives. At night Zareen sank her teeth into a thick slice of medium-rare roast beef and shut her eyes the better to savor it. Never had she tasted the natural flavor of meats, fish and vegetables quite this way: always eating them drowned in delectable concoctions of spices at home.

On Sunday — a day as scintillating and balmy as all the days she was to spend in Denver — they drove along winding roads through greenly rolling country to an abandoned mining town that had flourished during the gold rush, but was now mainly a tourist attraction.

Guiding her tour with enthusiasm, blossoming beneath the admiring yellow gaze of his beloved and the interest shown by the sophisticated woman in a sari, David gave Zareen her first taste for the history of the land. So tied up and tangled the day before, his tongue became fluent and he brought the Wild West vividly to life. His fumbling movements too were replaced by the surety that was natural to his compact body. And David, who had despaired in his dark bouts of gloom of ever impressing Zareen, was as surprised as she was.

When Feroza, agile in jeans, asked Zareen to climb the steep struts after her into an old steam engine, David tactfully suggested: "You'd better not in that beautiful sari."

"At least you have more sense than my daughter," Zareen said tartly: and intercepted a look between them — of David's delight at winning her favor and Feroza's bemused surprise. Zareen also caught a gesture she was not meant to see: Gloating at having scored over Feroza, David grinned, and though

Feroza tried to look hurt by the sudden switch in her mother's allegiance, it was plain to see she was pleased.

Each day the next week Feroza dropped her mother off at one or another of the gleaming shopping malls. To Zareen's dazzled senses they were pieces of paradise descended from the sky, crammed with all that was most desirable in the world. Shooting off at a tangent she darted between the garment racks and the cosmetics counters — the jewelry, linen, toy, shoe and furniture displays — like a giddy meteorite driven mad by the gravitational allure of contending cosmic bodies. Feroza fetched her late in the evening from some designated spot, usually an ice-cream parlor, and, eyes glazed by the glory of the goods she had seen and the foods she had tasted, Zareen climbed into the small car with large shopping bags.

The results of her first shopping spree were manifest that very evening. The tops of everything: counters, tables, window-sills, sprouted tissue boxes as if she had planted a pastel garden of fragrant Kleenex. She went from tissue box to tissue box plucking tissues with a prodigality that satisfied a deep sensual craving, and chucked them away with an abandon she had never presumed to indulge.

Feroza's dressing table and bathroom shelves blossomed in a dizzying array of perfume bottles and cosmetics, and the floor level of Feroza's two long closets rose by at least two feet in a glossy flood of packages containing linen, lamp-shades and gadgets. The hanging spaces were jammed with new blouses, trousers, skirts and jackets.

Feroza discreetly moved her clothes to David's closet.

Enchanted, Zareen made her daily debut in the kitchen, modeling her new clothes, and was as delighted as a child by the flattering comments from whoever happened to be break-fasting. She spent hours chatting with Laura and Shirley. They ferried her around occasionally when Feroza or David were busy, and she treated them to ice-cream cones, and the junk food she brought home. She bought small gifts for everyone.

....

David and Feroza, exhilarated by their success, relaxed some of their self-imposed restraints. David held Feroza's hand; and glancing at her mother, Feroza permitted it to be held. She rested her head on David's shoulder when the ride was long, and occasionally hugged him in a sisterly fashion in front of Zareen. Light-headed with delight, David let his hair, and even the stubble on his chin grow. His confidence too blossomed; and with it the gamin sense of humour that had so touched Zareen in the abandoned mining town when he had gleefully thumbed his nose at Feroza. At such moments, Zareen wished David was Parsee — or that the Zoroastrians permitted conversion to their faith.

Although Shirley and Laura occasionally roamed the house in shorts, David, warned by Feroza, kept his hairy legs modestly concealed. There were other strictures they prudently continued to observe: and David, nosing his way timidly on the surface of another culture, was entirely guided by Feroza. Neither smoked before Zareen: and both were careful not to give the slightest intimation of their more advanced physical intimacies.

And then, within three days of each other, in the third week of her visit, arrived a spate of anxious letters from Pakistan recalling Zareen to her mission.

Zareen's sleep became restless. As if prodded by an ominous finger, she sat bolt upright in bed one night, her pulse pounding. She looked at the watch on the side table: it was three o'clock. She felt something was terribly amiss and with a shock realized Feroza was not in her cot. For the first time Zareen suspected that her daughter probably slept with David. Tying her scarf round her head she began to pray.

Zareen knew what she must do. However useful and appealing David was, however natural to the stimulating and carefree environment, he would deprive her daughter of her faith and her natural element. Like a fish in shallow waters her child would eventually shrivel up.

The next day Feroza and David at once sensed the change in Zareen's mood. They were surprised how fragile their happiness was; how vulnerable they were. Linking Zareen's shift in temper to the bundle of letters that had arrived all together from Pakistan, Feroza wished the mail had been lost. Zareen's face grew more and more solemn as the morning advanced and a little frown appeared between her eyes. Feroza, after a few attempts to rally her mother had failed, became equally solemn. David's misgivings launched their customary attack. Racked by self-loathing and his usual gloomy doubts, he skulked about the garage and the backyard, trying to keep out of everybody's way. There were muffled sounds of an altercation from Laura and Shirley's room. Zareen's ill humour had contaminated the house.

Zareen waited for David to appear in the kitchen. Feeling he was deliberately avoiding her, she strode to the garage door and after ascertaining he was in his room, said, "David, can you come into the kitchen please? I want to talk to you."

David's spirits sank lower as he caught that elusive inflection that had so disconcerted him on the day of her arrival. Pulling his legs through his long pants David hurried into the kitchen and sat down before Zareen. Zareen gave him a quick cool smile and dispensing with courtesies said: "I am most concerned about Feroza. Do you intend to marry her, or are you just having fun?"

David felt the blood rush to his head and cloud his vision. At the same time, meekly lying on his lap his hands turned numb and cold. "Of course," he stammered, "We want to get married."

"Please speak for yourself," Zareen said, "And let my daughter speak for herself."

David was too stunned to say anything. He looked at Zareen with an expression of surprise and misery.

"Have you thought about the sacrifice you are demanding of my daughter?"

"I'm not demanding anything . . . Feroza does as she pleases:

pretty much . . ." Then, the slightest edge to his voice, he added: "She's an adult."

"An adult? I don't think so," Zareen said. "You are both too immature and selfish to qualify as adults . . . She doesn't care how much she hurts all of us. I'll tell you something," Zareen's voice became oracular with foreboding. "I look into Feroza's future and what do I see? Misery!"

David could not credit his faculties. The transition was too sudden. He could not reconcile the hedonistic shopper, the model swirling girlishly in the kitchen, the enthusiastic tourist and giver of gifts with this aggressive sage frightening him with her doom-booming voice, and a volley of bizarre accusations. "Could we talk about this later?" he mumbled, tripping over the chair as he got to his feet. "I'm getting late for classes . . ."

"Then go!" Zareen was imperious with scorn. "But please do think about the sacrifice you are asking of my daughter."

Feroza, who had retreated to her room and was nervously bracing herself for a quarrel, was not prepared for the ferocity of Zareen's attack — or its dangerous direction — as she marched into the room saying: "You are both selfish: Thinking of no one else . . . And don't think I don't know what you're up to!"

"What am I up to?" At once on her guard, Feroza adopted a haughty tone.

"Ask your conscience that! We have taught you what is wrong and what is right!"

"If you're referring to my virginity, you may relax," Feroza said attaching umbrage to her haughty voice. "I'm perhaps the only nineteen-year-old virgin in all America."

"You were not in your bed at three o'clock this morning! You expect me to believe you?"

"Believe what you want since you don't trust me!" Feroza said with scathing dignity and stalked from the room. Zareen followed her furiously. "Don't you turn your back on me! Look me in the eye!"

. . . .

They had the house to themselves. In the course of the row mother and daughter stormed in and out of rooms — raking up old quarrels — wrenching doors open and banging them shut. At the end of an hour Zareen, trembling with rage and exhaustion, raised her hand threateningly: "Don't think you're too old to be slapped!"

Feroza moved close to her parent, and caught her hand in a violent gesture of defiance. She stared at Zareen out of savage lynx eyes, her pupils narrowed. Zareen felt she had provoked something dangerous to them both. Tears springing to her eyes she jerked her arm free. She walked to the flimsy entrance door, pulled it open and swept out of the house.

Zareen had barely walked a block up the quiet, deserted street when she heard the angry whir of wheels as Feroza reversed the Chevette out of the drive. A moment later she whizzed past. Zareen felt drained and defeated. She turned round slowly and went back to the house.

Zareen sat brooding before the TV, searching her soul. She had acted exactly in a way calculated to push her daughter into the arms of this David. How could she have been so foolish? She was the mother, and yet Feroza had shown more maturity and restraint in her behavior than she had.

Late in the evening, lying on her bed, Zareen heard Laura and Shirley enter the house. She heard the garage door click: David had returned. Feroza must be with him. Quickly opening a magazine, she waited breathlessly for Feroza. The moments dragged by and she wondered if Feroza would show up at all: she wanted desperately to effect a reconciliation; wipe away the hurt in both their hearts. Feroza did not come. In fact the house was silent, as if it was empty. Tears sprang to Zareen's eyes and she put the magazine away.

Zareen heard the phone ring. A little later Shirley knocked on her open door and shyly, as was her way, said: "Feroza called. She asked me to tell you she is spending the night with a friend. She will see you after classes tomorrow."

....

Hesitantly, Shirley stepped into the room. "Are you all right? Can I get you anything?"

"I'm all right dear . . ." Zareen said, her voice thick. "Thanks a lot for asking. I'm just a bit tired . . . I was waiting for Feroza."

"You sound as if you're heading for a cold," Shirley said. "Let me get you a glass of warm milk."

Zareen felt soothed by the attention. She considered Shirley pretty. Shirley had high cheek-bones, a small nose and long blonde hair. The girls were not a bit like Zareen's preconceived notions of promiscuous American girls: even if Feroza had made that crack about being the only nineteen-year-old virgin in America. And these pretty girls did not have boys hovering round them.

Zareen stayed home the next day. She sorted out her shopping and packed a suitcase with gifts. It was expected of her: that she should return like a female Santa Claus. She did not see David or either of the girls all day. Feroza returned at about six in the evening, announcing: "I'm so hungry!" She was in high spirits. Zareen turned off the TV and followed her into the kitchen, saying: "I'm hungry too. I'll make us a *pora*."

Zareen rinsed a light plastic chopping board and collected the ingredients for the spicy omelette. "Only five days to go. By next Tuesday I'll be in Lahore," she remarked, expertly chopping onions and jalapeno peppers.

Feroza looked up from the mail she was reading. "Is that all? But you only just got here!" They could both hear David moving about in the garage.

Zareen sighed heavily and turned to Feroza. Holding the knife, plastered with cilantro and onion, she passed the back of her hand across her forehead in a weary gesture. "If you feel you must marry that man . . . I have only one request."

The induction of the subject was sudden. The capitulation unexpected. Feroza affected a visibly theatrical start, and asked: "What's that?"

This is what she loved about Feroza. Even as a child, after the red-faced shouting rages, the surly shut-ins, by the time she emerged from her retreat all was forgotten and forgiven. She rarely sulked: And even after their epic quarrel the day before, she was not above a little clowning.

"Get married properly," Zareen said. "The magistrate's bit of paper won't make you feel married. Have a regular wedding . . . Don't deprive us of everything!"

Feroza remained silent and raised questioning eyebrows.

"If you and David come to Lahore, we will take care of everything."

"Don't you think you might talk to David about it first?"

Zareen shrugged. "Then call him."

David came into the kitchen looking unkempt, unshaven and glum. Feroza noted the gold chain hanging from his neck, the Star of David prominent on his chest. She apprehended at once that her mother, by constantly flaunting their religion, had provoked this reaction. The top buttons on his plaid shirt were open, and part of it hung out of his pants. David turned the chair and straddling it, faced Zareen, surly and mildly defiant. Zareen was taken aback by the change in his behavior and appearance. His breath smelled of beer.

"Since you two are so determined to get married," she said, concealing her nervousness, and striving also to keep her tone light. "I want you to grant me a little wish."

David looked wary. "Feroza said you want me to come to Lahore . . . to get married?"

"Oh, not only you . . . Your parents, grandparents, aunts. They'll all be our guests. I want you to have a grand wedding!"

David remained silent and grimly unenthusiastic.

But marriages were the high point in Zareen's community life: and she was talking about her daughter's wedding. "We'll have the *madasara* ceremony first. You will plant a mango. It's to ensure fertility: 'May you have as many children as the tree bears mangoes.' In all ceremonies we mark your foreheads with vermilion, hang garlands round your necks and give you sugar and coconuts: symbols of blessings and good luck."

David, if anything, looked more wary. Zareen had expected him to at least smile, but his sense of humor had vanished with his courtesy and sensibility. She felt she was seeing him in his true colors. She recalled her initial reaction to his photograph.

"After that is done, we break a coconut on your head," she said with acid relish.

Feroza laughed. David blinked his eyes and looked profoundly hurt.

"She's kidding," Feroza said.

"Then we have the *adarnee* and engagement. Your family will fill Feroza's lap with seven saris. Whatever jewelry they plan to give her must be given then. We give our daughter-in-law at least one diamond set. I will give her the diamond and emerald necklace my mother gave me at my wedding."

"Don't look so worried," Zareen said, remarking David's ghastly pallor and compressed lips. "And tell your mother not to worry either: we'll be like sisters. I'll help her to choose the saris. We get a good selection in Lahore."

The more defensive and confused David appeared, the more Zareen felt compelled to talk. Feroza signaled her with her eyes, and when that did not deter her, with gestures of her hands and small amusing protests: "Mum, you'll scare him witless . . ." and turning to David: "It's a lot of fun really!"

"Of course it's fun. We'll give your family clothes: suit-lengths for the men, saris for the women. A gold chain for your mother, a pocket watch for your father. Look here: If your parents don't want to do the same, we'll understand . . . But we will fulfill our traditional obligations."

David was angry. He sat there exuding stubbornness: not mulish balking, but the resistance of an instinct that grasped the significance of the attack. He realized Zareen's offensive was not personal but communal.

And he knew that a Jewish wedding could be an equally elaborate affair — and though he didn't want to go through that either, he felt compelled to defend his position.

"My parents are not too happy about the marriage either . . . It's lucky we are reformed Jews, otherwise they'd go into mourning and pretend I was dead. We have Jewish customs too. I also belong to an old tradition."

"All the better," Zareen said promptly. "We'll honour your traditions."

Zareen felt an exhilarating strength within her, as if something very subtle was directing her brain: a power she could trust but not control.

David felt the subtle force in Zareen undermining everything he stood for: his entire worth as a person. He wasn't sure what it was — perhaps a craftiness older people achieved. His mother would be a better match: he had seen her perform the cultivated rituals of a closed society fending for itself in covert and subliminal ways that were as effective, but as difficult to pin-point.

"Next, we come to the wedding . . . If there is a wedding." Zareen said solemnly. "You'll sit on thrones like royalty, under a canopy of white jasmine. The priests will chant prayers for an hour, and shower you with rice and coconut slivers."

"I thought you said the priests refused to perform such weddings."

"I know of cases where such marriages have been performed," Zareen said, as if confessing to knowledge better left concealed. "That won't make you a Parsee, or solve Feroza's problems with the community, but we'll feel better for it. You'll have a wonderful time," continued Zareen compulsively. "Every day we'll sing wedding songs, smother you in garlands, and stuff you with sweets," she talked on and on. "I can just imagine Feroza in a white Chantilly lace sari with pearls and sequins . . ."

David folded his arms on the back of the chair and let his chin rest on them. He imagined his mother talking the same way. She'd want him to get married under the "huppa" canopy in the synagogue in which he'd had his Bar Mitzvah — and she'd want the same rabbi officiating.

David's blue eyes glazed over. Feroza glanced at him and felt bewildered and mortified by her mother's conduct.

Laura came into the kitchen in a boyish night shirt, apologized for interrupting and withdrew with her cup of coffee.

Zareen said: "Such decent girls. They don't have boyfriends to distract them from studies . . . They seem to know there is a time and place for everything."

"They don't need boyfriends," Feroza was complacent. "They're lesbians."

Zareen did not immediately register what she heard. She had read the word once or twice in magazines but never heard it pronounced. She became acutely uncomfortable.

"Lovers," Feroza added helpfully.

"But why? They're pretty enough . . . They can get droves of boyfriends."

"They're fed up. American boys change their girlfriends every two or three months. They're not all like my David. The girls want stable relationships: they can't stand the emotional strain. It takes them months to get over it. As Laura says: 'If Shirley gets my juices flowing why should I mess around with boys?' At least they get on with their lives."

Zareen wanted to throw up. She couldn't tell if Feroza was trying to impress her with her newly acquired worldly wisdom or deliberately insulting her. Feroza had been properly brought up to be respectful, sexually innocent and modest. That she could mention such things in her presence shocked Zareen.

Above all Zareen was dismayed at her own innocence: in all the time she had stayed with them she hadn't suspected the truth. What goings on. Feroza was living with a boy and a couple of lesbians. She wouldn't dare mention it to Cyrus or anyone. How could she face the disgrace of nurturing a brat who looked her in the eye and brazenly talked about the flow of bodily juices? She tried not to show how hurt she was.

But Feroza gauged the measure of her pain. Not able to do anything about her mother's attitude the past two days Feroza had helplessly watched David's slowly mounting perplexity, disillusion and anger. And suspecting that Zareen had just destroyed their happiness by her talk about diamonds and saris and superior Parsee ways, Feroza had instinctively hit back. The assaults were too vicious, the hurt too deeply felt, for either to acknowledge her wounds.

Zareen talked abstractedly for a while and stood up. "I've kept you long enough, David, you're almost asleep. Well, goodnight."

David nodded without looking at her or attempting to sit up. Feroza glanced at him surprised and reproachful. When Zareen left David swung himself off the chair and, avoiding her anxious and wistful eyes, stretching his back and rubbing his neck, went into his room. Feroza sat at the kitchen table for a long time, her face red and frozen. The tears came slowly.

Zareen had already checked her baggage. She stepped into the security section at the airport and placed her purse, a packed canvas carry-all, and three bulging shopping bags on the conveyor belt. After it passed through the X-rays she collected the hand luggage and turned to look at David and Feroza one last time.

David stood in his faded and torn denim shorts, his arms folded, his muscular legs planted like sturdy trees. Standing forlornly by him Feroza looked insecure and uprooted. As Zareen waved and smiled, an ache caught her heart and the muscles in her face trembled. Covering her head with her sari *pallu* to hide her crumpling face, she quickly turned away.

Once she was airborne Zareen opened her crocodile skin handbag. Its three sections had three thick wads of tissues. She picked one of each color and daubed her eyes. She wiped the tears from her cheeks, and gathering fresh tissues held their fragrant softness against her face. Her daughter was resilient: courageous in a way she could never understand . . . She would bounce back: like she always did . . .

And so would she, once she was with her family and friends. She needed desperately to be with them: to be assured she had done the right thing.

(From a novel-in-progress, *The American Brat*)

Birds of American River

JANE ROGERS

Kangaroo Island is separated from Cape Jervis, on the southern coast of Australia, by seven miles of warm blue sea. The straits are full of sharks, dolphins, seals, squid, and an abundance of smaller fishy life. On the ferry I read the "Whalewatch" notice, which told me that female whales and their pups pass this way in winter, en route for their northern feeding grounds. Here's one old female won't be passing this way in winter; I'll have to take the whales on trust.

I thought it would make a good prison. Probably did too, in the old days. Just the place for a penal colony: sharks come cheaper than a boundary fence.

They put me out of hospital (like you put out the cat at night, knowing it'll be back). My neighbour came in with meals. My son and his wife came to stay. My old friends rallied round. My daughters phoned from Sydney and said they had told their father, and please please would I talk to him. They heaped their grief and concern upon me like so many pillowcases of dry white feathers, till I was damned near suffocated. Each one had his or her own fondest imagining, of how I'd want to spend my last — six months? six weeks? They're cagey about giving you dates. It all depends. And the bargaining games that you play, like "swap you a month of bed-lingering for three good strong days on my feet and eating," are not with the doctors who seem to hold the key, but with some bastard who won't even show His face — never mind His hand.

Last year Arlene offered me and Matthew use of her holiday

shack at American River on Kangaroo Island. It was far enough away to shake them all off, but not so far that I wouldn't be able to get back if. When. The consultant was kind; he told me, full and square, and gave me time for questions.

"I don't know how fast it'll grow. Come back when you need us — there's no merit in suffering."

I'll go. I don't fancy pain.

So I rang Arlene and got the key. Begged her not to worry about the smallness, untidiness, bareness, general lack of suitability of the place for dying in. Declined all offers of companionship. And set off for American River.

A ferry always uplifts me. It's having my feet not planted firmly on the ground, that's the joy. I'd rather come back as a bird or a fish; wouldn't you? Call what we can do *motion*? Watch a dolphin, or a swallow.

Seal hunters named it American River a century ago. Knowing this, I imagined darkness, spicy with pine forest; an ice-cold river; silent, fur-wrapped men, their breath crystallising in the air.

I couldn't have been more wrong. American River, on the sheltered northern side of Kangaroo Island, lies warm and open as a child's palm. There is neither river nor forest; a lazy indentation in the coastline's formed a lagoon, where pelicans and black swans float like toy boats on a mirror. In the distance the far shore of the lagoon is white sand and green scrub, pretty as a pirate's island. The seal trappers have gone, and American River now boasts a hotel, a bottle shop, a deli and a post office. There's a single block of modern ranch-style houses, and, on the lagoon side of the road, a shanty village of holiday homes. They call them shacks: they're made of hardboard and corrugated iron, and either mint green paint was on special, or they had trouble getting any other supplies, but every crooked ramshackle lean-to is painted dirty mint green. Most sit in their own small yard of dust, it is too dry for grass; three or four big gums have been left between the tiny lots, and an

....

implausible row of three city neon lights grace the central dirt track.

Inside Arlene's shack I opened up the windows — it was stinking hot — and bashed a couple of the screens back into place. I checked there was rainwater in the tank; no need to turn the pump on. Then I drove to Kingscote for a boxful of groceries. By late afternoon I was done.

I walked down the dirt track towards the lagoon; the shore was only a few minutes walk away, but blocked from view by the huddle of shacks. Walking slowly past them, I realised that not all were holiday shacks. There was suddenly the interesting, poverty-stricken impression you always get where houses which were built to be temporary have become permanent: ramshackle additions and repairs, areas fenced off with chicken wire, a trough of glowing well-watered petunias sitting in the middle of a bare dusty yard. At the fronts, built in to the shabby plywood verandahs — or boxed in at the sides from uprights and chicken wire — were bird cages. At one, where a long-nosed, foxy dog came rushing to the fence to sniff me, there was a whole row of birdcages along the front. Topknot pigeons at the nearer end, galahs in the centre cages, white yellow-crested cockatoos at the far end. Nothing rare or strange; there were a bunch of galahs and cockies in the big gum behind the shack, they could've caught them in their own back yard. The yard was fully fenced — with an old fridge and the door of a car plugging weak spots — and the earth packed and trodden in a way which suggested poultry. I could see half a wooden railway truck behind the house, so I guess they kept chooks or turkeys there. But why the wild birds?

The pigeons were croop-cruuing, that close nostalgic sound which conjures the smell of autumn leaves burning (back in England, where it's safe to burn) and damp early-morning mist; neat grey slates on a church spire. The galahs and cockies sat hunched at the backs of their cages, staring balefully. I moved on.

Past the end two shacks the track widened into a dusty turning-cum-parking area, from which a footpath led on to the foreshore. I scrambled down and sat on a boulder. There were five pelicans floating close in to shore, and as I sat another pair came gliding in to splash down, hanging impossibly long that last inch above water, before their feet touched. Behind them the early evening sky was light blue paling to yellow, and the lagoon blue-green, darker where weed floated close beneath the surface. Above the silken lagoon floated the strip of opposite shoreline; above that, impossibly, more sea and an even further shore. A black dot in the sky, moving in from the other end of the lagoon turned into a dash, and then into the outstretched wings of a large bird. A primitive shape, like a pterodactyl — great pointed beak and broad oar-wings, gliding rather than flying; doing the occasional flap to lift it onto a higher air current, but mostly riding the thermals. An airborne pelican joyriding the sky with a wingspan wider than a man's arms, his great white back exposed to the sun and never a fear of Icarussing down.

I watched him a long time, half wanting him to head for water, to watch that impeccable glide-down to splash; and half wanting him never to come down, but to go on effortlessly gliding up and up the whorls of hot air, till he disappeared altogether.

As I walked back to my shack I glanced into the cages at the two end houses. The first was just one big batch of galahs — seven or eight in there together, with space enough to flutter round. The second had smaller birds; some honey eaters, a couple of topknot pigeons, other small bush-birds I couldn't name. There were empty stubbies on the verandah steps, in clusters of threes and fours, left where they'd been set down by their drinkers. I was going to cook myself tea, like any other holiday maker in the evening after a stroll. I was going to eat as if I meant to live. What else can you do?

But I didn't feel like it yet. I poured myself a beer, put on

....

some stinking mosquito repellant, and dragged an ancient armchair out into the yard. It was a funny place to sit, blocked in one side by a ramshackle weatherboard garage, and on the other by an ingenious system of four corrugated tin rainwater tanks, which provided tapwater in descending order. Above the roof of the next shack I could see the tops of two of the great gum trees. I sat down in my chair, took a mouthful of fizzy beer, nearly choked on the stink of Aeroguard, and thought, sod it. Sod it. Sod it.

I went back in, poured the beer down the sink, and had a shower. The shower was a home made affair with a water heater you had to switch on while the water was running. When I switched it off from under the water-stream a fair sized yellow spark streaked out at me and made me laugh aloud. You can't get me — I'm already spoken for!

When I was dry I felt clean and good. I put on my long skirt and blue silk blouse. I went in the bedroom and got what I should have got first, the bottle of Blackbush Matthew brought me for Christmas (what was I saving it for? the wake?) and a pack of cigarettes to keep the mossies off. The ice cubes I'd put in the antique fridge weren't quite frozen, but I picked off the top slivers of ice and floated them in my whiskey. Then I went back out to my chair. I'd only been ten minutes, but the sky was a lot darker; the gums above the shack roof were blackening now against the sky.

Suddenly there was a great squawking and kerfuffle overhead. A whole flock of galahs came wheeling in across the sky, did a couple of turns and settled heavily and clumsily into the gums, like fruit awkwardly re-attaching itself to trees it's fallen from. The dark pink undersides of their wings glowed hot against the sky, although the sun was already too low for colours. They filled the air with their excitable cries — flapping each other off their unstable perches, and gadding about to find another roost. A bunch of white cockies came in straight after, to perch in the gums; some came flapping down to the telegraph wires, where they squawked and screeched themselves into a fine old frenzy.

I lit another cigarette, and drained my tumbler: the sky was near black, I could see the first two stars. Birds still jockeying for position launched and twirled from the trees like exotic blooms; their racket crescendoed and I realised that an answering cacophony was coming up from the caged birds all along the track. Then, as suddenly as they'd started, they stopped. A single, indignant squawk from one: an answering shriek from another — and silence. Done.

I watched the sky as one by one then two by two then score on score the summer stars came out, and the good warm whiskey soaked through all the little holes in my body, and I felt more unimportant, and everlasting, than I had done for a while.

I slept late, it was hot when I woke up. I was hungry, and made a lot of scrambled eggs, which would have been nicer on toast, but there was no grill. Arlene had left an old exercise book of instructions on where to go and what to do, so I looked up swimming beaches and decided to head for the nearest. Nothing strenuous (I hadn't swum since the operation) but I was longing to be weightless again, and graceful. I walked down to the deli for a newspaper to take; at one shack, an old guy with a face like a dried apricot was pouring water into a dish in the galahs' cage. The door was wide open. I paused to watch and after a minute he looked at me.

"G'day."

"G'day."

He carried the water jug back to the steps, and picked up a bucket — there was food in it, fruit and household scraps. The galahs were hunched and motionless against the back wall of the cage.

"Won't they fly out?"

"Pardon?" He set the bucket down and turned slowly to deal with my question.

"The birds. Aren't you afraid they'll escape while the door is open?"

He grinned and moved his head very slightly to the left, a slow and energy-conserving no.

"Why not?"

"Scared. They scared to fly."

"Why?" Hunched against the wall and glaring, they looked like convicts waiting to be shot.

Without any perceptible movement the old man's mouth and shoulders indicated a shrug. The birds in all the cages were still and quiet. At last he said, "The space, mebbe. And the wild birds. They'd go for 'em, no worries. Mob 'em, peck 'em to death."

I looked at the birds, and they looked at me. "How do they know?"

"Ah." He seemed to smile. "They know." He turned to fill their food bowl slowly then stepped out backwards. The birds made no move.

"They aren't hungry," I said needlessly.

"This protects 'em, see," he said, tapping the chicken wire he had just pulled across. "Keeps 'em safe." He gave a single nod and moved back and up the steps to the flyscreen door.

While I waited there, not one of them moved; and they were as still when I came back that way with the newspaper in my hand.

An hour later I was swimming in the clear warm sea, watching shoals of small pale fish beneath me against the near-white sand. I saw two little puffer fish as well, and a kite-shaped ray idly flapping along the bottom. I should have brought a snorkel mask. Then I sat in the small shadow of my car, regretting the hot metal but lacking any better shade, and cut a hunk of hot bread and sweating cheese to eat with a couple of apples. I'd brought one of the knives from the shack, to cut the cheese; it was a surprising knife to be there, really. I guess the previous resident had left his cutlery behind. (Did he die there? If he lived there alone; if it was his only house. He would have died there. People die in houses. Babies are born in them. You buy a house and all you know is the number of bedrooms and the price.) The knife was old and solid, with a square yellowed bone handle. I read the name engraved on the blade; *Made in Sheffield for Richard C. Ford, Ororoo*. I wondered if the Sheffield cutlers knew that was Australia.

It was a good knife: the handle solid and comfortable to the palm; the long blade scratched and silvered thin with use and sharpening.

I was hot, even in the shade; hot and pleasantly exercised for the first time in weeks. On my shoulders and back the skin was prickling with dried salt water. I could feel each pore it expanded in. Quite soon I was too hot, so I went back to the shack which was even hotter and sat in the ancient chair on the shady side of the shack, and tried to read. But the book was boring and the chair not comfortable and I could taste the dust rising in the heat from the ground, and I thought for the first time that it was bloody stupid to be on Kangaroo Island pretending to have a great holiday alone.

There is something so sad and pointless about cooking for one in the evening. I've never been good at it. You start the morning full of life, full of joy — and as the day goes on — well, it just runs out.

At last the hot afternoon was done for, there was that scarcely perceptible shift in the atmosphere that means everything's changed, night's coming, and I found the energy to walk down to the lagoon again and watch the black swans and the pelicans gliding about like they'd been paid to do it. There was a cormorant too, diving for his supper. I tried holding my breath while he was underwater, but had to give up long before he reappeared. How come a bird's lungs can hold more than a human's? He always came up ridiculously far away, too, he could swim faster underwater than on the surface. He brought one fish up held sideways in his beak and tossed it — once — twice — before he caught it just the right way round to swallow; then down it went, head first, one gulp. At the edges of the lagoon the water was black silk; and in the centre, pearly grey, with the last reflected light of the sky. As suddenly as the previous night, the birds began to shriek and flap: I watched flock after flock of them come in across the lagoon, galahs, rosellas, cockatoos, all squawking and filling the quiet night with their mad racket. As I walked back along the track in the clear darkness I could hear the shrieks and squawks of the caged birds too; excited at their mates' party, even though they were too scared to join it.

Then I sat in the yard again, smoking and watching the stars come. The mosquitoes were hungrier than last night, queuing up for a stab at my neck and wrists and ankles. I was maddened to tears by them, "Leave me in peace you little bastards!"

There will be all the peace I can handle.

My first real fear. Not panic or irritation or unfairness. Real gut-fear. The shack wall behind me, the dark lean-tos on either side, the patch of black sky high above. A dark wooden box, measuring no more than your own height and width. Underground, forever.

I wanted to throw up but I couldn't. I couldn't stay in the yard, I was hyperventilating and my hands and feet were tingling. I got through the shack (small, dark, enclosed) out onto the track.

A swarm of moths around each of the three street lamps, flinging themselves against the light and falling. Dead quiet everywhere now, the birds are all asleep, the people all inside. Only the faint sound of laughter and voices from the other side of a lit window.

I pick my way, stumbling once, and squat beside the lagoon. It is hardly visible, but spreads a hundred soothing noises of its own into the darkness, lappings and ploppings and suckings at the shore, sounds I never even knew were there in daylight.

Swans and pelicans are floating out there, asleep on the black water.

I think of the scruffy captive galahs, hunched up against the back of their cage.

Like me. Angry, afraid.

I can't fly, no more than they can. I lack the — faith. Wouldn't you —? Wouldn't you have to believe in God and Christ and all the holy fucking angels, before you could take a leap into blind space?

Except I have to leap anyway. He's coming, to shake me out of the cage. To uncurl my toes from the perch.

If birds can fly . . .

If birds can fly . . . Can I begin to believe that death is freedom?

I find that I am laughing, in the noisy gentle darkness, laughing aloud. I can just hear my kids' disgust: "And you know what? She turned *religious*, for Chrisake, just before she died. She upped and told us she believed in God!"

Well, laugh. Why not?

Biographical Notes

....

THE EDITORS

Stephen Hayward was born in Hampshire in 1954; an Anglo-Irish background and an Anglican education combined to produce in him a fierce anti-clericalism, devout scepticism and a fondness for ecclesiastical architecture. Co-editor, with Sarah Lefanu, of *Colours of a New Day: Writing for South Africa*, he lives in London, where he works in publishing.

Sarah Lefanu was born in Aberdeen in 1953. Her Huguenot ancestry, Roman Catholic education and the influence of Scottish Presbyterianism produced an inability to believe in the concept of religious truth, but she remains fascinated by, and sceptical about, all matters religious. A freelance writer, she is author of *In the Chinks of the World Machine*, a study of feminism and science fiction. She has three children and lives near Bristol.

THE CONTRIBUTORS

Evelyn Conlon was born in County Monaghan and now lives in Dublin. She is the author of a novel, *Stars in the Daytime*, and a volume of short stories, *My Head is Opening*, and has recently completed a second collection entitled *Taking Scarlet as a Real Colour*. The founder of a crèche in the seminary at Maynooth, she has two children and has been active in campaigns which question the power of the Catholic church in Ireland.

Maureen Duffy was born in 1933, educated at state schools and the University of London. After teaching for five years, she has, since 1960, lived as a freelance writer of fiction and non-fiction, plays, scripts and poetry. Her novels include *Wounds, Capital* and *Gor Saga*. She lives in London. She is President of the Gay Humanist Association.

....